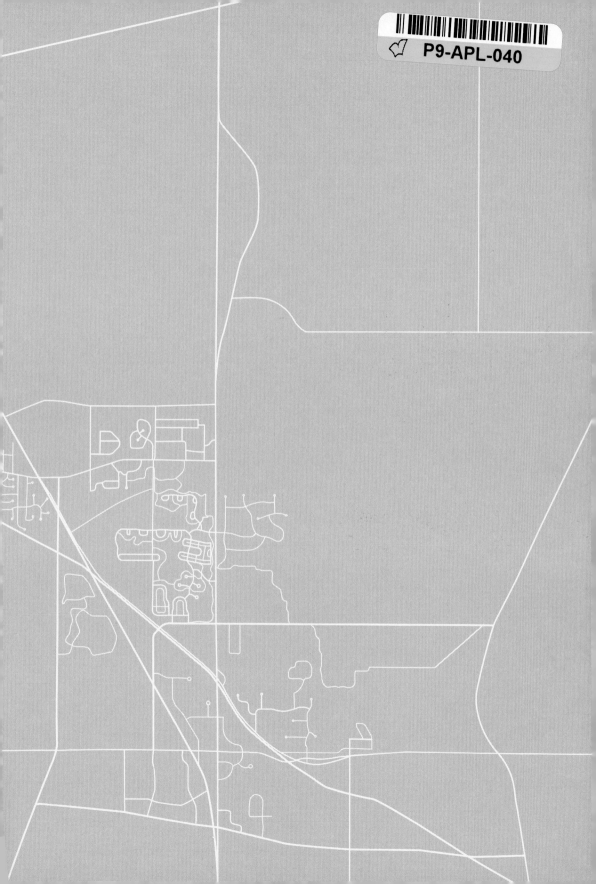

GREEN COMMUNITY

EDITED BY
SUSAN PIEDMONT-PALLADINO
AND TIMOTHY MENNEL

American Planning Association
122 S. Michigan Ave., Suite 1600, Chicago, IL 60603
1776 Massachusetts Ave., NW, Suite 400, Washington, DC 20036

National Building Museum
401 F St., NW, Washington, DC 20001

ISBN: 978-1-932364-74-3 (hardcover)
Library of Congress Control Number: 2009924917
Printed in the United States of America

GREEN COMMUNITY

EDITED BY
SUSAN PIEDMONT-PALLADINO
AND TIMOTHY MENNEL

CONTENTS

THE GREEN COMMUNITY IN CONTEXT

DENSITY AND TRANSPORTATION

CONSERVATION AND PRESERVATION

ENERGY AND RESOURCES

LOCAL HEALTH AND GLOBAL HEALTH

CONCLUSION

FOREWORD

CHASE W. RYND AND
W. PAUL FARMER, FAICP

The phrase "Green Community" is charged with promise and implications. As the chief executives of the American Planning Association and the National Building Museum, we strongly believe that this book and the eponymous exhibition at the Museum offer a new moment for reflection on the meaning of the term and the greater meaning of "sustainability."

One hundred years ago, in May 1909, 43 planners gathered in Washington, D.C., at the first National Planning Conference to engage in a conversation about what we now call sustainability. This book continues that dialogue and represents the most thoughtful and timely responses to core questions about the ways in which we live and work. What's more, these essays address the next 100 years of planning and beyond and serve as guideposts for creating communities of lasting value. Whether and how America can live up to the challenges and ideals set forth here is a critical question.

Many politicians, planners, architects, designers, and scientists in our global community are indeed leaders in sustainability. Others are still learning. Still others are just using the words. Sustainability must be about more than marketing, and "Green Community" must be more than an advertising slogan. Moreover, all of our existing goals, objectives, strategies, and tactics must be fine-tuned or even redefined if sustainability is to mean something other than simply good planning.

Together, we need to adopt and maintain a comprehensive viewpoint on the interrelated challenges ahead. As institutions with educational missions, APA and NBM must work to help political leaders and engaged citizens recognize that where and how we live has everything to do with reducing our energy consumption and our carbon footprint, and that meaningful higher density and compact development close to transit lines are basic elements of a green community. We must take the lead in developing state and local climate action plans. Most important, we must highlight the best practices in planning and sustainable design and the best examples of community engagement. Green technologies or trends should never eclipse the social equity issues that define and bind communities together.

As this book's essayists point out, the choices ahead are entangled in countless practical, political, and theoretical difficulties. To become convincing advocates of change, we must continually push the most viable work in the hard and soft sciences and in all related fields. We must also marshal the will and the resources to pursue the best policy options. Only then can we begin to ensure that each community is a green community, sharing space on an increasingly threatened globe.

W. Paul Farmer, FAICP
Executive Director and CEO
American Planning Association

Chase W. Rynd
Executive Director and President
National Building Museum

FUNDER'S
INTRODUCTION

THE HOME DEPOT FOUNDATION

The Home Depot Foundation is dedicated to building affordable homes for working families that are healthy to live in and affordable to own for the long term. Since our founding in 2002, we have helped build or renovate more than 65,000 homes for families across the country. A key part of our work is to encourage developers to incorporate responsible design and durable, efficient materials into their housing developments. Our focus extends beyond the four walls of a building, however, to make sure that these homes are part of a comprehensive approach to creating healthier, more environmentally responsible communities—close to schools, stores, and jobs so that transportation costs are low and commutes are short; and near parks and trees so that residents can enjoy a healthy, safe outdoor space.

That's why we are honored to sponsor the National Building Museum's Green Community initiatives, including the publication of this book. The challenges and opportunities regarding sustainability and urban planning presented throughout this book serve as effective discussion points and blueprints for policy makers and developers alike. The essays on seemingly diverse topics ranging from transportation and density to growth management and historic preservation effectively demonstrate that incorporating a multidisciplinary approach to building healthy, affordable homes in sustainable cities is critical to the long-term health of our cities and towns, our economy, and our environment.

To ground our priorities at The Home Depot Foundation, we always remember T. S. Eliot's statement: "Home is where one starts from." We firmly believe that having a healthy, secure home is an essential ingredient for the success of an individual, a family, and a community. As the sponsor of all of the National Building Museum's sustainability initiatives, we are proud to support its efforts to educate those in the building professions—as well as the public—about sustainable development and how buildings and land use have profound effects on the financial and physical health of the residents, on the sustainability of our environment, and on the social fabric of our communities.

Kelly Caffarelli
President
The Home Depot Foundation
www.homedepotfoundation.org

CURATOR'S INTRODUCTION

SUSAN PIEDMONT-PALLADINO

Health—our planet's, our communities', and our own—is inextricably bound to the ways we plan, design, and construct our buildings and cities. The *Green Community* exhibition, the third in the National Building Museum's green series after *Big and Green* and *The Green House,* explored the origins of our precarious ecological situation and featured a variety of communities where citizens, political leaders, planning and design professionals, developers, and government agencies have worked— usually together—to promote a more sustainable future. The exhibition demonstrated historical successes, present endeavors, and proposals for the future. Each featured community charted its own course based on its particular situation, but all drew on a growing collective body of cross-disciplinary research to support and inform their progress toward sustainable solutions.

These places may well provide templates for other communities and for a broader social engagement with the challenges of sustainability, yet the very phrase "green community" is full of assumptions and unartic- ulated expectations. What constitutes "green"? How do we define "community" in different contexts? Even if we can answer those questions, what then makes a community green? If a community is a place—as small as a neighborhood or as large as a megapolitan region—where people live, work, socialize, and participate in public life, then a *green* community must be all of that and more. It conserves its land, offers multiple options for transportation, provides open space for recreation and cultivation, and stewards its natural and cultural resources wisely. And yet com- munity is more than a place. Without people, there is no community. And without people who are committed to sustainable living, there is no *green* community.

63.7 GAL
The World

53.9 GAL
Germany

28.4 GAL
China

Groundwater
withdrawal per ca
1" = 3.5 gallons

THE WOR

COMMUNITIES-AT-LARGE

OF HOPE

Reshaping our communities, both new and existing, into healthier, sustainable ones is not a simple task, as it requires physical, social, and cultural transformation. The challenges of sustainability cut across several disciplines—planning, design, public health, and engineering, to begin with—but the difficulties arise not merely from the need for coordination or boundary drawing. Sustainability is inherently, in the words of Donald Schön, a problematic situation, one that is "puzzling, troubling and uncertain." He offers an example: "When professionals consider what road to build, for example, they deal usually with a complex and ill-defined situation in which geographic, topographic, financial, economic, and political issues are all mixed up together."[1] From each isolated perspective the task may appear to have clear goals and results, but the road itself leads, literally and metaphorically, to a new problematic situation, solving one problem while making a raft of new ones as it destroys ecosystems, severs social ties, enables sprawl, and so on.

Sustainability is a wicked problem—one that resists easy answers, in part because there is no single overarching solution, and every partial one engenders new complexities. And yet we must find solutions—and then more solutions—by culling problems from the situations we face, then testing, implementing, and evaluating solutions. To begin this process, we have here gathered a community of problem setters and solvers to speak from their own perspectives to the goal of a green community. This collection frames the problematic situation of sustainability and shares an array of sustainable solutions from around the world. Just as the communities in this exhibition together formed a mosaic of the diversity of approaches and issues that make a green community, so the essays together cover the expansive territory and diffuse boundaries of the green problematic.

Peter Hall's opening essay puts our contemporary problems into historical and global context, paying special attention to seminal proposals such as Ebenezer Howard's Garden City and various attempts to put its theories into practice. The political, economic, and industrial revolutions of the 19th century cast particularly long shadows onto the succeeding centuries as policy makers, planners, and designers wrestled with new technologies and a cultural infatuation with progress. Progress too often came in the form of the automobile.

With the rise of automobile ownership came regulations and planning strategies that have yielded countless low-density communities across the country. Mass transit needs density as much as density needs mass transit, but is there an ideal density? Even planning and design professionals tend to give a qualitative, rather than a quantitative, answer to the question. As Robert Lang and Mariela Alfonzo point out in their discussion of large-scale urban development, statistics alone, such as the number of housing units per acre, tell only part of the story. Equally important is the fact that well-designed, dense neighborhoods yield personal, social, and environmental benefits.

Jonathan Rose, who has developed compact and affordable communities, needs no convincing of the benefits. His concerns are logistical. Developing a truly green, sustainable community, he argues, cannot be accomplished compartmentally. Yet that is the structure of funding and programs that we have inherited. The public policy challenges for the future lie in operating across boundaries in a creative and productive trespass of older specializations.

As Rose argues for more conceptual mobility in the halls of government and financing, the other two essays in this section argue for more physical mobility within communities and between them. Both argue that the future of sustainable development lies in public transportation—including sidewalks. Technological innovations often seek to solve problems caused by earlier efforts. Zero-emissions automobiles may be solutions to greenhouse gas emissions and fossil fuel dependence, yet they offer no solution to the problems of low-density sprawl.

Kaid Benfield draws on the growing body of evidence supporting intra-urban and interurban accessibility. He challenges conventional thinking about greenness: is it building technology or location? Even the greenest, highest-performing building in an automobile-dependent location is no match for a typical building in a compact, walkable, transit-oriented city. Citizens are transportation opportunists. The opportunity to drive encourages driving; likewise, the opportunity to walk, bike, or hop onto a bus or streetcar encourages those behaviors.

But, we can't walk from one city to another, and a transportation choice is only as good as the system to which it connects. Fred Hansen uses the example of Portland and the Tri-Met regional government to illustrate the importance of interjurisdictional coordination. Portland's citizens benefit from a truly connected transportation system, where the places to change from one mode to the other are given as much thought as the modes themselves. Buses that accommodate bicycles, coordinated tram connections, sidewalks that connect residents to neighborhood services—these are all examples of a public transportation *system*.

Portland's successes illustrate the twin benefits of compact, transit-oriented development: walkable, vibrant streets within the city and conservation of green space outside for habitat, agriculture, and recreation. Douglas Porter surveys the array of tools available to jurisdictions to manage their growth. Communities from Sarasota County in Florida to Lincoln, Nebraska, deploy carrots and sticks to nudge development in certain directions and deflect it from others. Although these decisions directly affect the character and experience of towns and cities, they have often been made not in the offices of planners and architects but in legislatures and courtrooms. Whether branded as "growth management" or "smart growth," these strategies must link policy and design in both the vision and the implementation of development.

Tim Beatley suggests that our recent laissez-faire patterns of development reveal a too narrow definition of value. The wealth, and by extension health, of a community lies in its "durable stock" of natural and cultural resources. Only things with exchange value—that is, things which can be assessed relative to currency—are usually accounted for in metrics of prosperity. Put simply, the value of a forest cannot be reduced to the market price of its board feet of lumber, nor can the shade of a single tree be described solely by its shading coefficient.

Much of the success of the historic preservation movement can be credited to a successful shift in assessing value. Richard Moe and Patrice Frey of the National Trust for Historic Preservation argue that historic preservation is the natural and necessary ally of the environmental conservation movement. Stewardship of both natural and cultural resources underpins true sustainability. It may be a truism that the greenest building is the one you don't have to build, but like most truisms it is true.

In our section on Energy and Resources, four authors take on the problem of where we will get our energy in the future and with what consequences. Throughout history we have developed technologies to extract, harvest, and cultivate energy sources. In the process we have also continually redefined our relationship to the natural environment. Because modern technology now allows us to build almost anything almost anywhere, that relationship has lost its balance.

84,136 ACRES
of greater Denver

84,750 ACRES
Area of greater Atlanta

ISTED BASIN

300 ACRES
Area of listed brownfields

496 ACRES
associated brownfields
1994

Area of city : Area of brownfields
1" = 1508 acres

ATLANTA

HIGHLANDS' GA

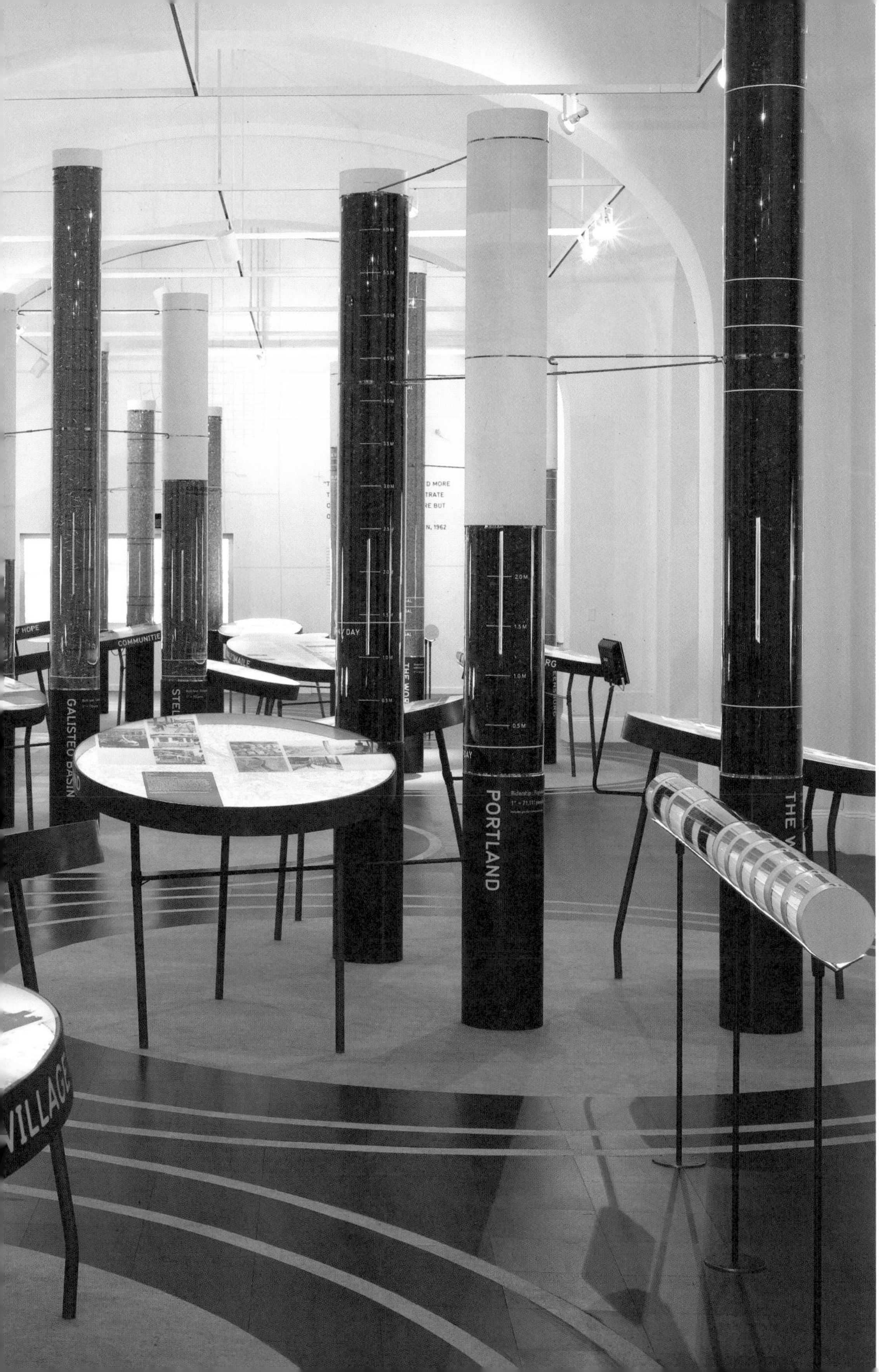
PORTLAND

Erica Heller and Mark Heller lay out a diverse range of choices: what each does best, along with its consequences, good and bad. They present the existential responsibility born from our hunger for power: technological freedom isn't free. Heller and Heller's assessment of the comparative burdens and benefits of these options emphasizes that such a complex problem has no single, simple solution. Any choice, whether nuclear or wind, has consequences—many unintended—for our personal health, the health of our planet, and the health of the flora and fauna of the hosting ecosystem.

Scott Malcolm and Marcel Aillery explore in depth one of those choices and its ripples of consequences. Focusing on the renewable fuel provision of the Energy Independence and Security Act (EISA) of 2007, Malcolm and Aillery reveal the sweeping changes that have and will continue to affect corn growers. Their essay offers an object lesson in the dilemma of creating a host of new problems while solving one. Our desire to grow our way to energy independence will change the lives of farmers, consumers, and residents of small towns, and it will put additional stress on water usage and soil conservation.

In her essay, Mary Rickel Pelletier takes on the relationship of water to communities, arguing for more attention to local waterways in community planning. Once considered marginal and unproductive land, wetlands are now seen as vital to the health of waterways. Draining wetlands and constructing canals and levees were once considered best practices to mitigate floods, but it has become clear that those approaches can have the opposite effect. Pelletier uses the example of West Hartford, Connecticut, to suggest that "blue urbanism" is essential to green urbanism.

What would a community look like that exercises green judgment in choosing its energy supply and cultivates both green and blue planning? William Browning offers a set of case studies to illustrate that far from bastions of sacrifice and asceticism, these communities are healthy, vibrant, and share a sense of common purpose. The unique character of historic cities such as Savannah, Georgia, or Siena, Italy, developed from just such close relationships among location, available material and energy, and the application of appropriate technology. One day tourists may flock to see the historic community of Village Homes in Davis, California, to marvel at the integration of building, agriculture, and energy.

With one foot planted in the Energy and Resources section, and one in Local and Global Health, Thomas Daniels stitches the policy choices to their consequences. He reinvigorates the aphorism "think global, act local" with examples of community action and straightforward suggestions for change. Much of that change, he suggests, must come first from our own behavior. A problem defined as technological yields only technological solutions. Changing behavior is a cultural, not technological, problem, and that must come first.

James LaGro looks at the dilemma that climate change poses for changing the culture of the planning and design professions. On the one hand, we must increase conservation and efficiencies at all scales to reduce our appetite for fossil fuels, but at the same time the realists recognize that we must also prepare. This dual strategy of mitigation and adaptation challenges both technological innovations and cultural values regarding private property and land use restrictions. LaGro points out the contradictions in educating the public about rising sea levels while federal flood-insurance programs continue to underwrite construction in vulnerable areas.

Our own health, and its connection to the built environment, is the subject of the final essays, each from a slightly different perspective. Esther Sternberg's research focuses on the human stress response and finds that the world we inhabit is rife with stressors. She reminds us that the history of public health lies in connecting disease to environmental factors and the "urban penalty" suffered by inhabitants of the crowded, smoggy industrial cities. She contrasts that with a "suburban penalty" suffered today in isolated, automobile-dependent developments. Our own bodies respond to environmental conditions, often in subtle ways after long exposure, but that response works both ways. If a polluted or badly designed environment can cause negative outcomes, it is equally true that we benefit, physically and mentally, from beneficial environments.

Nowhere is that more easily demonstrated than in our diets. Whether we have fresh local produce at a corner store or processed, packaged food from across the country in a big box outlet depends on a long chain of values and decisions. More than a question of "paper or plastic," our relationship to our food sources is, according to Carolyn Steel, among the primary shapers of human settlement, and therefore culture. Drawing on her own experience in Britain, Steel offers a vision of a different future for our cities, our food, and our selves.

In his essay "Healthy Communities, Green Communities," Howard Frumkin offers a compelling argument for improving our health not by ingesting more pharmaceutical products but by improving our environment. Green community design strategies can accomplish more to combat heart disease, asthma, diabetes, obesity, and injury than any single medical intervention, Moreover, Frumkin argues, the effect is generational; compact neighborhoods with trees, sidewalks—and places to walk to—are investments in the health of future generations. Knowing that, why would we not act?

Frumkin brings us back to the very essence of sustainability. While the United Nations Commission on the Environment and Development declared that sustainable development must meet "the needs of the present without compromising the ability of future generations to meet their own needs,"[2] the definition of the verb "to sustain" provides an even stronger foundation: "To strengthen or support; to keep (something) going over time or continuously; to confirm that (something) is just or valid."[3]

In his conclusion U.S. Representative Earl Blumenauer reflects on his own advocacy for livable communities and connects these efforts to 200 years of policies that tied transportation, conservation, and resources management to development. He assesses the legacies of those decisions, singling out particularly shortsighted policies of recent decades, to give context to the problems we face today.

History, even more than technology, offers a vast reservoir of sustainable solutions. We need not invent, so much as remember. Previous generations may not have used terms like "sustainable development" or "smart growth," but they knew that a healthy city enjoyed clean air, fresh water, fertile soil, and viable ways to move goods and people around. We used to build our cities as if it were a matter of life and death. It was—and despite our best efforts to conceal it from ourselves, it still is.

NOTES

1   D. Schoen, *The Reflective Practitioner: How Professionals Think in Action* (New York: Basic Books, 1983), 46.

2   The United Nations World Commission on Environment and Development, "Our Common Future: Report of the World Commission on Environment and Development," 1987. Available at www.un-documents.net/wced-ocf.htm.

3   See www.askoxford.com/concise_oed/sustain?view=uk.

LIVELY, DIVERSE, INTENSE
CITIES CONTAIN THE SEEDS OF
THEIR OWN REGENERATION...

—JANE JACOBS, 1961

Prairie Crossing, Grayslake, Illinois

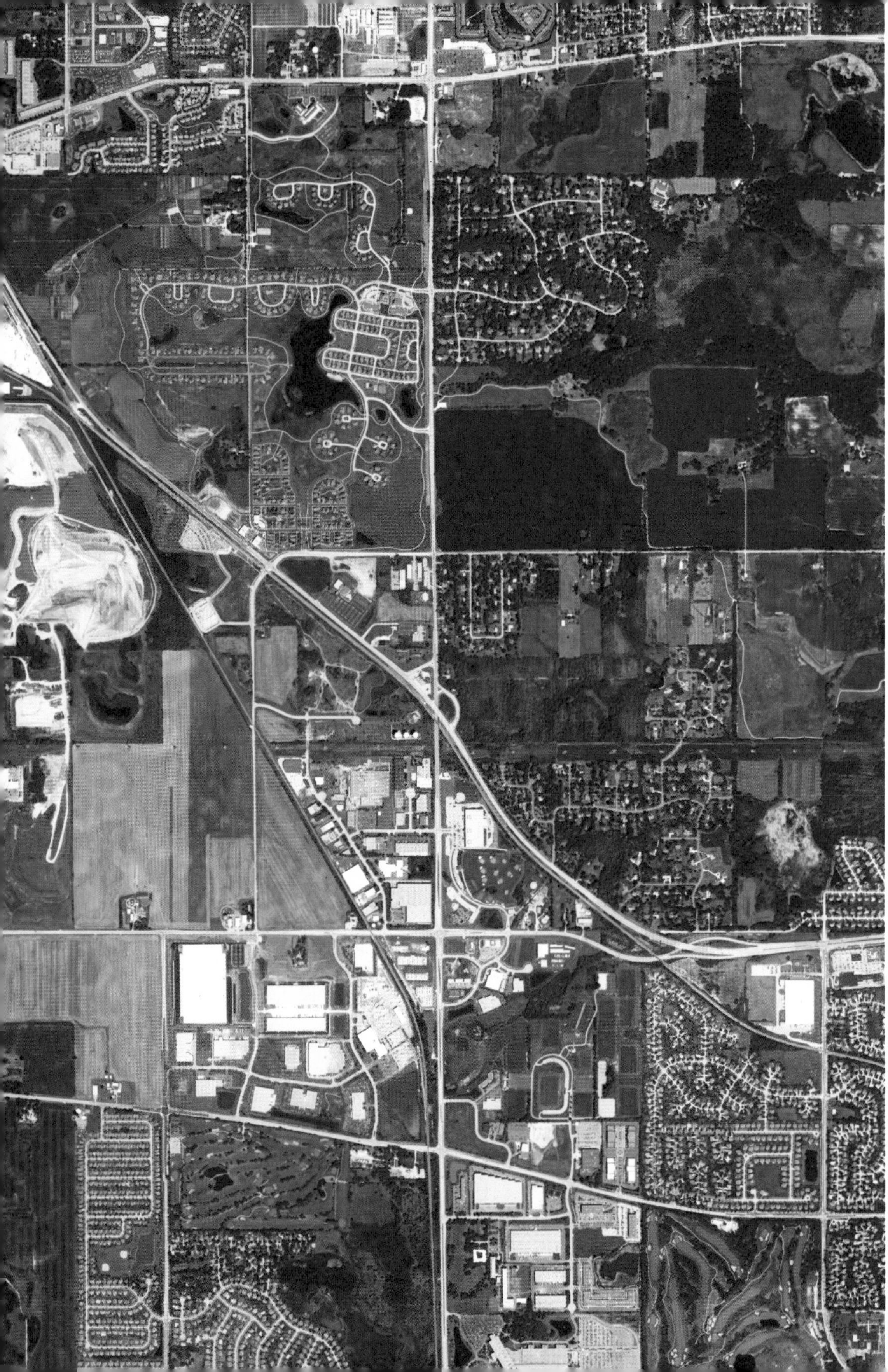

THE SUSTAINABLE CITY: A MYTHICAL BEAST?

SIR PETER HALL

Fifty years ago, James Thurber produced a wonderful fable concerning a gentleman who, having breakfast one morning, saw a unicorn in his garden.[1] He ran up to tell his wife of this and was told balefully by her, "The unicorn is a mythical beast." The question before us is whether the notion of sustainable urbanism is also a mythical beast.

A sustainable city or metropolitan area is one that does not rob the earth of fixed, nonrenewable resources—or if it does, it does so at only a minimal and decreasing rate. And to this end, it must comprise buildings that are highly energy efficient and low in energy use. And it must have a transportation system that minimizes the need for automobile traffic and maximizes access to jobs, schools, shops, social facilities, and leisure facilities without the need for long automobile journeys. Only a combination of land use and transportation policies will help secure this.

In order to pursue the question of whether this is an attainable ideal, I think we have to start with what has become almost conventional nowadays. We have known since the Brundtland Report, nearly 20 years ago, that the question is *how* we can realize the sustainable city, not whether we should.[2] And we now see that we can do it both in buildings themselves and in the relations among buildings, by maximizing accessibility, by encouraging travel on foot, bicycle, and public transportation, and by discouraging solo driving. We can and should develop activity centers around public transport nodes.

This is easy to say and more difficult to do, but we have done it before, and we have done it over a very long period of time, starting with Ebenezer Howard's Garden City and his concept of the social city. We did it in the UK, in the new towns inspired by Howard. We did it in Sweden, in the remarkable General Plan of 1952. We did it a little later on in France, in the Cités Nouvelles built around Paris from the middle 1960s onward, and we did it in the United States, in the layout of Radburn, New Jersey, and subsequently in Chatham Village, Pittsburgh, in Baldwin Hills Village, Los Angeles, and in Greenbelt, Maryland.

Now, if you look at Howard's social city, it is in fact a polycentric megacity region whose centers are linked by an "intermunicipal railway"—what we would call a light-rail system. And rather remarkably, 50 years later, the new towns in England did manage to realize Howard's social city, in Hertfordshire. We owe the existence of this and the other British new towns around London to Patrick Abercrombie and his Greater London plan. These towns were remarkable cases of relatively self-contained and socially balanced communities. The most spectacular of all were the ones built in the second generation, starting in the 1960s—in particular, Milton Keynes, 50 miles north of London. This plan is not very politically correct now, because it maximizes automobile use, but it is very well liked by the people who live in it. The town is now being expanded to roughly double its original size, with the goal of eventually reaching a population as large as half a million. These towns are successful, and although we did not know the word "sustainable" 50 years ago, we were planning sustainable communities in those towns.

At the same time, the Swedes developed around Stockholm a different concept of satellite towns linked by transit—in effect, a metro system. And from Vällingby, the very first in 1955, through to Skärholmen in the late 1960s, the standard recipe for building these was to surround a metro station with higher-density apartments, with a pyramid of density cascading away toward the edge. That was then followed, along similar lines but on a much larger scale, by the five Cités Nouvelles built around Paris after 1965 and linked by regional rail.

But long before all this happened, the United States had taken a remarkable lead at the end of the 19th century—through the efforts of the Regional Planning Association of America, led by such great, heroic figures as Lewis Mumford and Clarence Stein and Henry Wright—in planning the new town of Radburn. With its concept of segregated roads, pedestrian paths, and bikeways, especially for children to reach schools and play spaces without ever crossing a vehicular street, Radburn provided a model not only for Chatham Village and Baldwin Hills but also for postwar developments in Europe. The same can be said of the equally remarkable scheme for Greenbelt, the most successful of the relatively few towns that were built under the New Deal, with very much the same principles.

This high quality of planning has never been exceeded anywhere. We need to go back and learn from what was best about those towns. But we also need to fuse this with the best of what is happening in various parts of the world today. In the best examples—in the Netherlands, Germany, and Switzerland—we are

seeing compact transit-oriented cities; very large-scale pedestrianization of central business districts; traffic calming in the residential districts outside the central business districts; very high-quality public transportation and careful attention to integration of its different modes, especially between heavy rail, commuter rail, and light rail; and the constraining of traffic by congestion pricing.

In district after district in Europe, you see the prevalence of traffic calming. There is now this concept of shared space, essentially putting the car very much into second place behind pedestrians and children at play. You have to drive at a walking pace and with great care, because pedestrians and children are sharing the street space with you. This is especially true in cities that have strong public transportation, such as Amsterdam, which is near the summit of really effective integration of public transportation modes. In recent years, French cities have taken the lead in developing very strong tramway systems. In Grenoble, people are encouraged to use park-and-ride garages, where the ticket for parking is also a ticket for the streetcar, which can be boarded next door, in the same structure. You simply walk out of the garage onto the tram, and within five minutes you are in the pedestrianized city center.

Alongside the concept of traffic calming sits the notion that many different kinds of traffic can live in a civilized fashion together, even on very busy streets. This is apparent in Freiburg, Germany, one of the very few cities in the world that has registered an actual fall in automobile use over the last 25 years and an equivalent rise in public transportation not merely across the city but in the surrounding rural area. Perhaps the most remarkable city for integrated transit is Zurich, Switzerland, where an integrated commuter-rail system, which extends far out to the surrounding satellite towns, converges at the main train station with the intercity heavy-rail system and a light-rail, or streetcar, system. The ticket system is also integrated, and you can see the social integration that results: even the best-paid banker uses the streetcar.

Congestion pricing is a related concept with an interesting background. The first city to impose this was Singapore, in 1975, based on documentation from the Greater London Council's 1973 plans. Twenty-five years later, Singapore took the next step by introducing electronic road pricing. Individuals pay for use of street space in the city center via a smart card inserted into a transponder on the dashboard, which can be charged up at a number of places, such as 7-Eleven stores or ATMs. As this tool becomes more common worldwide, it is increasingly being used for other kinds of purchases, further simplifying its use.

Other cities have tried variants, among them Oslo, which in the 1990s introduced simple tollgates around the approaches to the city center. The most notable example is central London, where congestion pricing has cut traffic by 17 percent and congestion by 24 percent. There is now very little congestion, and traffic flows both smoothly and quietly, with great benefit to drivers as well as pedestrians. There is also a great deal of talk in the UK about a national road-pricing scheme, which would apply universally along major highways between cities, as well as within cities, and which would be controlled by satellite technology.

In the same period, Latin America—and Brazil in particular—has seen equally remarkable developments, notably in bus transportation. Even in cities where money has been lacking, bus systems have been implemented so successfully that they are emulated elsewhere. Brazilian engineers are taking the lead in spreading this technology throughout Latin America, most notably in Bogotá, Colombia. The key to this success is the integration of bus service and land use.

The first step was to develop high-capacity

bus systems through the use of smart boarding and unloading devices. The shelter itself actually minimizes the amount of time a bus has to stop. The second step was to develop three different types of bus—express, orbital, and local—and then integrate the three networks at key transfer points. The express buses in particular have very high capacities, up to 217 passengers, approaching the capacity of light rail. And, finally but critically, land-use planning has produced high-density corridors along the express-bus route corridors, which occupy reserved tracts in the middle of boulevards. This is almost as effective, in terms of integrating land use and transportation planning, as a full-fledged metro system like Singapore's.

Such busways are not a Latin American monopoly. Adelaide, in South Australia, some 15 years ago introduced a remarkable guided bus system developed by Mercedes, and this technology has been widely copied in other cities, including some English cities. Its remarkable feature is that the buses run at 60 miles an hour, express, along guideways; but when they reach transfer stations, they exit onto ordinary streets and zigzag through neighborhoods, with no stop farther than 550 yards from any given residential front door. Similar innovations have been put into use in Ottawa, Ontario. Edmonton, Alberta, emulating the system in Curitiba, Brazil, concentrates its buses at key hubs, so that they all arrive and leave together within a five-minute interval, and this gives a remarkably high level of service. As a result, even places such as the huge West Edmonton Mall, which you might expect to be completely car dependent, in fact is part of a very high-quality public transportation network.

So, it is possible to do bus cities, if we want to do them, and buses can deliver very good service, with high volumes, at very low cost. Can that service also serve low-density, peripheral sections of metropolitan areas, or are these areas inherently car dependent? I argue that they are not, because the growth of such areas is part of the process of our cities becoming more polycentric. Our cities and suburbs are effectively developing into megacity regions, on the original Ebenezer Howard prescription.

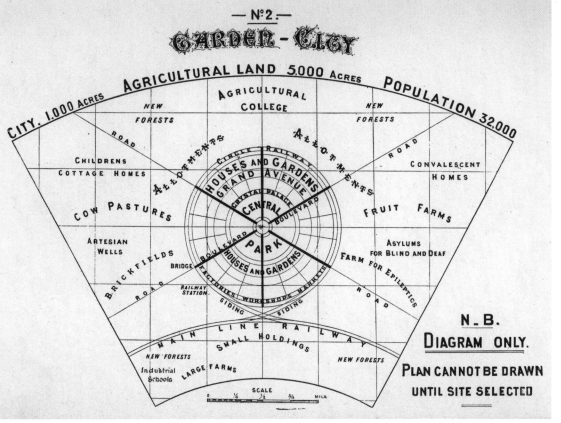

Ebenezer Howard's Garden City and his
concept of the social city

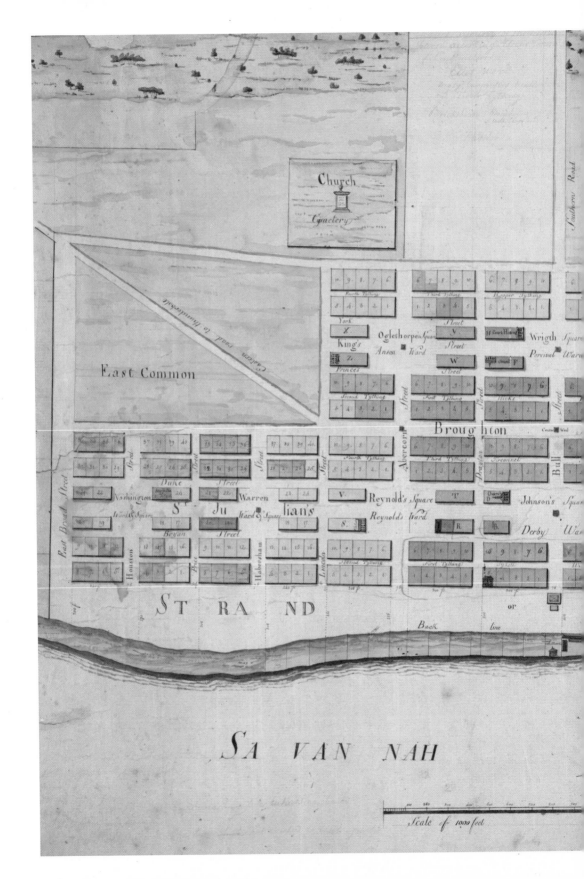

Church

Cemetery

East Common

King's

Oglethorpe Square

Wrigh Square

Anson Ward

Percival Ward

Princes

Broughton

St Julian's

Warren

Reynold's Square

Johnson's Square

Washington

Reynold's Ward

Duke

Derby Ward

Bryan

Houston

Haberfham

Lincoln

East Broad Street

STRAND

Back line

or

SAVANNAH

Scale of 1000 feet

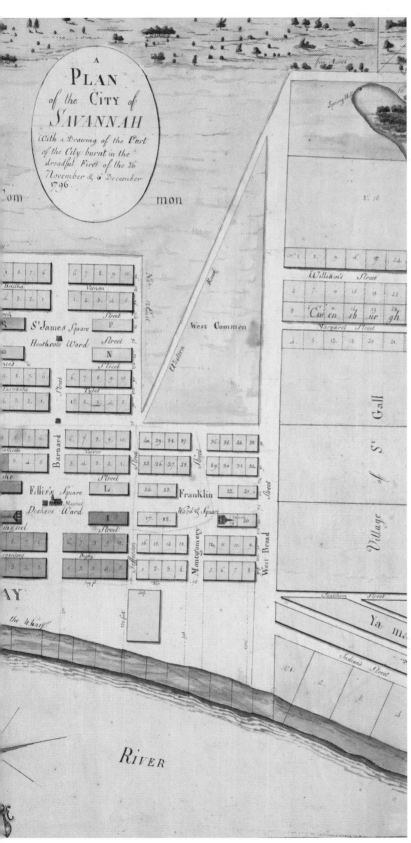

Trees and parks, often referred to as the "lungs" of the city, are among the essential ingredients of good urban design. James Edward Oglethorpe's 1733 plan of Savannah, admired by generations of urban planners for its integration of small green squares into a grid of streets, illustrates the long history of that principle. The squares are spaced no more than a few blocks' walk apart, yielding a rhythm of oases for pedestrians. The thick tree canopy also provides essential cooling in the city's subtropical climate.

The Green Community in Context

Present-day Savannah, Georgia.
From 1.81 km high.

With the application of these ideas anew, we have seen an urban renaissance in the centers of our cities. Birmingham, England, has been revitalized by canals that have been opened up on the edge of the city center; by a mixed use scheme involving a convention center, shopping, offices, and residential spaces; and, on the other side of the city center, by a new department store and a new cultural center. Similarly, in Manchester, which has had a problem of housing abandonment, the east side is seeing the development of a remarkable new medium-density neighborhood, as well as regeneration around the city sports center. Such successful repopulation can also be seen in Glasgow, Chicago, Amsterdam, The Hague, Rotterdam, and elsewhere.

But what densities should we be striving for if we are to make these districts fully accessible to public transportation? The typical suburban cluster—detached houses arranged very tightly around a cul-de-sac that gives onto a distributor road that gets gridlocked at peak hours, with effectively no possibility of being served by public transportation at all—is unfortunately still quite popular. This is a real challenge when designing a more permeable street system. We have to find a way of combining that preference with the need for a street system that is friendlier to public transportation. It is interesting to note that the Garden City planners were not planning low-density development; they were planning medium density, in part because of the preference in Anglo-Saxon countries for a private house with a private garden space. How do we bring all this together at the strategic level in terms of plans for metropolitan areas?

One solution in this context has come from the new urbanism, which promotes, among other things, higher-density neighborhoods that can be well served by high-quality public transportation. This was quite controversial when it was introduced, yet today this sort of development seems not dense enough. The ideal density for a new residential area is, in large measure, a factor of how well connected it is to public transit. Many new urbanist developments struggle with this issue—though some, such as the Crossings at Mountainview, in California, are connected to existing metro systems. Others, such as Laguna West, south of Sacramento, California, and Poundbury, outside the county town of Dorchester, in southern England, are not fully integrated with public transportation, and this compromises their success as urban design.

Some remarkable approaches to this problem are being taken up in Europe by combining the need for neighborhood density into a truly polycentric regional plan. Both Stockholm and Copenhagen have recently embraced the idea that they are regional metros that extend much farther out than previously conceived. The Stockholm transit system is now, in effect, a commuter-rail system that goes 60 or even 80 miles out in a ring and also serves the airport, 35 miles out. Even more remarkable is the Copenhagen system, which, thanks to the bridge crossing the Øresund into Sweden, is the world's first international metro.

Perhaps even more remarkable is what has been happening in London. As is well known, the London docklands were redeveloped starting in the early 1980s, culminating in the development of Canary Wharf. But this has now grown into the much larger-scale idea of creating new access to London from the east, down the lower Thames, as an extension of the docklands. This is intended as a counterweight to the growth of London toward the west, past Heathrow Airport, which has been the pattern of growth of the past 50 years. The key to this scheme is transit—specifically, the high-speed train lines that feed into the Channel Tunnel. As it was worked out in the 1990s, the strategy was to create two new train stations, one at Stratford, in East London, and the other at Edgefleet, just over the border from London in the county of Kent. These would serve as the hubs of new business centers and large-scale growth. Stratford, not many years ago, was a huge derelict area. By 2012 it is expected to be an enormous office city rather like La Défense: a secondary CBD astride the train station, with high-density apartments facing parkland. In addition, the 2012 Olympics are leading to the construction of a massive stadium right next to the station, along with the Olympic Village and other central facilities, which will remain after the games.

By such schemes as these and others, London

has been increasing its population very rapidly after decades of decline. It has gained half a million people since the 1980s, and it is expected to gain a million more over the next 15 years. It all ties together: the notion of a polycentric city, linked to a long, strong public-transport corridor, including the latest high-speed rail technology for both local and long-distance trains, plus high-quality busway transit, and increased densities to ensure that everyone has access. It is being done.

Is America different? Are these ideas completely inapplicable to the United States? Well, "Yes," you could say, "we have lower-density growth." But you do not have lower-density growth everywhere. Even Los Angeles is not a low-density city; it is higher density overall than New York is. And while America has over the last many decades seen exceptional losses of urban populations and jobs to suburban areas—to edge cities and "edgeless cities"—more recently population and employment have been growing again in most cities, and many cities have experienced renaissances. As Robert Fishman observed in his paper "The Fifth Migration," people are coming back into the cities because they want urban lifestyles again.[3] It has been happening, especially in the American West, just as it has been happening in Birmingham, Manchester, Glasgow, and around the world. And it has been happening in part because of the allure of sustainable urbanism.

We have done sustainable cities, and we must do them again. We did them 100 years ago. We did them 50 years ago and 30 years ago, and we have been doing them in the last decade. It can be done. It needs some government money—for infrastructure, in particular. It needs power, in some cases, to carry plans through. It needs imagination and determination.

Above all, we need to learn from best practice, from one another. So we need more practical research that compares cities worldwide: What do they do? How? With what powers and what funds? And the critical challenge will be in transferring successful best practice from one city, from one country, from one continent, to another. We must learn to map success and pick up on one another's successes, as well as one another's failures.

NOTES

1   This chapter is adapted and condensed from the American Planning Association and the National Building Museum L'Enfant Lecture on City Planning and Design, December 15, 2005, National Building Museum, Washington, D.C.

2   *Our Common Future: Report of the World Commission on Environment and Development* (New York: Oxford University Press, 1987). Available at www.worldinbalance.net/agreements/1987-brundtland.php.

3   R. Fishman, "The Fifth Migration," *Journal of the American Planning Association* 71, no. 4 (autumn 2005): 357–67.

THE FACT IS THAT EACH TYPE OF
TRANSPORTATION HAS ITS SPECIAL
USE; AND A GOOD TRANSPORTATION
POLICY MUST SEEK TO IMPROVE EACH
TYPE AND MAKE THE MOST OF IT.

—LEWIS MUMFORD, 1963

Central Station, Amsterdam, Holland

ROUND, ROUND, GET AROUND: REDUCING TRANSPORTATION BURDENS IN THE GREEN COMMUNITY

F. KAID BENFIELD

If you can tell a society's culture from its popular music lyrics, the 1960s were surely the golden age of the American automobile. On July 4, 1964, a new single became the first number-one song by that most American of bands, the Beach Boys. Performed with a driving beat and Brian Wilson's soaring harmonies, "I Get Around" celebrated the unequivocal freedom that cars provided, particularly on the group's home turf of Southern California:

We always take my car 'cause it's never been beat
And we've never missed yet with the girls we meet...
I get around
Get around, round, round, I get around
From town to town

Readers of a certain age may recall other hit songs of the 1960s that were paeans to the automobile, such as "GTO," by Ronny and the Daytonas, "Mustang Sally," by Wilson Pickett, and several more by the Beach Boys, including "Little Deuce Coupe" and "Fun, Fun, Fun."

By the turn of the 21st century, though, exuberant car songs were confined to oldies playlists, where they remain today.[1] One can speculate on the reasons, but surely one of the most compelling is that it has been quite a while since driving was "fun, fun, fun" for most Americans. Instead, it has become at best a matter of utilitarian point-to-point conveyance, far too often hampered by traffic congestion and stress—to say nothing of the havoc it has wreaked on our natural environment. While open convertibles were the most desirable cars of the 1960s, by the 1990s and early

2000s, sport utility vehicles—essentially complete family rooms on wheels that isolate their passengers as much as possible from the external world—had become the preferred vehicles.

The Transportation Challenge

What happened between the golden age of the automobile and today? Just as cars made it possible to expand our cities, suburbs, and regions far beyond traditional downtowns and rail corridors, the act of spreading out—suburban sprawl—placed increasing distances between the places where Americans live, work, shop, go to school, and worship. This inevitably led to a tremendous increase in driving: the number of miles driven annually by passenger cars in the United States has tripled since the 1960s, reaching a peak of just over three trillion in 2007.[2] In the same time period, our population increased by only around 50 percent.

As a result, traffic congestion has become an everyday menace of American life. According to researchers at Texas A&M University, congestion now drains $78 billion annually from the U.S. economy—in the form of 4.2 billion lost hours of productivity and 2.9 billion gallons of wasted fuel, which is equivalent to 105 million weeks of work or vacation time and 58 fully loaded supertankers.[3]

While the dramatic growth in driving has begun to reverse in recent years, we still have a long way to go in approaching anything near sustainability. With two-thirds of oil consumption in the United States going to transportation, the average American now uses over twice as much oil as the average person in other industrialized nations and over five times as much as the average person in the world as a whole.[4] As a result, carbon emissions from gasoline and diesel fuel use in the United States remain some 35 percent higher today than they were even as recently as 1990.[5] This is a major reason why the United States continues to lead the world in per capita carbon dioxide emissions, emitting about twice as much of the potent greenhouse gas per person as Germany, the United Kingdom, or Japan, and about three times as much as France.[6]

Given these sobering facts, the challenge in creating a green community is to maximize convenience and livability for the community's residents, workers, and visitors while minimizing the burdens placed on the environment by the basic need to, as the Beach Boys put it, get around. The task is an especially important one, given the relative importance of transportation to energy consumption and corresponding greenhouse gas emissions. A 2007 study reported in *Environmental Building News* demonstrated that otherwise "green" buildings may turn out to be not so green at all if they lack transportation-efficient locations: in fact, the amount of energy used (and greenhouse gases emitted) to run a typical office building is dwarfed by the amount that employees and visitors typically consume getting there and back.[7] Fortunately, there are tried-and-true ways of meeting this challenge.

Location, Location, Location

By far the most effective strategy to reduce the transportation burden of a neighborhood or community is to place it well within the existing development footprint of its metropolitan region and, as much as possible, on a centrally located site—central to either the region's downtown or one of its well-established suburbs. This is because of the principle of "regional accessibility": the proximity of the development site to other major destinations in the region such as jobs, services, and other neighborhoods. The greater the number of potential trip destinations within convenient reach of a location, the more accessible the location is said to be. Although there is considerable variation within metro regions, as a general matter,

locations that are more central tend to be close to more jobs, services, and other residents than outlying ones; they also offer a greater number of convenient alternatives to driving.

An often underreported effect of good regional accessibility is that it shortens driving distances. Research comparing two automobile-dependent neighborhoods in metropolitan Nashville found that households in the neighborhood closer to the center of the region drove 25 percent fewer miles per capita per year, emitting a comparably reduced amount of carbon dioxide than those in an outlying new suburb. This was the case even though the neighborhoods recorded the same average number of daily vehicle trips and there was no significant difference between the two neighborhoods in the number of trips taken on foot, by bicycle, or by public transit.[8]

Based on an exhaustive review of published studies, the transportation consulting firm Fehr & Peers has found that regional accessibility is a more important determinant of the amount of overall driving (measured by average vehicle miles traveled per household) than the other commonly measured factors—neighborhood density, diversity of uses, and walkable environment—put together.[9] The Fehr & Peers analysis confirms a widely reported research synthesis produced in 2001 by transportation experts Reid Ewing and Robert Cervero[10] and revisited in Ewing's 2008 book *Growing Cooler*, coauthored by Jerry Walters of Fehr & Peers.[11]

The effect of a good location on reducing greenhouse gas emissions can be dramatic. Consider the accompanying graph of per capita carbon emissions due to transportation from all locations in metropolitan Portland, Oregon, based on data from Portland's metropolitan planning organization. The locations with the lowest per capita emissions are those that are lightly colored on the graph; uniformly, they are within or close to the downtown area. Those with the highest per capita emissions are darkest in color; uniformly, they are in outlying areas. Consistent with the Portland data, additional analysis from the development and planning firm Jonathan Rose Companies shows that

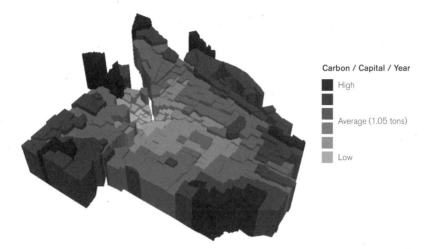

Carbon / Capital / Year

■ High

■

■ Average (1.05 tons)

■

■ Low

17

F. Kaid Benfield

even the most sustainably designed and constructed development cannot overcome the environmental shortcomings of a poor location. In particular, a state-of-the-art "green" household in an outlying location still consumes more energy and emits more carbon than an ordinary household in a more central location, because of its much higher rate of driving. This holds true even if the suburban household drives fuel-efficient cars while the urban household does not.[12]

To illustrate, the iconic brownfield redevelopment Atlantic Station (see page 121), in central Atlanta, has driving (and resulting emissions) rates far lower than the average rates of the 18-county Atlanta metro region as a whole. While the average resident of that vast region has been found to drive 34 miles per day, residents of Atlantic Station drive, on average, only 8.6 miles per day, a *75 percent* reduction. In addition, about half of all trips to, from, or within the development's site are made by walking, bus, rail, shuttle service, or carpooling; solo driving accounts for the other half.[13] Across the metro region as a whole, solo driving accounts for about 76 percent of trips.[14]

The reduction is exactly what one would expect from the development's relatively central location. On the accompanying map of the greater Atlanta region, the locations depicted in dark purple, including Atlantic Station, had an average driving rate of 10 or fewer miles per person per day at the time of the comprehensive 1998 regional travel survey. Note that these locations are concentrated mostly in the center of the region and in the center of the well-established older suburb of Marietta, to the northwest of downtown. Areas in lighter purple, where residents drove an average of 15 or fewer miles per day, include the traditional centers of older towns that are now effectively Atlanta suburbs, such as Jonesboro, Conyers, Roswell, and Lawrenceville. Areas in dark red, outside the region's center and outside traditional town centers, have an average driving rate of up to 44 miles per person per day. Even the best-designed community in these locations would not be able to come close to the green transportation performance of Atlantic Station.

The last point is particularly significant, since there is a large body of research showing that the parts of a metropolitan region with the densest development (measured by residential units per acre) also exhibit low driving rates.[15] This is because patterns of density tend to make very good surrogates for accessibility. Because we have built lower-density development in recent decades, the densest parts of a metro region tend to be those that are oldest and most centrally located. But building a new, internally dense development on a more remote site without good surrounding density and accessibility will have only a small effect on transportation patterns and could well result in driving rates that exceed the regional average.[16]

Neighborhood Pattern and Mix

Development density remains important, though. The Fehr & Peers synthesis of national research on neighborhood form and travel behavior concluded that, independent of other factors, a doubling of households or jobs per acre would lead to a 5 percent reduction per household in miles driven and a 4 percent reduction in vehicle trips, compared to a base case. And the firm found that, independent of other factors, mixing commercial and residential buildings, so as to double the ratio of jobs to housing, would also result in a 5 percent reduction in miles driven, along with a 6 percent reduction in vehicle trips. The effects are additive, so that doing both would lead to an expected 10 percent reduction in miles traveled and associated carbon emissions, on top of whatever benefits may be realized by the site's regional location.

The effect of density and mixed uses in encouraging walking instead of driving for some trips is now well established, and the benefits accrue to people as well as to the natural environment. A comprehensive multiyear study of land use, travel behavior, and health in metro Atlanta—the SMARTRAQ study, managed by Georgia Tech—found that people who live in neighborhoods where there is a mix of shops and businesses within easy walking distance are 7 percent less likely to be obese than those living where the mix is the same as the lower regional average. "Although this difference appears small," says the report, "the relative decrease in the actual probability of obesity is much greater—approximately 35 percent. A typical white male living in a compact community with nearby shops and services is expected to weigh ten pounds less than a similar white male living in a low density, residential-only cul-de-sac subdivision."[17]

Using a "walkability index" based on residential density, mix of uses, and street connectivity, SMARTRAQ rated precisely measured parcels of land within a 13-county Atlanta region. The report concludes that "the results show that the travel patterns of residents of the least walkable neighborhoods (those in the lowest quintile of the Walkability Index scale) result in about 20 percent higher CO_2 emissions [per person] than

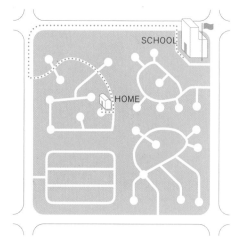

Traditional Cul-de-sac Neighborhood

travel by those who live in the most walkable neighborhoods. That comes to about 2,000 more grams of CO_2 per person each weekday."

Add a strong public transit connection and the transportation benefits go well beyond those highlighted by the SMARTRAQ study. Transit is partly a matter of location, of course, since choosing a development site on a transit line—or, even better, on multiple transit lines—can be a key factor in creating a green community. But it is also a matter of design, since placing the densest parts of a development, usually the commercial area or multifamily housing, closest to the transit will maximize the environmental benefits.

Transit-oriented development has become such an established part of the toolkit of city planners that the shorthand "TOD" is now commonplace in the lexicon. TOD works: a painstaking empirical study of 17 locations found that, on average, TOD around rail transit stations reduces car trips by 49 percent in the morning peak period and 48 percent in the evening peak, compared to what would be expected based on standard engineering estimates typically used by municipalities.[18]

One of the most stunning TOD successes is that of the recent mixed use development in Arlington County, Virginia, along the Washington, D.C., area's Orange

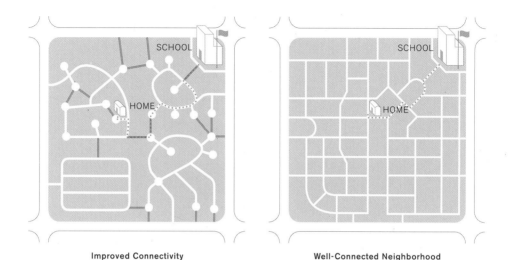

Improved Connectivity   **Well-Connected Neighborhood**

Line rail transit (Metro) corridor. Today, less than half of the residents in the five-station corridor drive to work. Thirty-nine percent use public transportation, nearly triple the rate of the region as a whole; and more than 10 percent walk or bicycle, also triple the regional rate; an additional 2.3 percent work at home.

Perhaps most significant, the additional 17 million square feet of office space and 24,000 homes built in the last two decades along the corridor have added only minimal automobile traffic. Mariia Zimmerman of the transportation policy analysts Reconnecting America (and an Arlington resident) reports that the daily traffic count on the corridor's main street, Wilson Boulevard, was around 15,000 vehicles in 1980; in 2004, it was 15,795. (In 1980, before the redevelopment began, the county had predicted that traffic on the street would soar to 36,900 vehicles per day by the early 21st century.)[19] The count on nearby Washington Boulevard actually *decreased* from 1980 to 2004, from 20,000 to 17,230.[20]

Connected, Complete, and Inviting Streets

If a community has a well-chosen site and the right mix of building and public transportation elements, the final design step to minimize automobile dependence is the creation of a streetscape that facilitates efficient travel by all users. The marker of a streetscape's efficiency that has perhaps the best grounding in travel research is street connectivity, measured by the number of a neighborhood's external and internal street connections. As the Federal Highway Administration puts it in *A Resident's Guide for Creating Safe and Walkable Communities*, "Streets that are not well connected can limit people's abilities to travel in the most direct path, increase distances to destinations, require larger intersections to move vehicular traffic, increase a pedestrian's exposure to vehicles (which increases the risk of being hit), and discourage walking."[21] Poorly connected streets also lengthen driving distances, increasing fuel consumption and emissions of greenhouse gases and other air pollutants.

Basically, the greater the number of connections there are, the better. And traditional street grids with small blocks do this much better than cul-de-sacs and subdivisions with only one or few entrances to and from arterial roads.

Consider the above illustrations from the Federal Highway Administration's guide. A resident living on a street in the lower left-hand corner of the typical cul-de-sac subdivision would have to walk, bicycle, or drive all the way around the perimeter of the subdivision to reach the neighborhood school in the upper right

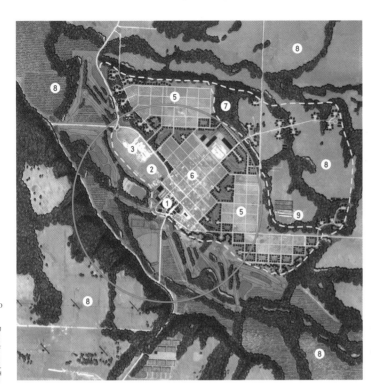

TOWN PLAN FOR STELLA, MISSOURI

1 Central activity space with attractive people-spaces.

2 Integrated school-community.

3 Enable school to evolve and develop to meet educational needs.

4 Narrow streets to reduce paving and runoff.

5 Grid block pattern to provide multiple routes through town.

6 Walkable community—short distances, multiple routes, sidewalks, shade.

7 Well-defined urban boundary within existing agricultural landscape.

8 Retain character of the agricultural landscape.

9 Use landscaping to screen large buildings.

– – Urban growth boundary.

—— Walkable radius from central activity.

corner. A resident of the well-connected neighborhood would have a variety of shorter, and probably safer, routes to choose from, as well as opportunities to stop at other houses or neighborhood features along the way.

Good objective measures of connectivity for a green community are the distances along the project's boundary between intersections with external through streets (the shorter the distances, the better) and the number of internal intersections per square mile (the more, the better). The LEED (Leadership in Energy and Environmental Design) for Neighborhood Development rating system—developed by the U.S. Green Building Council, Natural Resources Defense Council, and Congress for the New Urbanism—is the first comprehensive national set of technical standards to describe smart green development. LEED-ND proposes to disqualify from green certification any development lacking external connections at least every 800 feet along the boundary or failing to achieve at least 150 intersections per square mile. To earn credit toward green certification by having connected streets, a development would be required to have external connections every 400 feet and at least 300 intersections per square mile.[22]

Highlands' Garden Village in Denver (see pages 38

and 40) is a great example of connectivity done well. The 23.7-acre neighborhood is built on a traditional street grid with pedestrian-scale block sizes, as can be seen in its site plan. As a result, it measures a laudatory 792 intersections per square mile, indicating a very high degree of efficient walkability.[23] The site plans for the small rural towns of Greensburg, Kansas, and Stella, Missouri, also feature highly walkable traditional street grids with great connectivity.

New evidence indicates that compact communities with well-connected streets are safer as well as more walkable. Analyzing an accident database of 24 cities in California over a nine-year period, transportation researchers Norman Garrick and Wesley Marshall divided the cities into those with lower and higher traffic fatality rates. The researchers found that the cities with the fewest per capita traffic fatalities (averaging 3.2 traffic deaths per 100,000 people per year, compared to 10.5) were twice as dense in population (5,736 people per square mile, versus 2,673) and had about one and a half times the number of intersections per square mile as those with the most fatalities.[24]

Beyond connectivity, a concept that has been gaining favor among advocates for smart growth and green development is "complete streets." As explained by John LaPlante, longtime Chicago municipal

As explained by John LaPlante, "A complete street is a road that is designed to be safe for drivers; bicyclists; transit vehicles and users; and pedestrians of all ages and abilities."

planning engineer, and Barbara McCann, coordinator of the National Complete Streets Coalition:

> A complete street is a road that is designed to be safe for drivers; bicyclists; transit vehicles and users; and pedestrians of all ages and abilities. The complete streets concept focuses not just on individual roads but on changing the decision-making and design process so that all users are routinely considered during the planning, designing, building and operating of all roadways. It is about policy and institutional change.[25]

Sidewalks are a good place to start. LEED-ND recommends as a minimum requirement that continuous sidewalks "or equivalent [all-weather] provisions for walking" be provided along both sides of all newly constructed streets, at least 4 feet wide on residential blocks and at least 8 feet wide on commercial blocks. To earn credit toward green certification, the proposed minimum widths are 5 and 10 feet, respectively. The Fehr & Peers research demonstrates that a combination of good connectivity and good sidewalks has a measurable effect on behavior: isolated from other factors, a doubling of walkable design measures, including street connectivity, density of street and pedestrian networks, and completeness of sidewalks, would reduce miles driven by 4 percent and vehicle trips by 2 percent.

LaPlante and McCann recommend a context-sensitive approach to street design—for instance, urban downtowns need different features than quiet residential streets—and design speeds for vehicles in urban areas no higher than 30 miles per hour. Other techniques used to create complete streets include sidewalks buffered from cars; frequent, convenient crosswalks; bus pullouts or special bus lanes; traffic-calming features, such as sidewalk bulb outs and on-street parking; and the use of bike lanes.

Putting the elements together, a complete street might have automobile traffic lanes that are narrower than those on a high-speed thoroughfare, to encourage drivers to choose appropriate speeds for a mixed user environment; bicycle lanes on both sides, each wide enough to make cycling safe and convenient; pleasant sidewalks on both sides; a landscaped median in the center; slightly raised pedestrian crosswalks made of pavers, to delineate them from the portion of the street where cars have priority; and stoplights and walk signals where appropriate.

Finally, to create a successful walkable streetscape, shade trees, street furniture, and building heights and facades need to be placed and scaled in a way that is inviting to walkers and transit users. Again, LEED-ND is instructive. Based on historical models, practice, and research, LEED-ND proposes to exclude from green certification any development without a minimum of 20 percent of its street frontages having a building-height-to-street-width ratio of 1:3 or greater. A development may earn credit toward certification by ensuring that 40 percent or more of its street frontages meet or exceed the ratio. This is to discourage wide barren expanses and encourage a sense of enclosure that helps make pedestrians feel comfortable and safe.

Through its credit-point system, LEED-ND also encourages the placing of building facades close to the sidewalk, within easy reach of walkers; frequent building entries along the street; ground-floor retail in office and mixed use buildings; clear windows on retail, service, and trade use buildings; on-street parking to buffer pedestrians from moving traffic; elevated building entrances such as steps to ground-level residences; road design speeds of 20 miles per hour or less; and transit shelters. Additionally, the system credits streets that are lined with trees or functionally equivalent shading and sheltering such as arcades.

Especially in warm climates, shade trees can make a big contribution to the encouragement of walking rather than driving for short trips. In his paper "22 Benefits of Urban Street Trees," walkability expert Dan Burden contends that "for a planting cost of $250–600 (including the first 3 years of maintenance), a single street tree returns over $90,000 of direct benefits in [its] lifetime." Those benefits include more appropriate traffic speeds (research shows that drivers slow when passing along a shaded street); safer walking

environments (by creating visual walls and distinctions between pedestrian and vehicle spaces); increased security (due to more people on the street); improved business returns (with 20 percent higher income along shaded streets); increased property values; and reduced temperatures of five to 15 degrees, compared to exposed pavement.[26]

Fun, Fun, Fun Revisited

Can we, as a society, regain the optimism and exuberance of the early 1960s? Maybe not: we have done some environmental damage to the planet since then, and these are more sobering times for other reasons, too. If we recapture those feelings, it is unlikely to be because of cars and driving. But we can start down the road, so to speak, and being more thoughtful about our built environment can surely help improve our outlook.

It can definitely help the planet. Using Fehr & Peers's estimates, by doubling performance measures in all the four categories studied—location (regional accessibility), density, mix of uses, and walkable environment—we can reduce miles driven per household by 34 percent compared to a base case and reduce the number of vehicle trips by 15 percent. Emissions of greenhouse gases and other pollutants would be reduced accordingly. Where we can more than double performance on the key factors compared to the base case, the results will be even more dramatic, as with Atlantic Station. Research by PB Placemaking and others, along with the experience of Arlington County, confirm that transit-oriented development can further improve traffic- and emissions-reducing performance.

Not all of this will be possible to achieve in suburbs and smaller towns, but there we can still plan and design our communities more thoughtfully, to encourage walking and reduce driving distances, and make a difference, as in Greensburg and Stella.

Given the massive increases in population expected in the United States and elsewhere over the next half century, we had better get to it. And, yes, it will be fun for those of us fortunate enough to be working on it.

NOTES

1   In *The Washington Post*, J. Freedom du Lac notes: "Today, there are still automotive references in popular music, particularly in hip-hop. But they're usually brief mentions that often aren't about cars at all; instead, they're sexual metaphors ('Girl you look just like my cars; I wanna wax it,' R. Kelly sings) or status signifiers ('I deserve to do these numbers/The kid that made that deserves that Maybach,' Kanye West raps)." See J. Freedom du Lac, "Rollin' On Empty—In the World of Rock Music, Songs About Cars Have Lost Their Way," *The Washington Post*, September 7, 2008, p. M1. Arguably, Jimi Hendrix's 1968 "Crosstown Traffic" was a precursor to the use of cars in hip-hop. See Songfacts, "Crosstown Traffic by Jimi Hendrix," www.songfacts .com/detail.php?id=5051.

2   U.S. Department of Transportation, Federal Highway Administration, "Traffic Volume Trends—September 2008," www.fhwa.dot.gov/ohim/ tvtw/08septvt/08septvt.pdf.

3   Texas Transportation Institute, "2007 Annual Mobility Report" (press release), http://mobility.tamu.edu/ums/media_information/press_release.stm.

4   U.S. Department of Energy, Energy Information Administration, "World Oil Demand per Capita by Region, 2003," www.eia.doe.gov/pub/oil_gas/ petroleum/analysis_publications/oil_market_basics/dem_image_cons_per_ cap.htm.

5   U.S. Department of Energy, Energy Information Administration, "Emissions of Greenhouse Gases in the United States 2007," ftp://ftp.eia.doe.gov/pub/ oiaf/1605/cdrom/pdf/ggrpt/057307.pdf.

6   United Nations Statistics Division, Department of Economic and Social Affairs, "Carbon Dioxide Emissions: Metric Tons of CO_2 per Capita (UNFCCC)" (all countries), *Millennium Development Goals Indicators* (July 2008), http://mdgs.un.org/unsd/mdg/Data.aspx.

7   "Driving to Green Buildings: The Transportation Energy Intensity of Buildings," *Environmental Building News*, September 1, 2007, www.buildinggreen.com/auth/article.cfm?fileName=160901a.xml.

8   Natural Resources Defense Council and Criterion Planners, "Environmental Characteristics of Smart Growth Neighborhoods," *Natural Resources Defense Council* (2003), www.nrdc.org/cities/smartGrowth/char/charinx.asp.

9   Fehr & Peers, "Forecasting and Measuring the Impacts of Smart Growth," *smartgrowthplanning.org*, www.smartgrowthplanning.org/ForecastMeasure .html (accessed December 5, 2008).

10 R. Ewing and R. Cervero, "The Influence of Land Use on Travel Behavior: Empirical Strategies," *Transportation Research, Policy and Practice* 35 (2001): 823–45.

11 R. Ewing et al., *Growing Cooler: the Evidence on Urban Development and Climate Change* (Washington, D.C.: Urban Land Institute, 2008).

12 Jonathan Rose Companies, "Environmentally Responsible Development," *Developing Times*, 2004, http://rosecompanies.com/resources/images/ Spring_04_News.pdf.

13 Center for Transportation and the Environment and Lanier Parking Solutions, "Atlantic Station Monitoring and Evaluation Update Annual Assessment (Year Three) Summary" (February 2008).

14 Atlanta Regional Commission, "Regional Snapshot: Travel Patterns in the Atlanta Region, 2004" (based on 2001–2002 household travel survey), www.atlantaregional.com/documents/travelpatterns.pdf.

15 J. Holtzclaw et al., "Location Efficiency: Neighborhood and Socio-Economic Characteristics Determine Auto Ownership and Use: Studies in Chicago, Los Angeles, and San Francisco," *Transportation Planning and Technology* 25 (2002).

16 A. Khattak and D. Rodriguez, "Travel Behavior in Neo-Traditional Neighborhood Developments: A Case Study in USA," *Transportation Research Part A* 39 (2005) 481–500. There is yet another way of looking at density: comparing the densities of metropolitan *regions* to each other. Regions with high concentrations of households and jobs per unit of area exhibit significantly lower rates of driving and associated emissions. See, e.g., K. Bartholomew and R. Ewing, "Land Use–Transportation Scenarios and Future Vehicle Travel and Land Consumption: A Meta-Analysis," *Journal of the American Planning Association* 75 (December 2009): 13–27.

17 D. Goldberg et al., "New Data for a New Era: A Summary of the SMARTRAQ Findings" (January 2007), www.act-trans.ubc.ca/smartraq/files/smartraq_ summary.pdf.

18 PB Placemaking et al., "Transit Cooperative Research Program Report 128: Effects of TOD on Housing, Parking, and Travel" (limited use document, final draft, August 1, 2008), www.reconnectingamerica.org/public/download/ tcrp128.

19 M. Zimmerman, "Creating a Transit Oriented Community... a New Future for Northern Virginia" (presentation to the Dulles Area Transportation Association, September 28, 2005), www.datatrans.org/9-28-05DATATOD.pdf.

20 U.S. Census Bureau, "Means of Transportation to Work, 2005–2007, American Community Survey 3-Year Estimates: Washington-Arlington-Alexandria, DC-VA-MD-WV Metro Area," *American Fact Finder, Detailed Tables*, no. B08301, http://factfinder.census.gov/servlet/DTTable.

21 U.S. Department of Transportation, Federal Highway Administration, "A Resident's Guide for Creating Safe and Walkable Communities" (report FHWA-SA-07-016, February 2008), Chapter 4, http://safety.fhwa.dot.gov/ ped_bike/ped/ped_walkguide/residentsguide.pdf.

22 U.S. Green Building Council, Natural Resources Defense Council, and Congress for the New Urbanism, "LEED for Neighborhood Development Rating System" (first public comment draft, October 31, 2008), www.usgbc .org/ShowFile.aspx?DocumentID=5094.

23 E. Allen, "Analysis of Post-Pilot Version of Rating System" (unpublished, January 2009).

24 N. Garrick and W. Marshall, "Network, Placemaking and Sustainability" (presentation to the Congress for the New Urbanism Transportation Summit, Charlotte, N.C., 2008), www.cnu.org/sites/files/network_placemaking_ sustainability.pdf (accessed February 5, 2009).

25 J. LaPlante and B. McCann, "Complete Streets: We Can Get There from Here," *Institute of Transportation Engineers Journal* (May 2008), www.completestreets .org/documents/CompleteStreets_ITEMay2008.pdf.

26 D. Burden, *22 Benefits of Urban Street Trees*, Walkable Communities/Glatting Jackson Kercher Anglin (November 2008), www.walkable.org/assets/ downloads/22%20Benefits%20of%20Urban%20Street%20Trees.pdf.

Portland, Oregon

INTRODUCTION TO CONNECTIVITY

FRED HANSEN

All too often in the transportation sector, professionals act as if the entire goal of the system is to get people and goods from point A to point B. That is an overly narrow and potentially negative approach to the role of transportation, particularly public transportation. Rather than thinking of transportation in terms of moving people and things from point A to point B, we should view the role of transportation as providing access to the goods, services, and experiences that enrich communities' lives.

Looking through this lens of access, public transportation is and can be a transformational infrastructure investment. It provides an opportunity to transform existing neighborhoods by making new connections within and between communities, or to create new neighborhoods that are connected in ways and patterns that are very different from what has historically been the case.

The experience of the greater Portland, Oregon, region serves as a useful case study to illustrate the results that are attainable when we make those investments with a focus on accessibility and connectivity. By connecting transportation investments with land use and design standards, building on what communities and neighborhoods want, we are able to transform the whole urban landscape into a connective infrastructure.

Connectivity means making communities and neighborhoods work for people on a human scale. Citizens want the option of being able to walk to the corner to get a cup of coffee, go to the grocery store, or reach other essential services, in a very compact environment. They want it because it is a more convenient way to live their lives; it means spending less time stuck in traffic. We need to transform existing neighborhoods to establish this type of connectivity and ensure that new communities and neighborhoods are instilled with these attributes from their beginnings.

Historically, many of the largest transportation investments in urban areas, namely highway construction projects, split apart and destroyed the fabric of neighborhoods. While these investments may have enhanced mobility, it came at a very high price in terms of the character of cities, the nature of suburban communities, and our ability to create places where people want to live.

Transit and Connectivity in the Portland Region

As a result of a focus on connectivity, the public transportation system in the Portland region has become a very important part of the community— a part of its identity and a component of its lifestyle. That is, people use transit not just for the commute trip but for all sorts of activities. In fact, the fastest-growing segment of ridership in the Portland region has been non–work-related trips. Ridership on weekends, although still less than weekdays, is much higher compared to that in Portland's peer cities, reflecting the fact that people use the system for recreation, shopping, meeting friends, and generally getting around.

This is a situation that other communities are seeking to emulate, as indicated by the fact that barely a week goes by without a group from somewhere around the country or around the world visiting the Portland region to see specifically how land use has been successfully connected with transportation. When travel magazines write about coming to the greater Portland area, they invariably recommend using public transportation as a way to enjoy the region. Connectivity also results in usability, for residents and visitors alike. Many visitors are introduced to transit as soon as they leave the airport, boarding the MAX light rail, which enables them to get to the middle of the central business district within half an hour; others use it to access parks, shopping venues, a Trail Blazers basketball game, or other events.

As a result of the accessibility and usability that come from a focus on connectivity, Portland ranks seventh in the nation on a per capita basis for transit ridership. The rest of the top ten regions are generally older, well-established cities that developed around public transportation systems, such as New York, Chicago, Philadelphia, Washington, D.C., and San Francisco.

The Role of Statewide Planning Requirements

All this has come about not by accident or luck, but by a history of extensive and comprehensive planning to pull the various pieces of the transportation and land-use elements together, to provide that connectivity. In the Portland region, as is the case throughout the state of Oregon, there are comprehensive land-use and transportation planning requirements aimed at protecting fertile forest and agricultural lands in rural areas, while seeking to concentrate urban development within existing urbanized areas. These requirements not only limit sprawl that disrupts and transforms our landscape, but they also help to foster efficient and affordable infrastructure development such as roads, sewer systems, water supplies, schools, and other necessary services.

It is important to note that Urban Growth Boundaries (UGBs), which are dealt with below (pages 70–75), are a central tenet of the Oregon Land Use Planning Program, adopted in 1973. The main intent of the boundaries was to ensure the preservation and viability

of farmland by limiting city growth and preventing leapfrogging suburbs. The Portland metropolitan area boundary encompasses 24 cities and the urban portions of three counties. The Portland UGB is administered by Metro, the area's regional government.

This comprehensive planning approach has resulted in a very aggressive effort in the Portland region to take those statewide land-use plans and focus them in a more urban setting. This is known as the Region 2040 Growth Concept Plan. Before exploring the 2040 Growth Concept Plan, it would be instructive to describe more of the statewide foundational framework for these regional efforts.[1]

In the early 1990s, two key transportation measures were established that have substantially accounted for Portland's success in integrating transportation and land-use planning. The Transportation Planning Rule (TPR), adopted by the Land Conservation and Development Commission in 1991, clarifies the relationship between transportation and land use. It defines the characteristics of acceptable transportation plans, establishes standards for transportation system performance, and requires explicit links between local land use and transportation planning processes.

One of the major requirements in the TPR is that metropolitan areas adopt specific targets and plans to reduce reliance on the automobile. Metropolitan areas must either meet the state mandate to reduce vehicle-miles traveled (vmt) by 5 percent during the 20-year planning period or obtain state approval of an alternative standard. Plans to achieve the target must include: a combination of measures to improve the availability and convenience of alternative modes, including transit, walking, and cycling; transportation demand management measures; and parking management plans.

The TPR also directs metropolitan areas to implement land-use changes to promote compact, mixed use, pedestrian-friendly development as a way to achieve reduced automobile reliance. The TPR requires cities and counties throughout the state to prepare and adopt transportation system plans to meet long-range transportation needs. These must include planned roadway improvements as well as plans for bike and pedestrian facilities. Larger communities must include planning for transit.

The other key measure is the Oregon Transportation Plan (OTP), the state's long-range multimodal transportation plan. The OTP considers all modes of Oregon's transportation system as a single system and addresses the future needs of Oregon's airports, bicycle and pedestrian facilities, highways and roadways, pipelines, ports and waterway facilities, public transportation, and railroads through 2030.

The current OTP, adopted in 2006, supersedes the original plan, adopted in 1992. The original OTP established a vision of a balanced, multimodal transportation system and called for an expansion of the Oregon Department of Transportation's (ODOT) role in funding non-highway investments. With the benefit of 14 years of experience and technological advances behind it, the 2006 OTP provides a framework to further these policy objectives. The emphasis is on maintaining the assets already in place, optimizing the existing system performance through technology and better system integration, creating sustainable funding, and investing in strategic capacity enhancements.[2]

The OTP's commitment to multimodal planning is further enhanced by the Oregon Bicycle and Pedestrian Plan, which is one of the modal elements of the OTP. As such, the plan carries considerable authority, as it establishes ODOT's policies regarding bicycling and walking. It sets construction standards for ODOT and offers guidelines to local jurisdictions in establishing their bicycle and pedestrian networks. The plan also directs ODOT to establish funding programs to pursue improvements outside of modernization projects. These funding programs include grants to cities and counties for projects along local streets or state highways. Under the direction of the plan, ODOT provides training programs for engineers and planners, advises cities and counties on their programs and projects, and develops maps for touring bicyclists.

Planning in Practice:
The 2040 Growth Concept Plan

All of these statewide planning elements have created a solid foundation on which the Portland region has been building a green community in a way that reflects the philosophy of connectivity. As suggested above, the Portland region's 2040 Growth Concept Plan is the region's growth management policy; it defines development in the metropolitan region through the year 2040. The 2040 Growth Concept Plan guides how the region's UGB is managed in order to: protect the community characteristics valued by the people who live here, enhance a transportation system that ensures the mobility of people and goods throughout the region, and preserve access to nature. It outlines a vision for concentrating growth around regional and town centers. It is designed to ensure that the transportation system provides connectivity between and among those regional and town centers.

This approach has been essential to creating the density of development in those regional and town centers that can support a vibrant public transportation infrastructure. Put another way, it has helped create a community where getting a gallon of milk doesn't take a gallon of gas. In advancing these goals, the 2040 Growth Concept Plan encourages efficient land use, directing most development to existing urban centers and along existing major transportation corridors; promotes a balanced transportation system within the region, which accommodates a variety of transportation options, such as bicycling, walking, driving, and traveling on public transit; and supports the region's goal of building complete communities by providing jobs and shopping close to where people live.

Two plans, the Regional Framework Plan and the Urban Growth Management Functional Plan, both adopted in 1997, implement Metro's 2040 Growth Concept Plan. Their purpose is to translate the broad concepts into individual decisions made at the block-by-block, neighborhood-by-neighborhood level. These plans ensure that mixed use development occurs. For instance, in higher density neighborhoods with multistoried residential facilities, there will be commercial retail activity on the first floor, thus creating neighborhoods where essential services are close at hand.

The Regional Framework Plan contains the policies that direct our region's future growth. The plan provides specific guidelines that city and county governments will use to create and preserve livable communities. The Regional Framework Plan brings together these elements and contents of previous regional policies to create an integrated framework and ensure a coordinated, consistent approach. Issues addressed in the Regional Framework Plan include:

- Managing and amending the UGB
- Protecting natural resource lands outside the UGB
- Determining urban design, settlement patterns, and housing densities
- Planning transportation and mass transit systems
- Protecting and acquiring parks, open spaces, recreational facilities, water sources, and water storage facilities
- Coordinating plans and details with Clark County, Washington
- Integrating planning responsibilities mandated by state law
- Other issues of metropolitan concern

The Urban Growth Management Functional Plan is where "the steel meets the rail"; it is where the principles of the 2040 Growth Concept Plan are implemented. The functional plan contains very specific land-use and transportation requirements, which must be addressed by the 28 jurisdictions within the Portland metropolitan area. These include standards and guidelines for protecting streams and riverbank vegetation; implementing new minimum and maximum parking standards for particular uses; limiting big box retail in industrial areas; allowing accessory dwelling units in all single-family zones; and applying a minimum standard for the frequency of street connections.

In terms of specific transportation investments

and implementation, the regional framework and functional plans are supported by the Regional Transportation Plan (RTP). The RTP is a 20-year blueprint to ensure the ability to get "from here to there" as the Portland region grows. The RTP establishes transportation policies for all forms of travel—motor vehicle, transit, pedestrian, bicycle, and freight—and includes specific objectives, strategies, and projects to guide local and regional implementation of each policy. The plan was first adopted by the Metro Council in 1983 and is updated periodically to reflect changing conditions and new planning priorities.

The 2040 Growth Concept Plan provides the land-use direction for the RTP, with planned improvements closely tied to the needs of different areas. For example, areas with concentrated development—such as downtown Portland and the regional centers Gresham and Beaverton—are targeted with a balance of high-quality transit, pedestrian, and bicycle projects to complement needed auto improvements. In contrast, projects in industrial areas and along freeways and highways are largely oriented toward auto and truck travel.

In addition to focusing on strategies to improve everyday transportation needs, the RTP provides a vision for new ways to get around, such as commuter rail and van pools. This vision also includes telecommuting, ride sharing, and other programs designed to reduce demand on the transportation system. The plan includes specific policies related to street design, elderly and disabled transportation needs, and increasing the rate of walking, biking, and use of transit in the region. The policies established in the RTP guide local governments as they develop their local transportation plans. State law requires local transportation plans to be consistent with the RTP.

Integrating Transit into the Regional Growth Concept

In order to integrate public transportation into this regional effort, TriMet, the region's transit authority, has developed the Transit Investment Plan (TIP), the goal of which is to provide the framework to think about transit investments in a more comprehensive

In some respects, Portland's development philosophy is that more is better: more transportation options, more housing downtown, more retail, more civic amenities—more density. But is there an ideal density? Even planning and design professionals tend to give a qualitative, rather than a quantitative, answer to the question: density is good. Statistics alone, such as the number of housing units per acre, tell only part of the story. Equally important is the fact that well-designed, dense neighborhoods yield personal, social, and environmental benefits.

way. The TIP lays out TriMet's strategies and programs to meet regional transportation and livability goals through focused investments in service, capital projects, and the provision of customer information. The TIP shows how TriMet will implement the transit portion of the RTP over the next five years.

A central component of the TIP is building the "Total Transit System," which is TriMet's term for the elements that make transit an attractive choice for riders. These include frequent, reliable service all day, every day; clear customer information; easy access to stops; comfortable places to wait for transit; and modern vehicles. TriMet and its partners need to invest in building the Total Transit System not only to meet the current demand for service, but also to attract the level of ridership called for in the RTP.

Creating the Total Transit System also means ensuring individuals can get from their home or work to public transportation safely and comfortably. This requires sidewalks, safe street crossings, and bus stops and station platforms that are well lit and well

Trolleys and streetcars are familiar sights in many cities around the world, and were once common in the United States. Unfortunately, the mutually reinforcing trends toward low-density development and disinvestment in public transportation have left many Americans today with few mobility choices besides the car. Portland not only recently added streetcars and an aerial tram to its already diverse transit system, but also invested equally in pedestrian and bicycle infrastructure. Even frequent rain does not diminish the appeal of cycling in Portland; all of the city's buses, trams, and streetcars welcome bicycles on board.

protected from the elements. The transit system also needs to provide ways that individuals can access it easily. One key way to ensure this usability is through offering online trip planning. TriMet's online Trip Planner gives users step-by-step instructions showing how to get to a destination using buses, MAX, and the Portland Streetcar. The Trip Planner shows users where to board and make transfers, incorporates walking directions, and calculates how long the trip will take and how much it will cost.

TriMet also provides customers with real-time information about their transit trip, using a tool called Transit Tracker. The system can be accessed by computer or cell phone. By entering the location of the bus stop or train station, riders get the actual arrival time of the next bus or train. There are now more than 1.25 million calls per month to the Transit Tracker service, because people want to have greater control of their lives and be able to better manage their time, while still making use of the public transit option. It is a very important element in helping us create the Total Transit System.

While Google is at the forefront of providing mapping for all sorts of travel and locational needs, as they began developing their system to include transit options and looked at transit systems across the country, they chose TriMet as the pilot partner for their system. They did this in part because TriMet had the data necessary to provide the mapping, but also because TriMet's personnel are committed to providing tools to assist riders, making it easy and convenient for them to use the system. This reflects a commitment to ensuring transit becomes an integral part of people's lives, an element of how they operate day in, day out. Based on the model developed with TriMet, Google has now expanded that system to cover more than 75 cities and two states within the United States and more than 20 international cities and three countries.

The Role of Smart Street Design

As we seek to comprehensively integrate connectivity into our communities, we need to make transportation corridors places where people want to be. In this sense, streets are an important key to community livability. The Regional Framework Plan, the Regional Transportation Plan, the Transportation Planning Rule, the Intermodal Surface Transportation Efficiency Act of 1991, the Clean Water Act, and the listing of salmon and steelhead as endangered species have all elevated the importance of street design in the Portland area's regional planning.

Metro addressed these mandates with street design policies, adopted in the RTP, that support implementation of the 2040 Growth Concept Plan by linking the way a street is designed to the land uses it serves. Metro developed three handbooks that provide practical guidelines for designing safe and healthy city streets in the region. All of the guidelines are consistent with RTP street design policies, making the handbooks important tools for local governments, which will implement regional street design policies through state and local codes.

The first handbook, "Creating Livable Streets: Street Design Guidelines for 2040," describes how communities can design streets to better serve walking, biking, and transit, while also continuing to meet the region's motor vehicle mobility needs. Street design elements such as wide sidewalks, marked crosswalks, landscaped buffers, bikeways, on-street parking, street trees, pedestrian-scale lighting, bus shelters, benches, and corner curb extensions provide an environment that is not only attractive but that can slow traffic speeds and encourage walking, bicycling, and use of transit. The guidelines described in the handbook serve as tools for improving existing streets and designing new streets. They reflect the fact that streets perform many—often conflicting—functions and the need to reconcile conflicts among travel modes. A section of the handbook provides guidance for making trade-offs among design elements to respond to changes in land use or limited right-of-way.

The second, "Green Streets: Innovative Solutions for Stormwater and Stream Crossings," outlines basic stormwater management strategies and illustrates "green" street designs with features such as street trees, landscaped swales, and special paving materials that allow infiltration and limit stormwater runoff, helping protect stream habitats. The handbook also provides guidance on balancing the need to protect streams and wildlife corridors from urban impacts and the need to provide access across those streams as part of good transportation design. The design and construction of green streets is one component of a larger watershed approach to improving the region's water quality.

The third, "Trees for Green Streets: An Illustrated Guide," examines the role of street trees in managing stormwater. Appropriate tree species are illustrated in the handbook, with a list of major characteristics. The street tree guide focuses on the Portland region, but tree suggestions apply to any West Coast temperate climate from Vancouver, B.C., to parts of Northern California. It is intended to be used in conjunction with the other two handbooks.

Looking Ahead to the Next Major Planning Innovation

An indication of Oregon's likely next step in integrating land use and transportation is a concept the governor has proposed for consideration in the next legislative session: looking at transportation investments through the lens of least-cost planning. Some will be familiar with least-cost planning in the public power utility world. There, it is an effective tool for showing that an additional power need doesn't automatically mean a new power plant must be built. If, in fact, the least-cost way to meet the additional demand is by conserving power elsewhere—for instance, by installing weatherization treatments or cutting down on other power demands—then a new power plant is unnecessary. Investing in those alternatives produces a better, cheaper result.

If we think about applying the least-cost planning concept to transportation, it sets up a new paradigm for transportation planning in which planners do not just compare one highway project to another, or one highway project to a transit project. It forces transportation decisions to be made more comprehensively, including from a standpoint of land use as well. For example, the least-cost paradigm would empower planners to evaluate whether community needs can be met through a greater level of development in our regional and town centers, which can facilitate walking, biking, or transit use, rather than expand automobile capacity on our roadways. In this way, it could provide a new and powerful framework in which planners and the public can expand their thinking about how we can accomplish our connectivity goals by better integrating our land use with our transportation policies and investments.

In line with this emerging vision of least-cost planning is a concept that the City of Portland is just beginning to put into place in its jurisdiction: the 20-minute neighborhood. The idea is that rather than organizing transportation systems around going from point A to point B, they should be organized around people in those communities and the goods, services, and experiences they want to access. The goal is to make all the essential services people need and want to access in their communities reachable within 20 minutes by bicycling, walking, or catching transit. This approach causes planners to think differently about that neighborhood and the connectivity of those essential services. Effectively, it is a decision to make our transportation systems person-centric, rather than system-centric.

The Results to Date

In the greater Portland region, this comprehensive approach, this connectivity focus, has really paid dividends. We see these outcomes in the most recently developed new neighborhood. The Pearl District was built within walking distance of the central business district, on an old railroad yard, which had a low level of primarily warehouse activity. It has become one of Portland's most vibrant neighborhoods.

That vibrancy is in part a result of transformational investments in public transportation. In fact, the creation of the first modern streetcar line in the United States occurred through this district and helped it to develop. The results of that development are impressive. Since the streetcar alignment was chosen and construction begun, the area within one block of

the streetcar alignment is significantly denser than the areas that are two, three, or four blocks away. It is this density that has supported land use and transportation interconnections, resulting in a vibrant, mixed use, walkable neighborhood connected to the rest of the central city and the region by high-quality transit.

When comparing travel in this dense section of the Portland region with the rest of the Portland region (which most people recognize is further ahead than many suburban areas in terms of land use and transportation connections), there are dramatic differences. Specifically, people in the denser section are about 11 times more likely to take transit than they are in the region as a whole. They are four and a half times more likely to walk and about two times more likely to go by bicycle. The payoff of these trends is visible when looking at auto use. On average, individuals in these denser mixed use communities drive about half as many miles and have one-half the level of car ownership compared to the average in the rest of the region.

Another payoff is that we see that people want to live and work in a neighborhood that is walkable and has alternatives to the single-occupant vehicle. Walking, biking, or taking transit are not the only mobility options in these neighborhoods, but having those choices available offers a different set of opportunities and a better quality of life for residents and employees in those neighborhoods. This means you can meet a friend for a cup of coffee or glass of wine in a comfortable way that is conducive to sociability and reflects what we want our neighborhoods to be.

This desirability is reflected in an analysis of the development realized within two comparison geographies, before and after Portland's Blue Line light rail was introduced.[3] The geographies are: station areas, defined as taxlots within a quarter-mile radius of a light-rail station; and non-station areas, or taxlots within a two-mile corridor encompassing the Blue Line (excluding station area taxlots). A number of important results stand out:

• For MAX Blue Line light-rail transit station areas, development that occurred after light-rail investment indicates an average development density, or floor area ratio (FAR), of 0.65 more than the average FAR experienced for development outside of station areas. This means that for every 1,000 square feet of land area, station area taxlots that developed realized an additional 650 square feet of building area beyond the square footage realized in taxlots that developed outside of station areas.

- The station area capture rate of corridor-wide condominium development increased from 14 percent to 56 percent after light-rail investment was realized.

- The rate of development within Blue Line station areas was 69 percent higher than elsewhere within a one-mile corridor extending along the light-rail alignment. Rate of development was calculated as average annual square feet developed after light-rail investment, divided by existing building stock (in square feet) prior to light rail investment.

- Low- and moderate-value lots within Blue Line station areas redeveloped at twice the redevelopment rate reported for low-value lots outside of station areas.

Portland's experience suggests that this connectivity approach results not only in the vibrancy of neighborhoods but also in an ability to focus on the broad issues of sustainability as people work to create a green community.

In the United States, we utilize individual automobile travel for many of our transportation needs. In fact, 96 percent of passenger miles traveled nationally in 2005 were in cars or light trucks. From an environmental standpoint, specifically in the area of climate change, the impact is dramatic. In the United States, transportation is the second-largest and fastest-growing contributor of greenhouse gases of any sector. Between 1980 and 2005, the number of miles Americans drove grew three times faster than the U.S. population and almost twice as fast as vehicle registrations. If this trend were to continue, vehicle miles traveled would increase by nearly 60

percent from 2005 to 2030. This would overwhelm the greenhouse gas reductions generated by an increase in fleet efficiency called for under last year's energy bill and the reduction in the carbon content of fuels called for by California law, were it implemented nationally. A large portion of this growing travel demand has been a result of land-use patterns that require more driving. Across the United States, land was consumed for development at three times the rate of population growth between 1982 and 2002. Over the last two years, we have begun to see a reduction in the amount Americans are driving. While high fuel prices clearly have had much to do with this shift, the trend appears to be continuing despite the recent decline in gas prices (though this could also be attributable to current economic conditions). It may be too early to tell whether this signals a permanent shift away from the personal vehicle characterizing nearly all of American travel, but what we've learned in Portland over a longer period still offers valuable lessons as we look to green our communities.

Through coordinated transportation and land-use planning in support of connectivity, the Portland region has been bucking the trend toward sprawl and showing the nation a different way to develop. The result is more compact, efficient cities that are easier to serve with non-automobile transportation modes. Between 1996 and 2006, daily vmt per capita in Portland declined by more than 6 percent, from 21.7 miles a day to 20.3 miles a day, while the average length of a work trip decreased from 10 to 7 miles. In contrast, national vmt per capita rose by 8 percent in the same period. Reliable bus service, streetcar and light-rail lines, combined with attention to bicycle and pedestrian planning, ensure that residents who choose not to drive can take advantage of a variety of other travel options. Between 1996 and 2006, transit ridership in the area grew by 46 percent, while population only grew 16 percent. In addition to helping the region exceed federal air quality standards, these trends are reducing greenhouse gas emissions and helping address climate change. Between 1990 and

2007, community-wide greenhouse gas emissions for the City of Portland and Multnomah County, the area's most urbanized county, dropped 17 percent on per capita basis.[4]

The Portland region recognizes how important it is to address sustainability in its neighborhoods. The citizens want it, they are demanding it, and ways must be found to ensure that it can be accomplished. This is done by ensuring that people have walkable neighborhoods and that they are able to be closer to essential services. Ensuring that the investments made in transportation infrastructure—whether roads, when they're necessary, or public transit, bike paths, sidewalks, trails, and other amenities—are helping to make our neighborhoods more people-centric is essential to achieving greater livability.

All of this comes back to the unifying issue of connectivity: being able to connect people from where they are to where they want to be, in a way that really does provide for that neighborhood level of activity.

NOTES

1 Except where otherwise noted, the descriptions of the statewide and regional planning processes, plan, and policies provided here are drawn directly from TriMet's "Community Building Sourcebook," 2007, http://trimet.org/ pdfs/publications/community_sourcebook.pdf. The original authors and contributors of that work are hereby acknowledged for their content.

2 Oregon Department of Transportation, "What Is the OTP?" www.oregon .gov/ODOT/TD/TP/ortransplanupdate.shtml.

3 E. D. Hovee, Inc., for TriMet, memorandum, July 28, 2008.

4 City of Portland Bureau of Planning and Sustainability, "Portland / Multnomah County Climate Protection Strategy," www.portlandonline.com/ osd/index.cfm?c=41896.

CREATING THE PLANNING AND INFRASTRUCTURE FRAMEWORK FOR MIXED USE MIXED INCOME TRANSIT-ORIENTED AND URBAN-INFILL DEVELOPMENT

JONATHAN ROSE

Communities are complex systems that are nested within metropolitan regional systems. If we are to green our communities, we need to green the systems that frame, connect, and sustain them. So let us begin by looking at the larger planning, financing, and infrastructure issues that relate to creating the framework for greener communities, and at what makes communities vibrant, equitable, and livable.

America is projected to grow by 100 million people in the next 50 years. Either we will continue to sprawl, undermining the health of our environment and our economy, or we will use the opportunity presented by the current economic crisis to focus this population growth on our largest 100 metropolitan regions, which are the source of 80 percent of our nation's economy. By concentrating growth in existing metropolitan areas, we will invest our funds where they will generate not only the most economic benefit but also the greatest environmental and social benefits. But a comprehensive national strategy is essential to plan and coordinate our federal, state, and private investments so as to rebuild our communities in an era that demands immediate solutions to climate change.

Sprawl not only has environmental and economic impacts, but it is increasingly now generating social consequences. Currently, most American households spend more on transportation than they do on housing (see chart).[1] When we locate housing in walkable, transit-served communities, the percentage of household income spent on transportation drops from approximately 30 percent to approximately 9 percent,

freeing the remainder for other uses, such as education, health care, and savings.[2]

Today the working poor increasingly live on the edges of suburbs, where they have driven great distances to find more affordable housing. When, however, affordability is defined as the combination of (1) the cost of rent or mortgage payments; (2) the cost of the energy to heat, cool, and power a house; and (3) the cost of the energy to get to and from it, then a suburban single-family house consumes four times as much energy as a green multifamily home located near transit and neighborhood amenities (see chart).[3]

The solution to sprawl is to develop and redevelop compact, green mixed use mixed income transit-oriented development (TOD) communities. A neighborhood may be made of green buildings, which use less energy and healthier materials, but if it is located in a distant, disconnected place, by its very nature it is unlikely to be green. To transform our current development patterns to ones that are healthier for the environment, we need solutions that are built around an intentional—that is, planned—network of green infrastructure systems.

The good news is that there is tremendous market support for these greener, more compact communities. The two largest sectors of the housing market—the aging baby boomers and Generation Y, whose members are now in their early 20s—both want to live near vibrant urban downtowns. Developers recognize this, which is why for the last few years the Urban Land Institute's report "Emerging Trends in Real Estate" has

TRANSPORTATION V. HOUSING FAMILY INCOME SPENDING

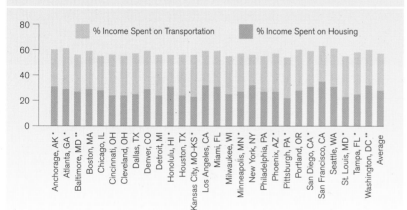

Note: All areas are Consolidated Metropolitan Statistical Areas except as follows. Those marked * are Metropolitan Statistical Areas and those marked ** are Primary Metroplitan Statistical Areas. Combined totals may reflect slight differences due to rounding.

URBAN V. SUBURBAN SINGLE FAMILY HOUSEHOLD ENERGY CONSUMPTION

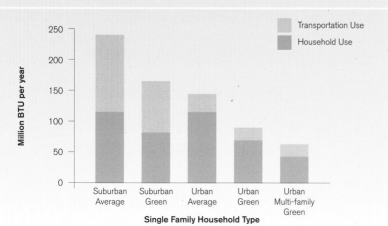

Above: Sprawl not only has environmental and economic impacts, but it is increasingly now generating social consequences. Currently, most American households spend more on transportation than they do on housing.

Below: When affordability is defined as the combination of (1) the cost of rent or mortgage payments; (2) the cost of the energy to heat, cool, and power a house; and (3) the cost of the energy to get to and from it, then a suburban single-family house consumes four times as much energy as a green multifamily home located near transit and neighborhood amenities.

identified urban infill as the top investment product of the real estate community. Many of the characteristics that make urban-infill projects appealing to the market are the very characteristics that also make the pursuit of them sound public policy. For example, residents of New York City, which is rich in transit and where walking is common, drive fewer miles than their suburban compatriots, and as a result generate 75 percent fewer greenhouse gases per person and weigh less because they walk more.

No individual community on its own can reverse the extraordinary human disturbance of the global ecology, but each can do its part. However, our large-scale ecological problems stem from the design of our large-scale systems. Our solutions must begin at the scale of large systems. Einstein noted that one cannot solve a problem with the same kind of thinking that created it. Just as sprawl was the result of a series of decisions that stemmed from a suburban view of the world, so we need to organize our decisions around a new green-community view of the world. And because the essence of a green community is to plan from the point of view of the whole, and not of the parts, integrated planning is essential to the development of greener communities.

A review of the origins and missions of just a few of the federal agencies involved in community planning illustrates this lack of integration. Created 40 years ago to solve problems in isolation, these agencies need to adjust to new challenges. For example, the National Environmental Policy Act (NEPA), signed into law on January 1, 1970, provided a basis for the integration of environmental policy. The act's first paragraphs state:

A. *The Congress, recognizing the profound impact of man's activity on the interrelations of all components of the natural environment, particularly the profound influences of population growth, high-density urbanization, industrial expansion, resource exploitation, and new and expanding technological advances and recognizing further the critical importance of restoring and maintaining environmental quality to the overall welfare and development of man, declares that it is the continuing*

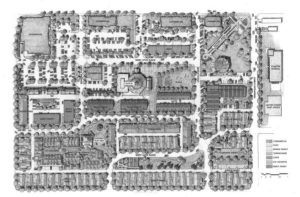

Surrounded by a residential neighborhood, the site of the once lively Elitch Gardens park could not be expanded and posed an adaptive reuse challenge for developers of Highlands' Garden Village. From the preservation of iconic structures to reusing demolition debris, recycling and reuse strategies were integrated into every aspect of the project. Demolition debris was reused in paving of new walkways and lanes. Developers also used recycled and recyclable materials to construct a dense range of affordable housing types, from single-family houses and town houses to senior housing and apartments.

policy of the Federal Government, in cooperation with State and local governments, and other concerned public and private organizations, to use all practicable means and measures, including financial and technical assistance, in a manner calculated to foster and promote the general welfare, to create and maintain conditions under which man and nature can exist in productive harmony, and fulfill the social, economic, and other requirements of present and future generations of Americans.

B. *In order to carry out the policy set forth in this Act, it is the continuing responsibility of the Federal Government to use all practicable means, consistent with other essential considerations of national policy, to improve and coordinate Federal plans, functions, programs, and resources…*

By the early 1980s, the Reagan administration's view that federal planning and regulation was an intrusion on individual and corporate rights and prosperity set back any hope of national planning for more than a generation. Since then, our federal system has been biased against the planning and coordination called for by NEPA. At the same time, the departmentalized structure of the federal government leads to the balkanization of public policy. Each agency answers to its own congressional oversight committee and has its own separate mandate and budget. As a result, the agencies have developed very separate planning processes, resulting in multiple uncoordinated plans.

For example, if a community wants to use HUD, CBDG, or HOME funds, it develops a community housing action strategy plan. To access transit dollars, its metropolitan planning organization, often controlled by road-building interests, develops a transit plan. To access water and sewer dollars from the EPA, it develops an SRF plan. National education, arts and culture, social service, and job training funds essentially have no physical or locational planning component. The Department of Commerce is responsible for agencies such as NOAA that monitor the climate, but the EPA regulates our impacts on the climate. And neither the Department of Commerce nor the EPA has a planning connection to the forest and agricultural practices of the Departments of Interior and Agriculture, which could preserve wetlands, forests, water and food sheds, and other critical natural resources. Without a clear national green-community goal, and a coherent planning and resource allocation system to achieve this goal, our agencies will continue to work at cross-purposes, no matter how well intentioned they are.

HUD was originally organized to revitalize many aspects of urban areas. At the time, there seemed no need for integration with the environmental policy of NEPA.

The congressional intent, identified in the first paragraph of the act creating HUD, says:

The Congress hereby declares that the general welfare and security of the Nation and the health and living standards of our people require, as a matter of national purpose, sound development of the Nation's communities and metropolitan areas in which the vast majority of its people live and work. To carry out such purpose, and in recognition of the increasing importance of housing and urban development in our national life, the Congress finds that establishment of an executive department is desirable to achieve the best administration of the principal programs of the Federal Government which provide assistance for housing and for the development of the Nation's communities; to assist the President in achieving maximum coordination of the various Federal activities which have a major effect upon urban community, suburban, or metropolitan development; to encourage the solution of problems of housing, urban development, and mass transportation through State, county, town, village, or other local and private action, including promotion of interstate, regional, and metropolitan cooperation; to encourage the maximum contributions that may be made by vigorous private homebuilding and mortgage lending industries to housing, urban development, and the national economy; and to provide for full and appropriate consideration, at the national level, of the needs and interests of the Nation's communities and of the people who live and work in them.

HUD began with the aspirations to build a Great Society. However, after the demise of the UDAG program in the 1980s, HUD became primarily focused on the development of housing, and neither it nor the EPA has achieved the metropolitan or environmental planning goals that Congress hoped for them.

But while planning was stifled on the national level, it gained vigor on the local level. As inner city communities were essentially abandoned in the 1970s—as embodied by policy proposals such as the RAND Corporation's "Planned Shrinkage"— community development organizations arose there, to protect existing affordable housing. Later, they became developers themselves. On the regional level, volunteer organizations such as New York's Regional Plan Association and 1000 Friends of Oregon gave rise to regional plans. As suburban communities began to oppose sprawl, community and regional land trusts were formed, first to purchase land, and then to develop open space plans. And thus, a citizen-based planning movement grew in many parts of the country, in part as a response to the absence of federal policy or national leadership on land use and growth issues.

In many ways, citizens groups are providing an "immune response" to the degradation of our ecosystems' health, just the way natural systems provide localized immune responses to insult. And it seems that when the federal government fails to act on an issue that has strong popular support, local and regional responses emerge. The leadership vacuum on global warming at the federal level has helped give rise to vigorous local, state, and regional efforts to reduce the contributing effects of human activity on climate change. A diverse range of solutions, designed to fit into the local political, ecological, and economic niches of their regions, has emerged. These responses will inform the national policy. But our climate is global. Thus, local regulation and solutions are necessary but not sufficient. We need a green policy and infrastructure framework that works at the local scale, but it must also be integrated at regional, national, and even international scales if it is to be truly effective.

Out of citizen-led local movements—which

"Not to see Elitch's is not to see Denver." This slogan once accurately reflected the park's popularity in the community. Among its many diversions, Elitch Gardens was most famous for its octagonal theater—home to the first summer stock company in the country—which remained a prestigious venue for traveling companies until the park closed in 1994. Now restored, the Center for American Theatre at Historic Elitch Gardens and the Carousel pavilion are linked by a new village green, standing together as a centerpiece of Highlands' Garden Village and a reminder of the site's history.

brought together planners, environmentalists, land preservationists, historic preservationists, community activists, architects, engineers, and even developers— a clear land-use planning paradigm began to emerge. It became clear that density was actually part of the solution, not the problem, and that higher-density communities needed to be thoughtfully designed and served with appropriate infrastructure. These were not new conclusions; many found models of this paradigm in the train station villages of the early 20th century and in some of our nation's most valued downtowns and neighborhoods.

These models of compact development show us how we might accommodate more people on less land even as we improve their overall quality of life. At the same time, this pattern of higher density provides greater return on infrastructure investment. For example, a road with water, sewer, gas, electrical, and phone lines provides four times the return on investment if it services 32 units per acre versus eight units per acre. And so density, thought of as an environmental problem in the 1980s, came to be recognized as an environmental solution in the 2000s.

We can really unleash the power of the higher-density green community when we combine it with restored natural systems. The result is a compact community with a mix of uses to serve its residents, a range of housing types and prices to support the diversity of the community, and green buildings to provide healthier living environments. We can reduce the transportation costs of residents, workers, and visitors, and increase their disposable income by serving the community with a range of transit options.

For decades, federal transportation policy, again lacking integration with urban or environmental policy, has attempted to mediate the tensions between transit interests and road interests, with highways and roads receiving approximately 80 percent of our federal funding and transit receiving approximately 20 percent. The fallacy of this funding model is evident in its failure to provide integrated results. Imagine a street repair project that integrates tracks for a streetcar, bike lanes, tree-lined sidewalks, natural swales for stormwater absorption, and safer parking, protected by bulb outs. Is such a transformed street a road project, a transit project, a livability project, a retail-enhancing economic-development project, or a stormwater infrastructure project? It is all of them.

Congress is expected to soon pass a new transportation authorization bill, known as T-4 because it will be the fourth major multiyear federal transit program, following TEA-21, ISTEA, and SAFETEA-LU. Since 1982, these bills have set our nation's transportation policy by creating dedicated pots of funding, with 80 percent going to roads and bridges, and 20 percent for mass transit. It is time that we opened up our transportation paradigm and also funded smart streets, which can accommodate not only cars and trucks but also bicycles, pedestrians, bus rapid transit, and other alternatives. Through T-4 reauthorization, we can develop transportation planning and funding models that provide for the integration necessary to develop smarter streets and more livable communities.

Why are green communities often mixed use communities? Economic, ecological, and social health all stem from diversity. Healthy cities are diverse cities. Diversity is also a key to economic, ecological, and social resiliency. Our communities will need greater resilience to respond to the stresses related to impending population growth, globalization, and climate change. Mixed use developments and diverse communities can draw from a broader range of resources to provide this resilience. For example, during recessions, multifamily rental rates typically decline, but mixed use apartment buildings that also have retail and office components are more likely to maintain steady cash flow and thus are more reliable assets. This principle works at larger scales. As we know, if the economy of a town is based on the prosperity of one company, if the company closes, the town suffers deeply. Communities are healthier when they include local retail, commercial, recreational, and cultural facilities and educational services ranging from preschool to lifelong learning.

The more walkable and well served by transit that communities are, the greater will be the mobility of

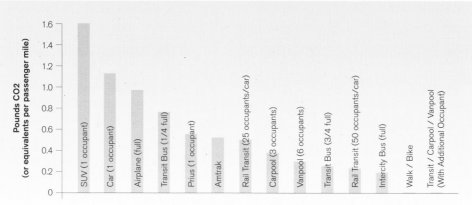

GREENHOUSE GAS EMISSIONS OF TRANSPORTATION OPTIONS

Pounds CO2 (or equivalents per passenger mile)

1.6 · 1.4 · 1.2 · 1.0 · 0.8 · 0.6 · 0.4 · 0.2 · 0

SUV (1 occupant) · Car (1 occupant) · Airplane (full) · Transit Bus (1/4 full) · Prius (1 occupant) · Amtrak · Rail Transit (25 occupants/car) · Carpool (3 occupants) · Vanpool (6 occupants) · Transit Bus (3/4 full) · Rail Transit (50 occupants/car) · Intercity Bus (full) · Walk / Bike · Transit / Carpool / Vanpool (With Additional Occupant)

Transportation Option (per Number of Passengers)

all residents. Many people have medical, job training, and other needs and often have difficulty accessing resources to meet their needs. Affordable and senior housing is best located with close access to schools, libraries, social services, health services, job training, and jobs. This social, cultural, and educational infrastructure is essential for the health of any community. The facilities for these services often can be built as components on the lower floors of affordable or senior housing projects, or within walking or short transit distance.

However, most of our federal and state housing programs finance housing only and make it very difficult to include these neighborhood-scale developments, especially in the same building. Our current HUD programs can be modified to provide financing for the holistic solution to meeting the needs of a community. There are two key impediments to mixed use and mixed income development: mono-use zoning and lack of mixed use and mixed income financing instruments. To encourage communities to develop mixed use zoning, HUD should incentivize communities that receive CBDG and HOME funding to create mixed use compact development zoning codes tied into green multielement mass transportation plans.

Because mixed use financing is more complicated

to underwrite, the financing market, until recently driven by Wall Street underwriting guidelines, has preferred single use products. In fact, most FHA products discourage a mix of uses, as do most federal affordable housing programs such as the Low Income Housing Tax Credit (LIHTC). HUD and the FHA, along with Treasury, Freddie and Fannie (now under federal control), and other sources of federal financing need to develop new mixed use credit enhancement programs, and to eliminate barriers to mixed use and mixed income development inherent in existing programs.

American communities also need new mixed income financing and credit enhancement programs to achieve their visions for their future growth. The HUD HOPE VI program, which redeveloped and revitalized public housing projects and surrounding communities around the country, illustrated the economic and social benefits of income mixing to communities and residents. However, most of our federal housing and community development programs are either aimed at specific income brackets and qualified census tracts or have no income focus but do have cost limits. The first policy often results in the concentration of low-income households, and the second policy tends to support market-rate sprawl development. We absolutely need to develop more affordable housing.

But income targets within most housing financing programs, typically set at 60 percent or below of the area median income, restrict communities from providing or incentivizing development of affordable housing for the broader household types and income brackets living in our communities. Housing policies and programs to address the growing housing crisis, as metropolitan-area populations increase, are critical, particularly in regions with expensive land and construction costs. New rental and for-sale housing finance instruments are needed to target families earning between 60 and 130 percent of the area median income. In high-cost census tracts, this workforce housing often requires some form of subsidy, even for households earning up to 175 percent of the area median income.

Green multifamily buildings in transit-oriented or walkable locations generate only 25 percent of the greenhouse gases that are generated by single-family homes located in sprawling developments. Sprawl also has economic costs: lower-income residents now spend as much on transportation as they do on housing costs. Thus, we must move HUD and FHA programs away from supporting single-family sprawl and toward multifamily mixed use mixed income TOD, which is a better solution for both residents and the environment.

HUD and state programs that set low cost-per-unit limits favor suburban sprawl, for which development costs are lower. Every HUD and FHA program needs to be reviewed and either made location neutral or refocused to support TOD and urban infill. For its existing and new programs, HUD needs to set locational priorities that coordinate with the administration's proposed transit infrastructure programs (T-4), which intend to create a linkage between the funding of new and expanded transit systems and mixed use mixed income development. For example, HUD, DOT, and the EPA could join together to fund a coordinated infrastructure block grant program to support the higher cost of structured parking, improvements to water and sewer utility, and other improvements needed to make TODs work.

No one federal agency currently controls or has the ability to integrate all of the financing and regulatory tools needed for urban revitalization. The LIHTC, New Market Tax Credit (NMTC), and Community Reinvestment Act (CRA) programs lie in Treasury. Economic development programs are in the Department of Commerce. Brownfield cleanup and water and wastewater programs are in EPA. If we are to have an effective coordinated policy to develop our metropolitan regions, either these programs need to be transferred to a reorganized HUD, or there needs to be a clear federal mechanism for program coordination and planning. If we are effectively to coordinate federal resources into comprehensive metropolitan regional strategies that really address our environmental, social, and economic issues and give rise to greener communities, we need a planning framework to create integrated metropolitan regional plans, and to have these summed up in a national plan to rebuild and renew America.

America has reached a crossroads, a time of tremendous opportunity and peril. Both our economy and our ecology are floundering. In the past, we have been misled to believe that each was in opposition to the other. It is now clear that our prosperity depends on both. Building green infrastructure, restoring natural systems, greening our existing buildings, and enriching our communities with social, cultural, and education resources will lead to greener communities, and these will lead to a more prosperous, resilient, and robust future.

The dogmas of the quiet past are inadequate to the stormy present. The occasion is piled high with difficulty, and we must rise with the occasion. As our case is new, so we must think anew and act anew.

—Abraham Lincoln

NOTES

1   See Center for Neighborhood Technology, www.cnt.org.

2   See Center for Neighborhood Technology, www.cnt.org.

3   Jonathan Rose Companies.

43

Jonathan Rose

Ballston, Virginia, overlooking Washington, D.C.

SUSTAINABLE MEGAPOLITAN: HOW LARGE-SCALE URBAN DEVELOPMENT CAN HELP GREEN AMERICA

ROBERT E. LANG AND MARIELA ALFONZO

The United States is increasingly a "megapolitan" nation. Sixty percent of Americans now live within 20 megapolitans—super regions that combine at least two metropolitan areas—which account for just 10 percent of the land area of the United States. This trend is expected to grow, with two-thirds of U.S. population growth over the next 30 years occurring in megapolitans. Thus, megapolitans face the biggest sustainability challenges in the nation. But what exactly does "going green" mean in the megapolitan era? How can we cultivate sustainable communities in the context of ever-growing large-scale urban regions?

Megapolitans have two or more urban cores that are between 50 and 200 miles apart. Megapolitans are larger than both metropolitan areas and combined statistical areas, but smaller than what are now described as megaregions (see the table on page 46). Megapolitans have more than just physical connections, however. They share economic, transportation, ecological, and cultural linkages.

Megapolitan growth becomes even more significant when you consider that the United States is the only developed nation in the world projected to make major population gains to mid-century.[1] The United States reached a population of 300 million residents in 2006 and is on track to reach 400 million in 2039. To put this growth in context, consider that not even China will add 100 million residents by that date. Only India and Pakistan are expected to add more people than the United States by mid-century. The majority of these new U.S. residents will be added to megapolitan areas. In the coming decades, just in its megapolitans,

the United States will gain almost the same number of people as the current population of Germany, the largest European Union nation.

The massive expansion of the United States presents a major sustainability challenge, but megapolitan growth does not have to translate into sprawl. In fact, the current metropolitan development pattern of excessive land and resource consumption will likely have to adapt to a new, more constrained ecological reality. The sustainable urban form response to an increasingly megapolitan United States will be a series of larger nodes and more intensely traveled paths rather than sprawl. These paths and nodes will not be just a practical response to sustainability and energy needs, but also to changing demographic structures and preferences, as only one in five households will have children by 2020. When the nation's population jumped from 150 million in 1950 to 300 million in 2006, most new residents were accommodated by suburban greenfield development at the expanding edge of the metropolis. In contrast, the coming generation of growth, which will add another 100 million people, will mostly be deflected back to built-up places in the form of infill development.[2] A major policy implication of this new urban form is that many of the country's biggest regions now face build out on an unprecedented scale.

Nodes

Some metropolitan areas within megapolitans have already begun to establish and intensify their nodes, and several regions in the United States are rapidly

THE NEW REGIONAL HIERARCHY

Type	Description	Examples
Metropolitan Statistical Area	An urbanized area or principal city with at least 50,000 people plus surrounding counties with a 25% Employment Interchange Measure (EIM) in 2000	Pittsburgh, Denver
Combined Statistical Area	Two or more adjacent micro and metropolitan areas that had an EIM of at least 15% in 2000	Washington/Baltimore; Cleveland/Akron
Megapolitan Area (Defined by Virginia Tech Metropolitan Institute)	Two or more metropolitan areas with anchor principal cities between 50 and 200 miles apart that are projected to have an EIM of 15% by 2040	Sun Corridor, Arizona (Phoeniz/Tucson); Northern California (San Francisco/Sacramento)
Megaregion (Defined by the Regional Plan Association and the Lincoln Institute for Land Policy)	Large connected networks of metropolitan areas that maintain environmental, cultural, and functional linkages	Piedmont; Texas Triangle

approaching the point where they are built out. For example, denser development is already the norm in Southern California. One of the surprising facts in recent discussions of sprawl is the finding that Los Angeles has the highest population density of the census's urbanized areas, exceeding even New York in this measure.[3] San Diego, a region now merging with Los Angeles, is not far behind. The reality is that Southern California is nearly out of developable land.

The area called the Inland Empire—east of coastal Los Angeles—still booms with greenfield growth. But even in this once wide-open space, lot sizes have shrunk to postage stamps, and compact growth is becoming the norm rather than the exception.[4] The problem is that much of the West features what author Bill Fulton refers to as "dense sprawl"—a condition where places achieve high density but are not spatially organized to benefit from concentrated development, as are areas with transit and mixed land uses. But some changes are coming. At Victoria Gardens, in the Inland Empire—a mixed use project in one of the last remaining undeveloped patches of Rancho Cucamonga—residences have pedestrian access to retail. In even more built out Orange County, there are now mixed use lofts in Santa Ana, high rises near the entrance to Disneyland in Anaheim, and transit-

oriented development in downtown Fullerton.

This development pattern is likely to continue as the Southern California megapolitan area squeezes millions of new residents into the urban space that exists today. Southern California, once the poster child for sprawl, is being remade into a vast multicentric urban complex that mixes densities and land uses in a way that resembles neither traditional cities nor suburbs.

Similarly, South Florida is something of the Eastern tropical version of Southern California, at least in terms of its growth patterns.[5] Broward County, north of Miami, has been one of the fastest-growing areas in the United States in the past few decades. County officials estimate that less than 10 percent of its land area is available for future development. In response to its approaching build out, the county "upzoned" much of its remaining open space. The county's long-range planning assumes that only a tiny fraction of new development will take the form of conventional suburbs with large-lot subdivisions and single-family detached homes. After that, Broward will become one large infill project.

The same is true throughout much of South Florida. Given that the region's population could increase by more than 70 percent by 2040, there remains only one option: denser growth. This is already happening.

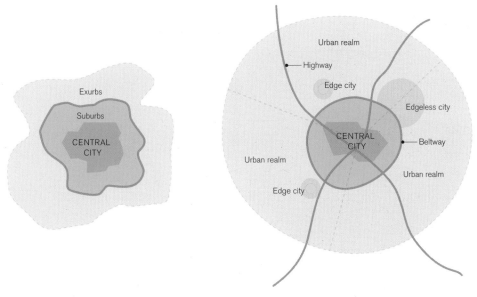

MODERN INTEGRATED METROPOLIS
1930–1970

POSTMODERN
QUASI-INTEGRATED METROPOLIS
1970–2010

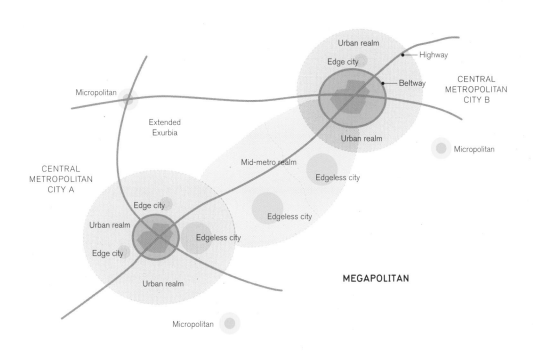

MEGAPOLITAN

At Victoria Gardens—a mixed use project in one of the last remaining undeveloped patches of Rancho Cucamonga, east of Los Angeles—residents have pedestrian access to retail.

Miami now has a forest of high-rise residences along its waterfront (although controversial due to the fragile ecosystem of coastal areas), and towers are under construction in booming suburbs such as Sunrise and Coral Springs, in western Broward County.

South Florida has significant reserves of grayfield space in the form of old malls and warehouse districts. Given the region's land constraints, new construction in these redeveloped spaces will be much denser and could include more mixed uses than existing developments. By 2040, South Florida will be transformed into an urban archipelago, where new cities arise among a sea of older low-rise subdivisions.

Some land-scant megapolitans have taken a proactive stance toward sustainable growth. Rather than solely relying on market trends pushing compact infill development, regions such as Portland, Oregon, and Seattle have implemented land-use regulations to facilitate sustainable development. Both Portland and Seattle have urban growth boundaries (UGBs) that set a higher density standard for inside the boundary and

limit development outside of it. As a result, both areas have been aggressive in utilizing infill opportunities and building more densely within their UGBs.

In fact, Portland's upzoning inside its boundaries, combined with the regional government's growth strategy that includes a transit-oriented development program, has led to several mixed use developments in the area's suburbs, such as the Round, at Beaverton; Central Point, in Gresham; and Esther Short Commons, in nearby Vancouver, Washington. Similarly, Seattle's UGB, together with its Vision 2020, which aims to establish a region of dense, pedestrian-friendly urban nodes linked by transit, has led to projects such as Alley24. It is a LEED Silver adaptive reuse, mixed use project in Seattle's South Lake Union neighborhood, which is linked to downtown by Seattle's streetcar.

Land-use regulations can aid in sustainable megapolitan growth. At the same time, some critics of regulations such as UGBs argue that they artificially limit land supply and inflate demand and hence decrease affordability. However, studies, such as a

Brookings Institution paper on the link between housing affordability and growth management, have concluded that the market is the primary determinant of housing prices.[6] The study also determined that well-devised land-use regulations could actually bolster affordability, compared to more traditional land-use policies. Often, regions with regulations such as UGBs ultimately green-light a greater amount of compact infill development, in contrast to the NIMBYism that typically arises in response to local government approval of large-lot subdivisions in the edge (see also Nelson et al.).[7]

Unlike the Southern California, South Florida, and Seattle-Portland regions, some megapolitans have plenty of room to grow. Megapolitan regions with limited supplies of land readily lend themselves to more-sustainable growth; indeed, land-scant megapolitans must implement creative, progressive land-use strategies, such as mixed use redevelopment. What about megapolitans where there is no built-in pressure for compact growth? What will incentivize megapolitans with virtually unlimited land supplies, where greenfields could technically be developed all the way until mid-century, to adopt sustainable community development strategies?

First, changing market and demographic realities will greatly reduce the amount of exurban development in the coming decades—even in places where no barriers to such growth exist. Also, the recent spike in energy prices drove up transportation costs, making commuting from the edge more costly. Despite the recent global plunge of oil prices, price volatility is to be expected, and ultimately, the long-term prospects of energy scarcity and rising private transportation costs will significantly dampen demand for conventional suburbs in the coming decades.

For example, even regions such as Atlanta, where plenty of land remains for sprawling development, are seeing a dramatic rise in urban living as households seek closer-in residences. Downtown Atlanta alone has added more than 10,000 housing units over the past 10 years and is projected to add more than 4,500 additional units by 2011. Additionally, Midtown

Atlanta, the area north of downtown, contains about 30 percent of the city's high rises. Midtown also houses Atlantic Station, the new multibillion-dollar mixed use transit-oriented development built on a former brownfield site. The development won the EPA's Phoenix Award for the Best National Brownfield Redevelopment in 2004 and was listed in the Sierra Club's America's Best New Development Projects in 2005.

The Dallas–Fort Worth region has also adapted to changing market trends. Dallas saw a dramatic increase in downtown housing, including luxury condominiums and trendy lofts. Over the past 10 years, downtown Dallas has added approximately 5,700 units and is projected to add another 800 units by 2011. Victory Park, located near the West End Historic District of downtown, is one of several large mixed use developments that have come on line recently. Victory Park is connected to two lines within the Dallas Area Rapid Transit (DART) system. Compact development within the Dallas–Fort Worth region is not limited to just its core. For example, the once low-density suburb of Plano, Texas, has a station stop on the DART system and dense transit-oriented development.

Paths

So far, we have discussed the various types of nodes within megapolitan areas and the differing techniques and rationales by which they are being intensified. However, promoting mixed use redevelopment and higher density, pedestrian-friendly development is only one part of how megapolitans can grow sustainably. New and intensified nodes have to be linked with alternative forms of transportation in order to effectively reduce our ecological footprint. The new Obama administration is pushing for major infrastructure investments. For example, we are likely to adapt European high-speed rail at the megapolitan scale. Plans exist for high-speed rail between Washington, D.C., and Baltimore, which would make the D.C. to Baltimore commute faster than that between D.C. and some of the more distant station stops on the Metrorail system, such as Gaithersburg, Maryland. This type of high-speed rail would create more effective and

Robert E. Lang and Mariela Alfonzo

efficient linkages between metropolitan areas within megapolitans and intensify already existing economic linkages within them. Moreover, a high-speed rail network would provide location advantages to station stops, which would serve as alternatives to airports as high-speed rail journeys replace short-haul flights. On the whole, high-speed rail networks would further promote sustainability.

Light rail is another way to link nodes within and between the metropolitan areas of megapolitans. For example, the Silver Line of the Washington, D.C., Metrorail System, which will extend to Tysons Corner, Reston, and Dulles Airport, in Virginia, has already been approved and could be completed as early as 2016. Additionally, a Purple Line that will connect two existing suburban stations—Silver Spring and Bethesda—in Maryland, is being pushed as a green commuting alternative. Both the approved Silver Line and proposed Purple Line would create new nodes, connect existing nodes, and most significantly, facilitate the intensification of various nodes within the metropolitan region. In anticipation of the metro system extension, Tysons Corner has already put together a plan that encourages mixed use, transit-oriented development. This will effectively create a larger-scale extended form of the Wilson Corridor, in Arlington—one of the most successful models of building around rail. As such, a county once synonymous with sprawl will take on a more complex and sustainable structure and include a more diverse mix of land uses and densities than was seen in a previous generation.

Implementation, Urban Design, and Community

Refocused development—in the form of intensified, compact nodes and alternative pathways linking them—is helping megapolitans "go green." But what are the challenges of creating denser compact growth? What do these nodes look like? What do they represent? How do they transform our ideas of community? There are many practical implications of, as well as more ethereal connotations related to, higher-density mixed use redevelopment, which practitioners, advocates, and policy makers must better understand in order

Arlington, Virginia, overlooking Washington, D.C.

to cultivate communities that are truly sustainable in ecological, economic, and social terms.

An increasing number of new, distinct nodes are emerging across many megapolitans, particularly in the form of mixed use projects. Many of these are redevelopment projects in core, inner suburban, and mature suburban counties. In numerous instances, mixed use redevelopment projects are transforming once derelict or economically blighted sites—such as grayfields (failing commercial centers and malls) and brownfields (contaminated sites)—into thriving and dynamic gathering places. Given Pricewaterhouse-Coopers' estimation that more than one in five U.S. regional malls are failing, grayfield redevelopment has taken hold over the past decade.[8] Dozens of obsolete suburban malls have been transformed. These developments, such as Santana Row in San Jose, California, typically cost from $50 million to $750 million and cover more than 50 acres; and they include a mix of residential (for sale and lease), retail, office, civic, hospitality, and entertainment uses. While not all grayfield sites may be suitable for mixed use redevelopment, viable sites provide the potential to create new neighborhoods within existing mature suburbs; in effect, they can aid the sustainable growth of megapolitans.

Both grayfield and brownfield mixed use redevelopment are certainly in line with the sustainable development strategies outlined here: promoting intensified, compact, pedestrian-friendly nodes that are linked by alternative transportation pathways, and taking advantage of megapolitan growth and market trends. It is important to note, however, that we do not yet know how these new mixed use centers will evolve.[9] With grayfields, for example, the assumption is that adding a residential or office component to previously single-use retail helps to increase the sustainability of these centers. But retail centers are notorious for requiring constant renovation and upkeep. Retail trends cycle approximately every five years, and the half-life of a retail center is said to be approximately 15 years. Lack of attention to retail trends is often what led to the demise of a retail center in the first place.

If a mixed use center were to fail, for residents it would be more problematic than if they just lived *near* failed shopping centers.[10] In the case of mixed use centers, there may be multiple residential (condo) owners living directly on top of the retail component, which is often held by one entity. Residential owners are likely to have a personal long-term stake in their property investment, but developers or real estate investment trusts (REITs) may have shorter-term property holding strategies, which can range from five to 10 years. For the former, it's a home; for the latter, it is an asset to be held or traded. If the retail component within a mixed use center changes hands or is mismanaged, it is likely that *all* the retail will be affected, as is the case with failing suburban regional malls—only now there will be people living directly above, making it more than just a property value issue.

The bottom line is that mixed use is not quite a de facto sustainability strategy. Despite potential challenges, mixed use centers still hold the promise of increasing the sustainability of growth, especially megapolitan growth as described here. As such, it is important for public officials and planners to take a proactive stance by anticipating and addressing potential challenges that redeveloped mixed use centers could face and establishing policies that address, and possibly avoid, potential difficulties that could arise as mixed use centers evolve.[11] For example, creating ordinances that establish standards for maintenance, signage, and design could help assure the upkeep of the center and ward off potential future disinvestment by owners. Additionally, establishing guidelines for flexible and responsive urban design—such as varied retail floorplates and diversity of uses—can help ensure the sustainability of new mixed use centers. Further, business owners and residents within the mixed use centers could forge formal or informal partnerships that could serve as open forums to discuss mutual interests and concerns. Such a partnership could be structured as a mix between a business improvement district and a home owners association that would protect both sets of interests. In the end, the sustainability of redeveloped mixed use centers will depend on the commitment by the developer and management, the "proactiveness" of public officials and planners, partnerships between businesses and residents, and the flexibility and upkeep of the design of sites.

Another potential challenge of redevelopment remains dense sprawl. Earlier we noted that a number of megapolitan areas are intensifying, including Atlanta, Dallas–Fort Worth, South Florida, and Southern California. But as with mixed use, density in and of itself does not automatically equate with sustainability. From the standpoint of sustainability, as megapolitans such as Atlanta and Dallas–Fort Worth continue to grow, it is not sufficient for development to merely be dense and compact. For example, in the case of some high-rise condo developments, residents may still be very auto-dependent, even for simple errands such as getting milk at a grocery store. Further, some dense developments have been criticized in terms of their built environment. Small residential lot sizes, while compact, can lead to garage-dominated, homogeneous streetscapes. Expanding megapolitans that are adopting compact growth strategies need to also create accessibility to shopping, employment, schools, and the public realm; provide a multimodal environment in which to access these diverse uses; and establish urban design guidelines that promote human-scaled, pedestrian-friendly, dynamic environments.

Beyond the question of implementation, both in terms of mixed use and density, there is the issue of what these newly formed or intensified nodes mean for sustainability and community. Many emerging nodes within megapolitans are walkable, livable, people-friendly places. The best nodes strive to establish both functional and emotional connections with the community, by serving practical needs as well as fulfilling social functions.[12] Retail has become a significant part of this equation, especially as far as establishing the appropriate, sustainable retail mix for the community. In fact, many of the retailers within these new nodes act as third places —not the home, which is the first place, or work, which is the second place, but the places where people can gather outside of the pressures of home and work.[13] These are not

Santana Row in San Jose, California.

necessarily third places in the way that Oldenburg originally envisioned, such as the early 20th-century English pub or Austrian tearoom. Instead, these third places may take on the shape of the local Starbucks, Barnes & Noble, bar, or simply a lively and active "public" space. They are quasi-public realms acting as new urban living rooms.

People may begin to experience a sense of "urban vitality," or dynamic, within these nodes,[14] akin to what Jane Jacobs described in *The Death and Life of Great American Cities*.[15] People go to these nodes to socialize and experience both planned and unplanned events and interactions, and they go often. People may start to recognize faces and have chance encounters with other people they know or spontaneous interactions with people they do not know. They may also start to recognize and casually interact with shopkeepers or become regulars at the local coffee shop. People may become attached to these nodes. Also, people *walk* within these places. Often, nearby residents walk *to* these places or take transit. These activities, feelings, and behaviors may move beyond sense of community, a residential phenomenon centered around homogeneity, to instead represent a reenergized "urban-ish" public life. The true meaning of these nodes may be more broadly related to creating a sense of liveliness or dynamic "urban" livability in intensified and emerging areas within megapolitans. To the extent that these places fulfill community and social needs, they are helping us to make great strides toward sustainable megapolitan growth. In the end, recognizing megapolitan emergence is not advocacy for sprawl or business as usual; regions that evolve sustainably will prosper over places that continue to sprawl.

NOTES

1 R. Lang and A. C. Nelson, "America 2040: The Rise of the Megapolitans," *Planning Magazine* (January 2007) 7–12.

2 Ibid.

3 R. Lang, "Open Spaces, Bounded Places: Does the American West's Arid Landscape Yield Dense Metropolitan Growth?" *Housing Policy Debate* 13, no. 4 (2002): 755–78.

4 Lang and Nelson, "America 2040: The Rise of the Megapolitans."

5 Ibid.

6 A. C. Nelson, R. Pendall, C. J. Dawkins, and G. J. Knaap, "The Link Between Growth Management and Housing Affordability: The Academic Evidence" (Washington, D.C.: The Brookings Institution Center on Urban and Metropolitan Policy, February 2002).

7 A. C. Nelson et al. "Growth Management and Housing Affordability—Do They Conflict?" in *The Link Between Growth Management and Housing Affordability: The Academic Evidence* (Washington, D.C.: Brookings Institution Press, 2004).

8 PricewaterhouseCoopers, "Greyfield Regional Mall Study" (2001).

9 M. Alfonzo, "A Mall in a Former Life: How Converting Failing Malls into Mixed-Use Neighborhoods Impacts Sense Of Community" (unpublished dissertation manuscript, University of California–Irvine, 2007).

10 Ibid.

11 Ibid.

12 Ibid.

13 R. Oldenburg, *The Great Good Place* (New York: Marlow, 1999).

14 Alfonzo, "A Mall in a Former Life."

15 J. Jacobs, *The Death and Life of Great American Cities* (New York: Random House, 1961).

Robert E. Lang and Mariela Alfonzo

CONSERVATION MEANS DEVELOPMENT
AS MUCH AS IT DOES PROTECTION.
I RECOGNIZE THE RIGHT AND DUTY OF
THIS GENERATION TO DEVELOP AND
USE THE NATURAL RESOURCES OF OUR
LAND; BUT I DO NOT RECOGNIZE THE
RIGHT TO WASTE THEM, OR TO ROB,
BY WASTEFUL USE, THE GENERATIONS
THAT COME AFTER US.

—THEODORE ROOSEVELT, 1910

Galisteo Basin Preserve, New Mexico

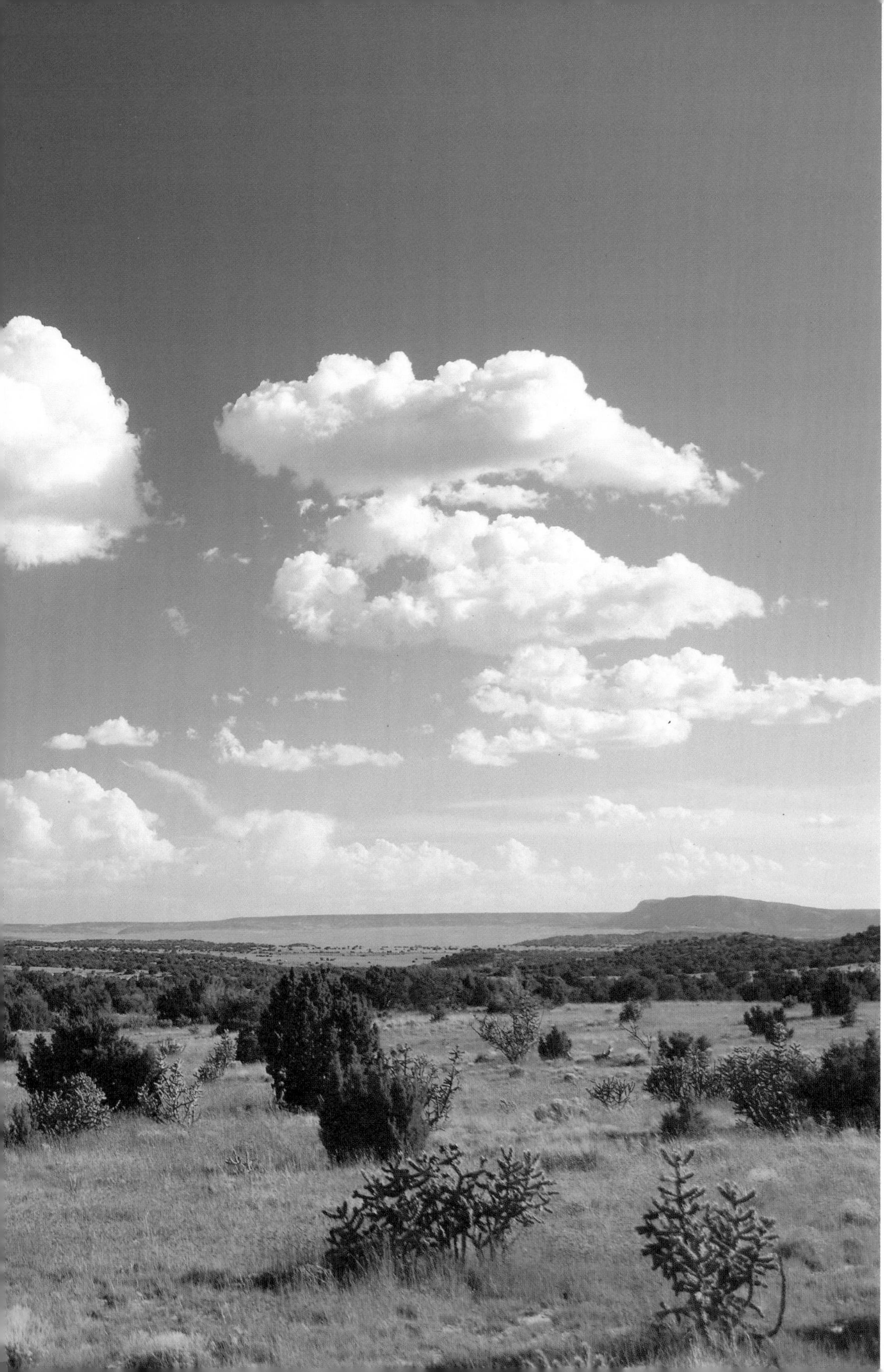

With its very large-scale mixed use development and innovative energy-generation systems, Viikii, Finland, is practically a laboratory for executing the ideas that underpin the concept of green community.

GREEN COMMUNITIES AND THE REDEFINING OF COMMUNITY WEALTH

TIMOTHY BEATLEY

One of the alarming dimensions of the current economic crunch is just how illusory our economic wealth and assets seem to be. Market systems that assign a value to things based on consumers' and investors' willingness to pay and highest and best economic use are always subject to such vagaries, but when the value of homes and stock portfolios and retirement accounts plummets so precipitously, and so unexpectedly for most, this shocks us to the core. And there are many real and tangible implications for the quality of life and life planning of the many individuals and families who have relied on these usual measures of wealth.

Should we begin to explore a different notion of assets, one that comprises the less illusory, perhaps less volatile and more resilient, stock of things, patterns, and relationships in our communities that have *lasting* and *enduring* value, irrespective of the more fleeting economic and market values that might be placed on them? Indeed, the essence of green communities, their essential qualities and design and planning elements, is about building this more *durable* stock of community and environmental assets.

The thinking here is analogous to the new thinking about macroeconomic measures such as the gross domestic product (GDP). Some years ago, Redefining Progress, a California-based think tank, unveiled an alternative calculation of macro-level progress, called the Real Progress Indicator (RPI). The RPI corrected for the perverse and undesirable things counted by the GDP, such as expenditures to clean up pollution, and added in good things not usually counted by GDP, such as volunteer labor. The result was a different

numeric peg and also a new and different way of thinking about progress itself. It turns out that rising GDP belies level, or even declining, real progress under an RPI calculation.

Perhaps there is a similar metric of community wealth—*true* or *real* community wealth—that might help us weather the economic shocks and global vicissitudes faced by communities today and better understand how green communities and green community planning can work to bring about the truly valuable elements that make up resilient and sustainable communities.

What would make up this portfolio of real, less transitory community assets? And how would the design and building of green neighborhoods and communities help in accumulating those assets that really matter, that provide enduring value?

We might start with healthy, functioning ecosystems and all the natural services provided by them. There are many services associated with these natural systems that can be valued in economic terms, of course. In economically difficult times, the services of a tree, a neighborhood forest, or a wetland and riverine system become even more important. Natural breezes and the shading and evapotranspiration benefits keep neighborhoods tolerably cool in times when the energy and dollars to run air-conditioning may be difficult to find. And a neighborhood wetland, urban stream, or series of rain gardens is especially important in times when more-expensive engineering-based solutions to flooding may be beyond reach.

These natural systems and features often harbor

immense biological diversity, and they are important neighborhood and community assets in themselves. As sources of wonder and amazement, they have the potential to reconnect us to larger systems of life, to insert a degree of wildness into our daily existence, and in the process to bring the human species together to cherish and celebrate this immense antiquity around us. These are not the usual assets taken into account, to be sure, but they are ones that have the most potential to elevate, inspire, and cultivate meaning and purpose beyond our own limited and narrow self-interest.

Perhaps, then, another more accurate way to gauge our real assets is to develop an understanding of how connected we are to the nature and landscapes that ultimately sustain us. "Biophilia," a term coined by Harvard myrmecologist and conservationist E. O. Wilson to describe the extent to which humans are hardwired to need connection with nature and other forms of life, ought to guide our design of neighborhoods and living environments in the future.[1] The evidence is mounting that daily contact with nature provides tremendous therapeutic and restorative benefits. Test scores are higher in schools with abundant natural daylight; worker productivity is higher in buildings with natural ventilation and other green features; a walk in a natural setting delivers tremendous benefits in mood enhancement.[2] We are happier and healthier the more we are able to live our lives in direct contact with nature. And the greener our neighborhoods are, the more nature there is around us, the more we are propelled to be active and outside creatures and the more socializing we engage in as well.[3]

Every neighborhood and urban district has the potential to be profoundly more biophilic. Many of the most impressive efforts have been in European cities and neighborhoods: the stream daylighting in Zurich, Switzerland; the extensive regional green network in Helsinki, Finland; the 80-kilometer-long Green Ring that encircles the City of Hannover, Germany, providing large blocks of forest and green space, in combination with a compact transit-oriented urban form, in close proximity to all residents. Investments in bike and pedestrian networks, moreover, make

access to the larger spaces and natural landscapes beyond neighborhoods remarkably easy, as in the case, for instance, of the Green Cycle Routes in Copenhagen, Denmark.

We often overlook the most important things around us. The sounds of birds and tree frogs and cicadas in the summer months, the ever-spectacular cloudscape, and the nighttime sky are among the most special. We commonly ignore or disregard the daily sights, sounds, smells, and other sensory cues that places are imbued with (not all of which are natural, of course). We lack the ability to name or even recognize common species of trees and birds and flowers. The features of the natural world tend to drop off the radar of things that we value; they rarely are tallied in any standard community asset statement or comprehensive planning map, nor is our disconnection from them. Yet in many ways, they are the building-block assets of community and place.

That children are growing up today in a denatured, mostly indoor world is fairly obvious to most. In his wildly popular book *Last Child in the Woods*, journalist Richard Louv documented the many causes of what he refers to as "nature deficit disorder."[4] Television is an old culprit, but there are also the computer, generally sedentary lifestyles, apprehensive parents (who have what Louv refers to as the "bogeyman syndrome"), and the trend of overscheduling the lives of our kids, among other factors. Can one measure the enduring value of a place by the extent to which it allows—indeed, encourages—kids to be outside and in close daily contact with the natural world? We design communities in part to protect our children from dangers; we strap our children into their car seats—yet we have failed to create places where they will develop a closeness with nature, a love for nature and for being outside, and a lifestyle that is active rather than passive. Green communities can and should be designed in ways that raise healthy free-range kids.

How much time residents of a community spend outside is perhaps another important dimension of wealth. There are many benefits—biophilic, emotional, and physical health, and greater connectedness to

Copenhagen, Denmark, which pedestrianized many downtown streets in the early 1960s, has become a model of a livable city.

people and place. At the same time that we acknowledge the importance of living in dense, compact cities and towns, we should also recognize that a form of measurable wealth can be found in places that value the outdoor life. Even in cities in relatively harsh climates, outdoor living is possible. Examples abound, in Australia and Scandinavia, for instance. Copenhagen underwent a transition to a walking, strolling outdoor city. Yet when plans were made to pedestrianize the Strøget, Copenhagen's initial walking street, there was much skepticism. "The Danes are not the Italians," it was said. But the naysaying was rebuked, and among other things, the city adopted a unique and effective policy of gradually but consistently converting downtown parking—at a rate of 2 to 3 percent each year—to pedestrian space. Today, the season of outdoor eating has been extended well into winter, and if you sit down at a restaurant in the pedestrian district, you are as likely as not to be handed a blanket along with your menu.

Another important community asset is time. Americans don't seem to have much of it, and we have trouble slowing down; green communities offer some hope of making this easier. It is perhaps not surprising that the Slow Food movement has its origins in Italy, where strolling and pleasurable eating are fine arts and

essential elements of community life. We may find it hard to fully emulate the Italian lifestyle, but there is something to be said for a sensibility that values time with family, time in the community, and time spent walking and strolling in the civic realm. One of the interesting offshoots of Slow Food is a network of Italian cities that call themselves Città Slow. While they are concerned with food, they have a broader agenda that emphasizes strengthening all things unique and special about a place, slowing cars and traffic, and the many ways in which communities can enhance quality of life. This philosophy and outlook lead to seeing and appreciating things in new ways.

Even the more work-oriented Dutch and Germans have a different set of priorities about time than do people in the United States. Vacationing is the most obvious example, with workers receiving a mandated and generous minimum number of weeks off. There is also maternity and paternity leave, generous leave to care for an ill relative or aging parent, and a life philosophy and perspective on time that attaches more validity to time spent in these economically less-productive ways.

The concept of "time-affluence" and time-affluent communities is promoted by organizers of the yearly Take Back Your Time Day in the United States and

Las Ramblas in Barcelona, Spain, reverses
the familiar hierarchy of the street. Here,
pedestrians dominate the center while cars
are pushed to narrow lanes at the edges.

Canada.[5] While time in many cases is money, the two are quite different. Many of the most enriching and enduring aspects of our lives cannot be purchased with anything other than time and interest. Being a good neighbor, helping an elderly member of the community, spending time with children and family, growing food in a neighborhood garden and then enjoying it in the form of a neighborhood dinner—all these things require time. Time-affluence is certainly a profoundly different outlook on community wealth.

There are many ways in which green design and planning can help to expand the collective pool of time. Reducing the dependence on car commuting and car trips generally can deliver time equity. If we can design new neighborhoods to discourage cars and car ownership, if we can invest in transit, pedestrian spaces, and bicycle facilities, if we can arrange communities to facilitate sharing, of both burdens and material goods, we will have more time for community, people, and nature. As L. B. Pierce notes, "Perhaps the most dramatic time savings in livable towns occurs in families with children. Parents can give up their part-time jobs chauffeuring their kids to school, extracurricular activities, and friends' homes. Children can walk, bicycle, roller blade, or use their scooters to get to where they want to go. This eliminates a dead activity (driving) for both parents and children, who then use their own motion power rather than ride in a car."[6]

Time often translates into greater ability to form personal relationships and become engaged in the communities in which we live. Robert Putnam has famously argued that sprawl, car dependence, and commuting have served to diminish the time Americans have available to spend on civic activities. He has even put forth a rough equation: for every 10-minute increase in commuting time, he believes there is a 10 percent drop in time spent on civic and community life. With the rise of car ownership and car-oriented culture, we've seen a form of mobility and commuting of a highly individualistic nature, not very conducive to conversation or social community building—or place appreciation, for that matter. If we

are able to emulate the design and planning of many of the best European green communities, the return in the form of collective, or civic, time may be considerable.[7]

The European models of green urbanism compellingly show the possibilities of lives lived with profoundly smaller ecological footprints, yet with a high degree of richness and fulfillment. In the neighborhoods of Freiburg, Germany, Vitoria, in Spain, and Leiden, in the Netherlands, the ideal of smaller homes with little or no individual garden space is embraced, and the trade-off for this kind of housing is the beauty and vibrancy of large public parks and civic spaces. The experiences of these towns show the possibilities of richer lives with fewer material things, and they show a way to transition from a life centered around things to a life centered around people, relationships, and community.

Perhaps there are ways to give tangible expression to these alternate perspectives on time? Erecting signs that declare that you are about to enter a Slow City might be one way, but there are others: displaying a metric of how many hours of volunteering have been given during the year in a particular community, or how much time on average kids are able to spend outside at play. We have been good at preparing pedestrian maps that draw the five-minute walk radius, but this is not very ambitious. Perhaps we need to develop wholly new concepts for displaying the time losses associated with living in particular types of neighborhoods and the time gains of green communities. This is a real community asset, but largely invisible and traditionally undervalued.

The value of programs and initiatives that nudge us to slow down and connect more deeply to the places we live in and the people around us are important to recognize. Again, cities and green neighborhoods in Europe have been more likely to do this, and there are abundant examples of the benefits. In Stockholm, for instance, there is now a program for training and certifying nature guides, and some 200 individuals have gone through this program. On any given weekend, residents there are tempted with a nature walk—a chance to learn about a special natural site, to learn more about their ecological home—guided by someone who has been trained not only about the environment but also in effective ways to convey this information. In the district of Hammarby Sjöstad, in Stockholm, an ecology center makes green living more interesting and fun, provides resources and workshops that help people to overcome inertia, and visits all new residents as they move in, subtly tempting and guiding them to consider the ease of car-sharing, bicycling, nature walks, and recycling.

These green communities can also help us to relearn the art of human sharing. This can take other forms than car-sharing and bike-sharing, common in European cities and now finding application in the United States. The common house in Danish cohousing, the sharing of tools in the Dutch *centraal wonen* (central living), and the sharing of common meals in both cultures offer physical forms and structures in which less is needed for a rich life. In Australia, toy libraries—run by either community groups or municipal councils, are a brilliant strategy for reducing the consumption and material flow associated with this particular aspect of Western consumption. There are toy libraries in every country: there are some 1,000 in the United Kingdom alone. There are not many in the United States, but there are some—for instance, in Pittsburgh and Cleveland. All of these examples show the possibilities of creating formalized systems for sharing things not usually shared.

Moderating the space demands of the car and designing communities around outside pedestrian living not only strengthens the social realm, it often creates spaces for important activities—such as growing food—that are also useful in enhancing the long-term resilience of these communities. The trend in green European neighborhoods has been to design-in from the beginning spaces for growing food in the neighborhood—for example, in Viikki, in Helsinki, and Oikos, in Netherlands. As the number of Americans utilizing food stamps has recently hit an all-time high, and as the price and availability of food become significant issues for many Americans, having spaces in which to grow food will become

another important aspect of the new understanding of our community assets. The move in the direction of pedestrian neighborhoods, then, will have the added benefit of enhancing resilience in the face of many different kinds of shocks: the rising price of food and growing insecurity of food supplies, rising oil prices, and the many impacts associated with global warming and a changing climate.

Even in dense urban settings, many green communities place high importance on the integration of gardens and food production in and around living environments. And they often do so in some creative ways. The ecological neighborhood GWL-Terrein, in the Westerpark district, in central Amsterdam, has been designed to minimize the impact of private cars, through commitment to transit and bicycling and walking, but also by making most of the spaces of this fairly dense neighborhood car free. The result is space for other things—including 120 community gardening plots—and both the opportunity and reason to be outside, interacting with other residents and other families. Such garden spaces can help to break down social and cultural barriers between people and can help to forge friendships and lasting social relationships.[8]

The extent and quality of the human relationships that exist in a community are another important kind of asset, an important stock of wealth, but again one not commonly highlighted or mapped in the planning process. We know, from increasing empirical evidence, that stronger and deeper and more extensive friendship patterns are helpful in weathering the trials and tribulations of life, and they are a major element in a meaningful life. Strong friendships and personal relationships actually make us healthier and better able to withstand the shocks and vicissitudes of life. The deeper and more extensive the network of close friends, the lower the mortality rate from cancer, for instance. Friendship patterns and social capital of various sorts have been shown to be important in recovering from disaster events. Yet just as evidence is mounting about the value and personal resilience friendships bring, we seem to be becoming even more socially isolated in the United States.[9]

While we should not overestimate the role of the physical environment, there is little question that sustainable urban design and planning can create the physical conditions and opportunities for socializing and for starting and building friendships. We perhaps need to rethink the larger networks and systems of pedestrian spaces in communities as another key asset, in terms of combating social isolation and providing spaces to support activities that tend to bind us together as a people and culture—the spaces for political rallies, parades, and civic events of many kinds, but also the spaces to just be together as fellow human beings. This is potentially an essential antidote to the aloneness that characterizes much of American society.

Green communities offer the hope of providing a new abundance of time, and a deeper perspective on time and on the steady arc of time over the ages. A longer temporal outlook may be an especially steadying asset in a period that seems economically and socially shaky. Most things in the natural world operate on long cycles and much of the planning we do—community and natural—requires a longer time frame than we currently adopt. We are too often treading water, it seems, lucky to have saved that building, improved that intersection, modified that development in some small way—without much sense of how or in what ways these small (though not insignificant) actions add up to something larger. A longer, wiser sweep of time allows us this perspective.

These, then, are not the usual ways to think about assets and wealth—individual or community—but they are really at the heart of the movement toward green communities. Resilience and self-sufficiency, ecological and personal health, connectedness to place, friendships, and public life, and ultimately, a greater, deeper meaning to life have always been at the core of sustainability. The paradigm of sustainability has always been about shifting our priorities from the more material—the quantity of things we possess, the size of our homes, the extent of our economic wealth—to the larger quality of our lives, the extent of our relationships, and the broader health of our communities. These perilous economic times have simply served to reinforce the illusory nature of conventional notions of wealth; the move toward green communities and neighborhoods might best be viewed as a profoundly cautious recalibrating of how we measure our well-being and security.

NOTES

1   E. O. Wilson, *Biophilia* (Cambridge, Mass.: Harvard University Press, 1984), and "Biophilia and the Conservation Ethic," in S. R. Kellert and E. O. Wilson, eds., *The Biophilia Hypothesis* (Washington, D.C.: Island Press, 1993).

2   For a review of the evidence, see T. Beatley, *Native to Nowhere: Sustaining Community and Place in a Global Age* (Washington, D.C.: Island Press, 2004).

3   E.g., Peter Schantz and Eric Stigell, "How Does Environment Affect Walking-Commuting in Urban Areas?" paper presented at 12th Annual Congress of the ECSS, 11–14 July 2007, Jyväskylä, Finland; see also Timothy Beatley, *Native to Nowhere*, Island Press, 2004, for a full review of the literature in this area.

4   R. Louv, *Last Child in the Woods: Saving Our Children from Nature-Deficit Disorder* (Chapel Hill, N.C.: Algonquin Books, 2005).

5   J. de Graaf, ed., *Take Back Your Time: Fighting Overwork and Time Poverty in America* (San Francisco: Berrett-Koehler, 2003).

6   L. B. Pierce, "Time By Design," in de Graaf, ed., *Take Back Your Time.*

7   R. Putnam, *Bowling Alone: The Collapse and Revival of American Community* (New York: Simon and Schuster, 2000).

8   L. Bartolomei et al., *A Bountiful Harvest: Community Gardens and Neighborhood Renewal in Waterloo* (Sydney: University of New South Wales Faculty of the Built Environment, 2003).

9   M. McPherson, M. E. Brashears, and L. Smith-Lovin, "Social Isolation in America: Changes in Core Discussion Networks over Two Decades," *American Sociological Review* 71 (June 2006): 353–75.

FURTHER READING

Brand, S. *The Clock of the Long Now: Time and Responsibility.* New York: Basic Books, 1999.

Dean, T. "Finding Devonian," in *Living with Topsoil: Tending Spirits, Cherishing Land.* North Liberty, Iowa: Ice Cube Press, 2004.

Kellert, S. *Building for Life: Designing and Understanding the Human-Nature Connection.* Washington, D.C.: Island Press, 2006.

Persson, B., ed. *Sustainable City of Tomorrow.* Stockholm: Formas, 2005.

Pyle, R. *The Thunder Tree: Lessons from an Urban Wildland.* Boston: Houghton Mifflin, 1993.

Sanders, J., and K. Van Lengen. "Making Sense: The MIX House," *Architect,* May/June 2008.

FINDING COMMON GROUND: HISTORIC PRESERVATION AND GREEN BUILDING

RICHARD MOE, WITH PATRICE FREY

While it is inarguable that we face a climate-change crisis, the reality is that we can't consume our way out of it—we must *conserve* our way out. Within the planning and design community, the field of historic preservation offers particular insight into the practice of resource conservation in the built environment. Historic preservation is primarily concerned with the protection of irreplaceable cultural resources, including buildings, monuments, and landscapes. What is perhaps less evident, however, is that historic preservation is also inextricably linked to the responsible management of *natural* resources. Our cultural treasures include everything from the majestic landscapes of the American West—no doubt falling into the natural resource category—to buildings and other structures whose construction required a significant investment of natural resources.

Over the past 25 years, the National Trust for Historic Preservation's Main Street Program has led the preservation-based revitalization movement by serving as a clearinghouse for information, technical assistance, research, and advocacy. Between 1980 and 2005, local main street programs rehabilitated 96,283 buildings and yielded $18.3 billion in total reinvestment. In the past 10 years alone, federal tax credits for historic rehabilitation have incentivized the reuse of over 217 million square feet of commercial and multifamily residential buildings. This represents a significant reinvestment in our nation's older buildings and communities.

Yet there is a widespread perception that historic preservation and conservation of the environment have little in common and that in fact preservation is an obstacle to going green. For example, preservationists typically advocate the retention of original features of buildings such as historic wood windows, which may run afoul of efforts to install new energy-efficient replacement windows. And in some instances, efforts to increase density, particularly near mass transit, can conflict with the protection of smaller historic buildings.

The National Trust launched its Sustainability Program in 2007 in order to address these challenges. The program is guided by four principles of sustainable stewardship. First, the reuse of existing buildings reduces the amount of demolition and construction waste deposited in landfills, lessens the demand for new energy and other natural resources needed to construct new buildings, and conserves the energy originally expended to create the structures.

Second, reinvestment in older and historic communities has numerous environmental benefits. Older and historic communities tend to be centrally located, dense, and walkable, and are often mass-transit accessible—qualities promoted by smart growth advocates. Reinvestment in these communities also preserves the energy expended in creating the existing infrastructure, such as roads, water systems, and sewer lines.

Third, retrofits of historic buildings can and should be undertaken to extend building life and better capture the energy savings available through newer technologies. Such retrofits can be done with great sensitivity to the existing historic fabric—for example, research indicates that historic wood windows can be

Restored buildings in Rivers Park, in Troy, New York

repaired and weatherized to be nearly as efficient as new energy-efficient windows.[1]

Finally, respect for the lessons older and historic buildings and communities teach us is an important component of the Sustainability Program.

Accompanying these principles is a commitment to reconsider long-standing preservation practices as they relate to sustainable development efforts.

Reuse of Buildings

While the transportation sector accounts for 32 percent of America's carbon emissions, 43 percent come from building operation. This percentage does not even include the carbon that is generated by extracting, manufacturing, and transporting building materials.[2] Since nearly half of the carbon sent into the atmosphere comes from buildings, any solution to climate change must include being wiser about how we design and use buildings.

We often think of the environmental impacts of buildings in terms of the power needed to heat, cool, and light them. The energy needed to power buildings is significant. But constructing buildings is also an energy- and resource-intense activity, and for this reason we can think of buildings as vast *repositories* of energy. It takes energy to manufacture or extract building materials, more energy to transport them to a construction site, and still more energy to assemble them into a building.

Many assume that the energy and carbon expended in manufacturing building materials and constructing a new green building is offset by its efficient operation.

In fact, a recent study from the United Kingdom found that it takes 35 to 50 years for an energy-efficient new home to recover the carbon expended in constructing it.[3] No matter how much green technology is employed in its design and construction, any new building represents a new impact on the environment. The greenest building is very often the one that already exists.

Reinvestment in Older and Historic Neighborhoods

While building reuse represents an important means of reducing carbon emissions and the use of natural resources, reinvestment in older neighborhoods offers a means to capitalize not only on the embodied energy and carbon in existing buildings but also on the infrastructure that serves buildings. Older and historic neighborhoods offer additional environmental advantages as well.

In recent years, land has been developed in the United States at a rate approximately three times that of the population growth rate. And for much of the post–World War II era, Americans have built communities that are accessible *only* by vehicle.

Communities that were established prior to World War II and the widespread adoption of the auto-mobile offer a valuable alternative to the sprawling suburbs of more recent years. As with new transit-oriented development, reinvestment in older urbanized areas takes advantage of existing and inherently sustainable features and reduces pressure for sprawl on the urban fringe.

Retrofits of Older and Historic Buildings

There is a common misconception that historic buildings are energy hogs. In fact, some older buildings are as energy efficient as many recently built ones. When the General Services Administration examined its nationwide buildings inventory in 1999, it found that utility costs for historic buildings were 27 percent less than for more modern buildings.[4] Data from the U.S. Energy Information Agency suggest that buildings constructed before 1920 are actually more energy efficient than those built between 1920 and 2000.[5]

The relatively superior performance of historic buildings is due largely to difference in construction methods. Many historic buildings have thick, solid walls with thermal mass that reduces the amount of energy needed for heating and cooling. Buildings designed before the widespread use of electricity often feature transoms, high ceilings, and large windows for natural light and ventilation, as well as shaded porches and other features to reduce solar gain. In the past, architects and builders also paid close attention to siting and landscaping as methods for maximizing sun exposure during the winter months and minimizing it during warmer months.

Nonetheless, there are many instances in which historic buildings do not use energy efficiently or cause other environmental impacts that must be addressed. In some cases, alterations made over the years to historic buildings have made buildings less energy efficient than they were originally. Sometimes, older heating and cooling systems simply do not perform as well as their modern counterparts. But an increasing number of green rehabilitation projects demonstrate that older and historic buildings can go green.

Respect for Heritage Buildings and Communities

We can learn a lot from heritage buildings and communities, which were constructed using traditional practices that allow man-made places to exist in harmony with the natural environment. With the advent of new materials and technologies, we have lost touch with many of the building lessons of the past.

Unlike their more recent counterparts that celebrate the concept of planned obsolescence, older buildings were generally built to last. Most older buildings were constructed so that their individual components, such as windows, could be easily repaired or replaced when necessary. Because of their durability and repairability, these buildings have almost unlimited renewability. This is not a feature of many buildings constructed today. There is also much to be learned from traditional communities that were constructed before the automobile took over our roads. These places offer a

Historic Millwork District, Dubuque, Iowa.

vision for how our cities and towns could function in a post–auto-dependent world.

A spirit of innovation and enthusiasm is evident among green building professionals, which is both exciting and encouraging. It is clear that lessons from history, however useful, will not be enough to solve all of today's problems. But innovation in the green building and planning arena must be grounded in the hard-learned design lessons of the past.

Local Innovation in Sustainable Preservation
A number of cities lead the way in developing policies that acknowledge the vital role building reuse and neighborhood reinvestment must play in efforts to reduce carbon emissions.

Perhaps no single city is doing more than Dubuque, Iowa, to reuse older buildings, reinvest in urbanized areas, and retrofit buildings as part of its sustainable development policy. Through the Sustainable Dubuque Program, the city has launched the Dubuque Historic Millwork District project to revitalize a 17-block neighborhood that once served as the city's mill-working area. The district contains approximately one million square feet of space, much of it in warehouses, that are currently underutilized and energy inefficient.[6]

The project includes the development of an Energy Efficiency Zone (EEZ) pilot program. The EEZ program, similar to the establishment of an Enterprise Zone, will make assistance available to an existing defined neighborhood to encourage energy-efficient redevelopment of the area. Building owners in the EEZ will be eligible for technical assistance on greening their buildings, as well as grants and low-interest loans. The EEZ will also be home to a Zero Solid Waste pilot project, which will seek to dramatically reduce waste deposited in landfills.

There are significant economic and social dimensions to the Millwork project, as well. The city and its partners see revitalization of the district as key to attracting high-quality jobs and new residents to the area. According to the City of Dubuque, "this pedestrian friendly, urban cultural atmosphere creates a 'Live, Work, and Play' product that will promote the values of economic development, workforce recruitment, and energy efficiency to the growing number of individuals that place value on these components."[7] Social and cultural values are also promoted by the retention of the rich historic fabric of the neighborhood.

San Francisco is unique in directly addressing the density-preservation dilemma described earlier. The city touts its green building ordinance, introduced in 2008, as the most progressive in the country. It requires LEED Gold certification of every private project over 5,000 gross square feet, beginning in 2012. Developers who demolish buildings and build new structures must meet additional, more stringent requirements. For example, if an owner demolishes a building, the project must earn 10 percent more LEED credits than would normally be required. When a new building triples the density of the demolished structure, 8 percent more credits are required under the LEED system. If density is quadrupled, the point penalty is 6 percent of total LEED credits.[8]

Above: Adobe Building, South of Market, San Francisco. Below: The Garretson, Woodruff & Pratt & Co. Building, a reused warehouse on the University of Washington campus, Tacoma, Washington.

The point penalties for demolition are somewhat arbitrary since they are not based on a rigorous assessment of the relative environmental benefits of building reuse versus density increase. However, San Francisco appears to be the first community to begin to grapple with the value of reuse relative to density. The city offers a model to other communities that will inevitably face the challenge of balancing increased density with the value of conserving the existing building stock.

The City of Tacoma, Washington, is among the more progressive in developing policy that is favorable toward reuse.[9] The city recently released a climate action plan that establishes the reuse and recycling of buildings as a strategy for addressing global warming. It noted that "using older buildings for new purposes should be encouraged by city policy."[10] While more is needed in the way of substantive recommendations to implement this strategy, Tacoma remains a leader among cities in calling out the reuse of buildings as a goal.

Tacoma's focus on reuse may be reinforced by a stronger demolition ordinance, now in development. This ordinance will require review of all permits issued for buildings over 50 years of age and provide an opportunity to determine whether a structure is historically significant and should be listed on the Tacoma register. Structures listed on the register cannot be demolished. This proposed policy change is designed to reduce the number of teardowns of historic homes and other buildings. As they have in other cities in the United States, many homeowners in Tacoma have decided to demolish their older homes in order to build new, usually much larger, homes.[11]

While teardowns present an enormous challenge for those concerned with retaining community character, they also present environmental concerns. Tacoma's demolition ordinance is therefore motivated not only by an interest in historic preservation but also by concerns about landfill waste and the negative environmental impacts associated with new construction.

Conclusion

Preservationists are often accused of being sentimentally fixated on the past and out of touch with modern needs. Yet by its very nature, preservation is strongly future oriented. Preservation's goal is to ensure that the historic built environment—our legacy from the past—survives so that future generations can experience it, learn from it, and be inspired by it.

This focus on the future is at the very core of sustainable development, which will drive the remaking of towns and cities in the coming decades. While preservation does not hold all of the answers, the tradition of sustainable stewardship, which preservation has always embraced, and the knowledge that preservationists have gained from decades of experience can be of enormous help in the sustainability-oriented transformation of the built environment.

NOTES

1   B. James et al., "Testing the Energy Performance of Wood Windows in Cold Climates: A Report to the State of Vermont Division for Historic Preservation and the Agency of Commerce and Community Development" (Burlington, Vt., 1996), p. iv.

2   Pew Center on Climate Change, "Building Solutions to Climate Change," *In Brief* (November 2006), www.pewclimate.org/docUploads/Buildings-InBrief.pdf.

3   Building and Social Housing Foundation and Empty Homes Agency, *New Tricks with Old Bricks* (London, 2008).

4   U.S. General Services Administration, *Financing Historic Federal Buildings: An Analysis of Current Practice* (Washington, D.C.: Office of Business Performance, Public Building Service, General Services Administration, 1999).

5   U.S. Energy Information Agency, "Consumption of Gross Energy Intensity for Sum of Major Fuels for Non Mall Buildings" (2003), www.eia.doe.gov/emeu/cbecs/cbecs2003/detailed_tables_2003/2003set9/2003pdf/c3.pdf.

6   C. Steinhauser and T. Goodmann, "City of Dubuque, Iowa, Power Fund Pre-Application" (2008).

7   Ibid.

8   "Chapter 13C: Green Building Requirements," San Francisco Building Inspection Commission Codes (2008), www.sfenvironment.org/downloads/library/sf_green_building_ordinance_2008.pdf.

9   Green Ribbon Climate Action Task Force, "Tacoma's Climate Action Plan" (Tacoma City Council, 2008), www.cityoftacoma.org/Page.aspx?nid=674.

10   Ibid., 18.

11   For more detail about teardowns, see www.preservationnation.org/issues/teardowns.

MANAGING DEVELOPMENT TO CREATE SUSTAINABLE COMMUNITIES

DOUGLAS R. PORTER, FAICP

Growth Management: A Viable Framework?

Today's revolutionary campaign for achieving sustainable development rivals the late 1960s onset of innovations in community planning and regulation that became known as "growth management" programs. Traditional planning and zoning efforts had proved inadequate for guiding the development of desirable communities and urban regions. Many American cities and towns had originated with planned layouts that promised grandiose versions of old-world urbanity but more often served as marketing tools for selling platted lots. Few founders of such places paid much attention to long-term, changing needs as communities grew. As urban areas matured, civic leaders made sporadic attempts to improve roads and build parks, civic buildings, schools, and other accoutrements of urban life.

The bill for lax control of development came due during the 1960s, when backlogs of infrastructure improvements put pressure on local tax bases and raised taxpayer animosity to continuing development. Rachel Carson's *Silent Spring*, published in 1962, sparked environmental concerns that eventually led to passage of the National Environmental Policy Act, which became law in 1970. In 1973, the report of the national Task Force on Land Use and Urban Growth concluded that "It is time to change the view that land is little more than a commodity to be exploited and traded."[1] Dissatisfied with ineffectual zoning and lax implementation of planning goals, public officials sought greater influence over the development process by inventing and applying more powerful techniques for controlling urban growth and change. Innovations such as zoning for open space conservation, drawing boundaries to contain growth, and requiring developers to contribute to public facility systems allowed public officials more opportunities to affect the direction and quality of community expansion. "Growth management" became the mantra for guidance of community development in the public interest.

The term "growth management" may now seem outmoded, superseded by popular new models of planning and design, such as "smart growth" and "new urbanism." However, as conceived, the term described a comprehensive, decisive public process for guiding development in a strategic, hands-on manner. "Decisive," in the sense of replacing vague, poorly enforced plans and easily amended regulations with more-focused public requirements: "Build here, save natural resources there"; "cluster near available or planned public services"; "provide basic infrastructure as part of developments." (The Smart Growth tenets widely propounded in recent years represent restatements of common aims of growth management.) The strategic, hands-on approach of growth management called for shaping a comprehensive policy consensus on the composition, qualities, and locations of future urban development, linked directly to regulatory and action programs to implement that policy framework.

Simply put, growth management programs represent a proactive, more nuts-and-bolts form of development control than conventional comprehensive planning and regulation represented. Briefly, such programs propound a dynamic public, governmental process that aims to plan for development and change and act on those plans; an inclusive process for anticipating and determining an appropriate balance among competing development goals, to accommodate future needs; and a forum for addressing and reaching agreement on local and regional interrelationships.

Typically, growth management programs encapsulate a rich heritage of public measures for guiding growth and change, which have multiplied over the years. The programs aim for firm governmental exercise of local powers to guide future development, through various types of policies and techniques.

One technique is to guide locations of expected development by designating areas within existing neighborhoods and at the growing edge of jurisdictions where plans for urban development will be supported by zoning and subdivision provisions, infrastructure improvements, revitalization efforts, and other public actions. For example, jurisdictions such as Sarasota County, Florida, Lexington-Fayette County, Kentucky, and Lincoln, Nebraska, have adopted growth or urban service boundaries to serve this purpose.

Targeted development can be supported by identifying centers of development and redevelopment, and by pursuing public actions to assemble developable sites and provide financial and other incentives for development, especially in declining neighborhoods, obsolete or brownfields areas, and desirable nodes of activity at the urban edge. Pittsburgh is one of many cities and towns that carry out ambitious revitalization programs.

Another option is to shape future development

by requiring its phasing according to available public services and infrastructure, and by influencing the location and quality of development in extra-jurisdictional areas through annexation policies and interjurisdictional agreements. The intergovernmental agreement between Boulder, Colorado, and Boulder County exemplifies actions by many Colorado jurisdictions to coordinate annexation and development policies.

Open space and natural resources can be protected by preserving and restoring environmental qualities within and outside urban areas, through planned land acquisition, set-asides within developing areas, and programs such as transferable development rights. Other steps include protecting production qualities of agricultural and forested areas and establishing environmental threshold standards by which to evaluate proposed developments. Anne Arundel County, Maryland, Lincoln, Massachusetts, and Bellingham, Washington, are protecting open space by these methods.

Green building practices can be encouraged by establishing standards to guide design and construction of new and renovated properties—including public buildings—to improve energy efficiency, water and landscape conservation, indoor air quality, use of recycled and durable materials, and locational qualities that promote sustainability. Austin, Texas, and Pasadena, California, have been particularly successful in promoting green building practices through incentives and requirements.

Timely, efficient provision of infrastructure can be

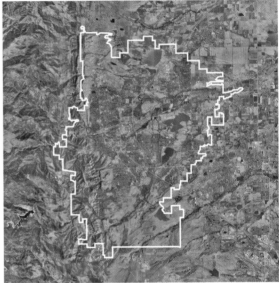

facilitated by preparing plans and identifying financing sources to maintain adequate infrastructure systems to meet capacity standards as development takes place. This includes evaluating potential use of exactions, impact fees, special taxing districts, and tax-increment financing to augment public infrastructure investments. The Denver region is funding and carrying out a dramatic program of rail transit construction linked to development, and Arlington Heights, Illinois, has employed a variety of financing techniques to revitalize its downtown, centered on a new train station.

Another step is to retain, improve, and restore community qualities by preserving and improving desirable living and working environments through techniques such as mixed use zoning, allowance of planning and design options and incentives, preservation of historic districts, design review procedures, economic revitalization, and social equity programs. Arlington, Virginia, and San Jose, California, operate successful programs to spur use of many of these techniques.

Finally, collaborative relationships with regional and state agencies can be improved by establishing representative, functional, and coordinative connections between local jurisdictions, regional agencies, and state programs. For example, the Denver and San Diego regional agencies play important roles in guiding development by establishing close working relationships with local jurisdictions and state agencies.

In structuring growth management approaches, communities pick and choose among these types of programs, tailoring them in accordance with their particular concerns. They may weave them into comprehensive or special plans and incorporate them in zoning and subdivision regulations or separate laws. Also, many, if not most, of the initiatives require close interaction with other departments and jurisdictions and with organizations such as housing and conservation groups. Watchwords for effective growth management are: *connections* (across jurisdictions and among economic, social, and physical components of communities); *choices* (to meet needs of a variety of people, households, businesses, and organizations);

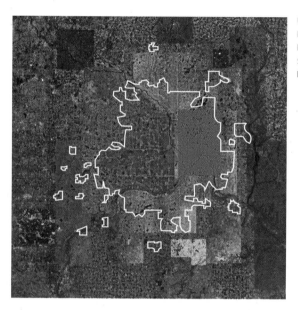

Urban Growth Boundaries: Portland, Oregon (from 67.16 km high), Boulder, Colorado (from 27.84 km high), Twin Cities region, Minnesota (from 180.98 km high).

Douglas R. Porter, FAICP

and *collaboration* and *coordination* (among those people and organizations).

Leaping the Legal Hurdles

Examples of these growth management initiatives came into being in the 1960s, through individual efforts by local governments to curb or control rapid development. However, since the U.S. Supreme Court's finding in 1926 that upheld zoning as a valid form of regulation by the Village of Euclid, Ohio, the balancing of governmental powers to regulate land use and private property owners' rights remains controversial. Local governments had gained legal authority for zoning from state legislation to regulate real estate development by use of the police power to protect the health, safety, and general welfare of citizens. Under the police power, local governments can severely limit private property owners' rights to use of property, although courts have established legal constraints to safeguard private property rights. In the late 1960s, communities such as Ramapo,

New York, Petaluma, California, and Boca Raton, Florida, expanded their legal control over the timing, phasing, and amount of development, testing the outer limits of the police power. A string of supportive court decisions laid the foundation for widespread use of growth management practices. But attempts to ratchet up public requirements for development still generate push-back legal challenges by property owners and developers, some of which have curtailed certain practices.

Court cases offer only one side of the story, however. Although legal challenges persist, increased regulation of development is resisted as much or more through political arm-twisting—over zoning changes, for example—or by property-owner resistance to upping tax rates to pay for new schools or infrastructure expansion, or rezoning to allow construction of affordable housing in certain neighborhoods. The old truism still holds: political will is the main driver of effective growth management.

Moving into the New Age

Over almost a half century, many communities across the nation have honed and refocused growth management programs and practices to deal with contemporary issues of urban and metropolitan growth and change. As the nation's concern for developing in a more sustainable manner has escalated, two strong concepts for managing growth have gained attention from urban designers, planners, and policy makers. One is the importance of conserving and restoring natural resources as development rebuilds existing cities and continues to surge into the countryside; this requires a conscious search for a sustainable future. Although the green movement may falter for a time as the economy supports less construction, green seems here to stay as a factor in sustainable development—and has become an important goal in managing growth.

The second important concept is a renewed respect for fostering memorable urban design—a turning toward the creation of pleasing, multipurpose urban environments. This move recognizes urban design as an important, even *the* important determinant of satisfactory urban development.

The two trends are interrelated, of course. They respond to issues of global warming, species preservation, economic and social equity, and other aspects of a sustainable way of life. And both trends benefit from significant shifts in the makeup of urban populations, which have generated millions of small and older-aged households interested in city rather than low-density suburban living environments.

Meshing Environmental and Urban Values

Decades ago, Ian McHarg's *Design with Nature* called for maintaining the ecological integrity of growing urban areas by limiting the impacts of development on the natural functions of landscapes, habitats, and hydrologic systems. Many designers have followed this maxim, especially in planning for small- and large-scale residential and office park developments, where designers take care to preserve and make accessible for human enjoyment stream corridors, woodlands, and other natural features. Architect William McDonough's firm carries this practice even further, essentially integrating the form, character, and infrastructure of proposed developments with the area's ecology, as revealed by his design for the village of Coffee Creek, in Indiana.

Certainly, conservation of natural features is in the air. Planners and nature lovers in many urban regions are advocating the creation of green infrastructure systems threading through urban areas and into the countryside—such as hiking and biking trails along natural corridors linking to parks and other open areas—creating access to green spaces for urban and rural dwellers. Conservation organizations have succeeded in raising funds to preserve large natural areas outside growing cities, and national, state, and local programs require protection of other natural areas and features. Still, it seems that much more can be done to acknowledge the significance of resource conservation.

Rediscovering Growth Management

For planners and designers, recent decades have been exciting times. The nation's changing demographics and apparent wealth are attracting residents back to cities, sparking revitalization in many communities. New development projects in cities and older suburbs, many of them superbly designed, demonstrate the economic viability of a fascinating variety of living and working environments. From this experience has come an impressive number of attractive models of development for emulation elsewhere. However, the prevailing patterns of continuing suburban development are increasingly viewed as unsustainable in a world challenged by increasing pollution and climate change. Following historic patterns, growth continues to spread into jurisdictions unready and often unwilling to control it—until it is too late.

Furthermore, the prescriptions offered to address unsustainable development patterns should not be viewed as cure-alls. Smart growth principles and regional visions that look impressive on paper are effective only when defined into actionable measures. For example, the admonition to build "compact, mixed use" development must move beyond a one-size-fits-all simplicity to interpret the terms for the specific place and time. Frequently this is where the process disintegrates, as differences resist agreement. Green development standards have been seriously implemented in only a minority of communities and for a small proportion of development; moreover, most standards are still evolving, and few give much attention to locational issues. Supporters of new urbanist design appear to insist that function follows form; they discount matters such as interjurisdictional interests and social and economic equity as virtually irrelevant to the built environment. Nevertheless, these concepts add strength to the discussion of the ways and means to manage urban development.

However, the plenitude of evolving approaches to guiding growth reconfirms the importance of constructing strong policy and implementation frameworks for community and regional development—frameworks that connect the dots of individual initiatives. This is the job of the growth management paradigm. The arduous, finicky process of managing growth may seem inadequate to address sustainability in a time of rapid change, especially when some communities apply growth management devices—for example, moratoriums due to infrastructure inadequacy—mainly to limit or avoid growth. But with few exceptions, sustainable design and development seldom flourish in poorly managed development environments.

The undeniably critical but difficult task of providing strong direction for community development requires that community leaders be energized to think boldly about guiding development and to insist on design qualities that will promote sustainable goals while meeting the market, thus harnessing growth in the cause of creating great communities.

NOTES

1   W. K. Reilly, ed., *The Use of Land: A Citizen's Policy Guide to Urban Growth*, task force report sponsored by the Rockefeller Brothers Fund (New York: Thomas Y. Crowell, 1973), 6.

PETROLEUM SPRINGS AND COAL
MINES ARE NOT INEXHAUSTIBLE BUT
ARE RAPIDLY DIMINISHING IN MANY
PLACES. WILL MAN, THEN, RETURN
TO THE POWER OF WATER AND WIND?
OR WILL HE EMIGRATE WHERE THE
MOST POWERFUL SOURCE OF HEAT
SENDS ITS RAYS TO ALL? HISTORY WILL
SHOW WHAT WILL COME.

—AUGUSTINE MOUCHOT, 1870

Middelgrunden, Denmark

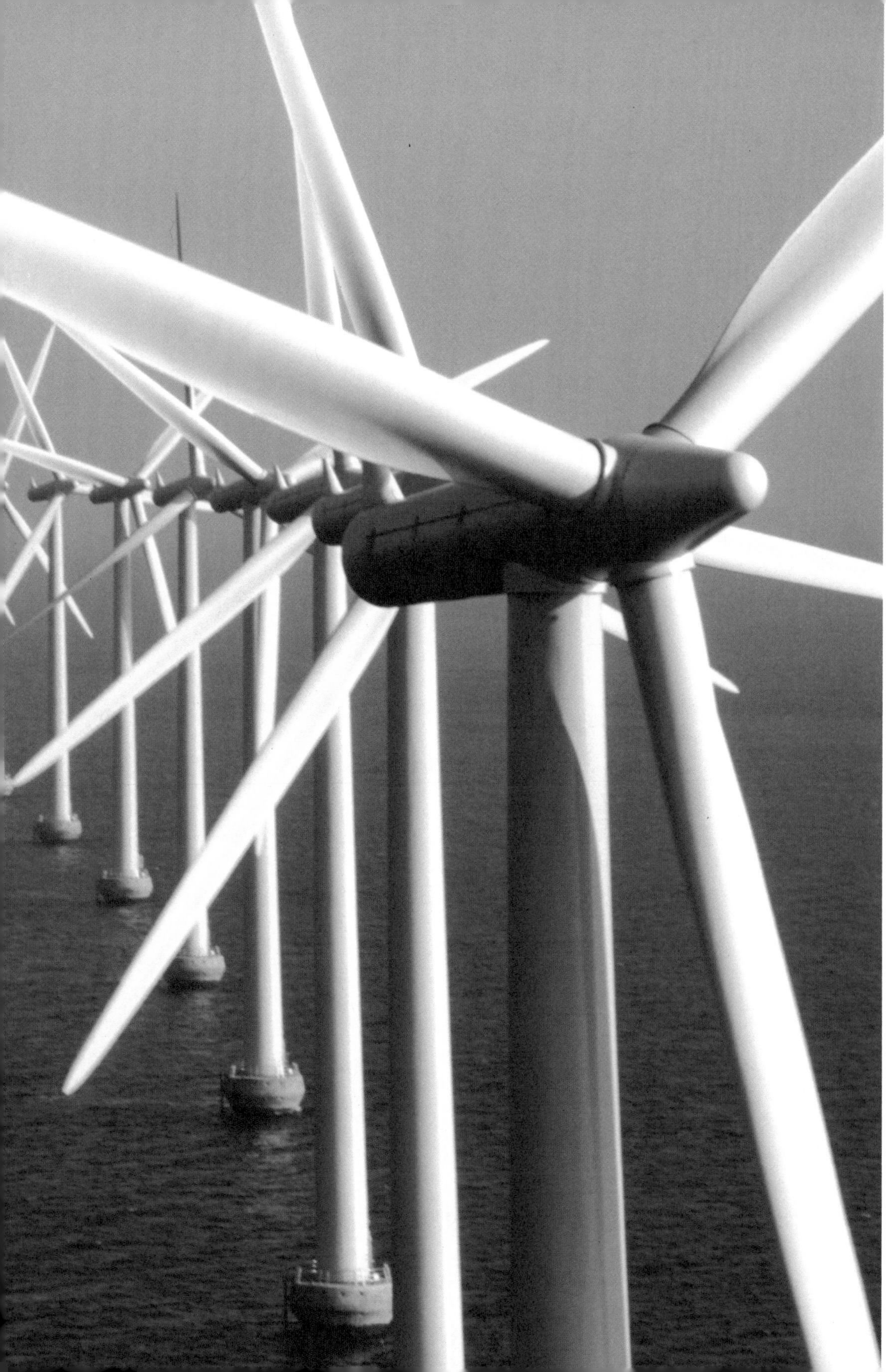

ENERGY AND COMMUNITIES

WILLIAM BROWNING

The form of communities is intimately tied to energy. Our towns and cities rely on energy for the modern essentials of lighting, heating, and cooling, but also to provide the basic services that make dense settlements possible, including clean water, sanitation, and transportation. Prior to the extensive use of fossil fuels, the energy for these services was predominantly supplied by the sun, wind, flowing water, wood, or muscle. While issues of energy have become an urgent theme in modern community planning and design, their influence on urban forms can be observed in ancient cultures around the world.

More than 2,500 years ago, citizens of the Greek city of Preine decided to move their community to higher ground after it had been flooded multiple times. The new city was planned with streets aligned along an east-west axis, giving all homes an equal opportunity for solar access. Buildings were designed to capture maximum solar heating in the winter months, with south-facing courtyards and two-story structures along the northern side of the courtyard that blocked winter winds; in the summer, shading was provided by overhangs and high walls.[1] A nearly identical configuration can be seen in the streets and houses in the *hutongs* (older neighborhoods) of Beijing and other communities in northern China.

Many ancient cities were dependent on wood as a primary fuel—so much so that deforestation triggered severe energy and ecological crises, ultimately contributing to the collapse of civilizations such as the Maya in Central America and the great cities along the Tigris and Euphrates rivers. In ancient Rome, as locally available wood became scarce, the Romans made increasing use of *heliocaminus* (literally "solar furnace") rooms: south- or southwest-facing rooms that used mica or glass as glazing to trap heat. The heat generated by these rooms was so crucial to the comfort of their homes that laws were created to guarantee that no home could shade a neighbor's *heliocaminus*. The evolution of solar technologies has made this principle relevant again: in the early 1980s, solar access laws were enacted in communities in California and Colorado to protect solar panels from shading.

Designing communities for effective solar heating requires thinking in three dimensions. Urban setback codes, such as those written in the 1920s for Manhattan skyscrapers, usually address sunlight access to the street but stop short of providing for passive or active solar energy strategies. Addressing this gap, Ralph Knowles at the University of Southern California School of Architecture has developed the concept of solar envelope planning, the aim of which is to produce a three-dimensional space over a lot that will capture at least three hours of midday sunlight and not block the sun for adjoining lots. Using computer simulations of the development of Indian pueblos, such as Taos in northern New Mexico, he and his students have found that the larger multifamily structures exhibit forms that roughly match a computer-generated solar envelope.

Just as heating requirements can drive the form and development of communities, the need for summer cooling can be influential. Connected, covered walkways occur in many cultures' vernacular architecture, and street trees have long been prized

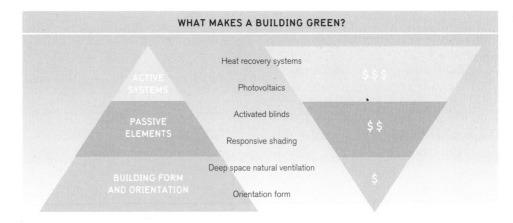

WHAT MAKES A BUILDING GREEN?

ACTIVE SYSTEMS

PASSIVE ELEMENTS

BUILDING FORM AND ORIENTATION

Heat recovery systems

Photovoltaics

Activated blinds

Responsive shading

Deep space natural ventilation

Orientation form

$ $ $

$ $

$

for both aesthetics and their cooling effects. Perhaps more intriguing are built features that channel wind as a natural cooling mechanism. In many regions of Iran, wind-catching towers called *bâdgir* have been constructed for about 500 years, based on earlier "wind scoops" from more than 2,000 years ago. Traditionally made of mud brick, the towers catch wind from one or more directions, absorbing heat in their walls as the air descends. Some towers channel the breeze through underground passages, to be further cooled by the surrounding earth and then released in plazas with fountains, which provide additional evaporative cooling. Examples of this passive cooling strategy can still be found in use in Middle Eastern communities today.

Some modern communities are revisiting these ancient passive strategies to effectively temper the built environment, while saving energy. In Hangzhou,

China, Xihu Tiandi is a "festival marketplace" under construction on the shore of the historic West Lake. The development includes the adaptive reuse of historic buildings and the addition of four- and five-story restaurant and retail structures. To temper the outdoor spaces, air is moved through underground earth tubes and then delivered into courtyards, where it interacts with multistory water features. The falling water creates a breeze and further moderates the temperature. This design strategy lowers the outdoor air temperature by 10 to 15 degrees Fahrenheit during the summer and increases it by about 10 degrees in winter. It also uses 80 percent less energy than would have been required to enclose and air-condition the entire complex.

On a larger scale, municipal codes in Freiburg, Germany, regulate new buildings to preserve passive cooling opportunities for the community as a whole.

The city, located in the Rhine River valley, experiences a regional wind pattern known as the *Hoellentaeler,* which arises from the nearby Black Forest. To ensure that these cooling summer breezes are not blocked by new development, the size and shape of buildings on certain key streets have been regulated since the 1990s.[2] Likewise, in Hong Kong, the international engineering firm Arup is working with the city's housing authority to create new high-rise models that preserve natural ventilation opportunities. As typically built, the city's dense skyscrapers tend to create a windbreak for the coastal breezes that would provide natural cooling in this tropical climate. The use of computational modeling techniques is now giving designers the ability to experiment with the orientation and configuration of buildings, allowing them to maximize wind benefits. This project in the Upper Ngo Tau Kok estate will inform future development strategies by the housing authority, which provides public housing for 50 percent of Hong Kong's residents.[3]

In the 1980s, a number of solar developments were able to greatly reduce the energy use of individual homes, notably La Vereda Compound in downtown Santa Fe, New Mexico, and Wonderland Hills, a solar subdivision in Boulder, Colorado. While highly commendable for reducing energy use, in general these developments did not challenge conventional land planning. One community that did embrace modern solar design at the core of its town planning was Soldier's Grove, a small rural town of 600 people in southwest Wisconsin. Like Preine, the town had experienced catastrophic flooding, prompting the community to move to a new site in the early 1980s. With local ordinances requiring solar access protections, stringent thermal performance, and 50 percent solar heating for commercial buildings, the town was the nation's first solar village and for a while, had one of the highest concentrations of solar buildings in the United States.[4]

One of the earliest private developments to be shaped by an intensive neighborhood-level energy program was Village Homes, in Davis, California, developed by Michael and Judy Corbett starting in 1975.

Village Homes' plan minimizes energy consumption through integrated transportation, landscaping, and infrastructure strategies.

The neighborhood's drainage system, also the first of its kind in California, uses passive strategies that require minimal pumping energy, while also conserving water.

With 240 homes on 70 acres, Village Homes took a comprehensive approach to conservation and renewable energy. Homes were oriented on an east-west axis for maximum solar potential, and solar heating was used on every building in the neighborhood, with impressive results: these systems provide 50 to 80 percent of the annual heating load of each home, even using 1970s technology.

Beyond the utilization of solar, the planning of Village Homes minimizes energy consumption through integrated transportation, landscaping, and infrastructure strategies. The pedestrian-oriented master plan was based on Radburn, New Jersey, a 1920s "new community" that explored the separation of cars and pedestrians. The plan of Village Homes resembles two sets of fingers interlaced: one a network of pedestrian paths, the other a network of streets. All houses face onto pedestrian greenways, and it is possible to reach any point in the neighborhood without crossing more than one street. There are 23 acres of parks, vineyards, orchards, and community gardens sprinkled throughout the neighborhood fabric, as well as community buildings and playgrounds. In addition to providing open space, the landscape plan includes pedestrian commons where all landscaping is edible: fruit- and nut-producing trees and shrubs. The neighborhood is bounded to the west by organic community gardens, which sell produce to restaurants in the nearby cities Sacramento, San Francisco, and Berkeley. This neighborhood-based food production, both commercial and small scale, indirectly lowers the development's total energy footprint by reducing transportation energy consumption.

In addition to reducing the emphasis on cars, the innovative planning of Village Homes' street network had ancillary benefits in terms of energy. Instead of building streets to the Davis standard of 32 feet wide, streets in the neighborhood were narrowed to 24 feet, the width required for two fire engines to operate side by side in the event of a major fire. By narrowing the street, less impervious surface was created, with more room for planted areas. Within ten years, mature trees already shaded the streets and lowered the ambient air temperature by 10 to 15 degrees Fahrenheit. In a climate that reaches 113 degrees Fahrenheit during the summer, the significant difference means that less energy is needed for air-conditioning in the neighborhood.

The neighborhood's drainage system, also the first of its kind in California, uses passive strategies that require minimal pumping energy, while also conserving water. Integrated with the street and landscape plan, the system consists of shallow surface swales with small check dams and infiltration basins located in the pedestrian greenway zones. The system is designed so that water cycles through within a six-day period—an important length of time to prevent mosquitoes from hatching. By keeping stormwater out of the wastewater treatment plant, the system indirectly conserves energy. With about one-third of stormwater percolating into the ground, the development also uses about half the irrigation water of a normal subdivision in that area; in a state where 20 percent of annual energy consumption is attributed to the pumping of water, the impacts of this "upstream" conservation are significant.

At the time, the city engineer for Davis did not think such an alternative system could work. In fact, he initially rejected it, saying that it would attract vermin—to which the Corbetts responded that if "vermin" was the engineering term for wildlife, they hoped they would succeed. The city required the Corbetts to put up a performance bond to prove that their drainage system would work. The proof came three years later, when Davis had a hundred-year storm event. Village Homes' was the only drainage system that actually functioned correctly; all the others failed. The system not only worked but also saved $800 per lot, which enabled the neighborhood's vineyards, community gardens, and community spaces to be built at no additional capital cost.

Village Homes was built for middle-class residents; houses were initially priced at $40,000 to $60,000 and ranged in size from 800 to 1,800 square feet. In 1976, however, the local real estate agents thought that the neighborhood was just too strange and refused to show homes there, claiming that the houses would not hold value. Twenty years later, these houses sold for a premium of $23 per square foot. In recent years, when houses have come on the market, they have sold in less than a third of the market average time. The development is now seen as an enlightened model of pedestrian-oriented, low-energy town planning.

While we continue to learn from past models, the most exciting new community developments will literally rewire the relationship between buildings and energy. In Sydney, Australia, Newington is a community built to serve as the Olympic Village for 15,000 athletes and coaches during the 2000 Summer Olympic Games. It consists of three neighborhoods each within a five-minute walk to a village green as well as a 300,000-square-foot commercial center. Located on the site of a former munitions depot that was restored to its native savanna ecology, the buildings at Newington were built not as temporary structures but as permanent houses to be occupied in stages after the Games. Great care went into the choice of building materials and energy-efficient design, with integral rooftop photovoltaic systems on many of the homes. These systems, financed by the New South Wales Sustainable Energy Development Authority and Pacific Power, each generate one kilowatt of electricity. As a result, Newington as a whole is one of the largest building-integrated photovoltaic systems in the world and is being used as an experiment in "distributed generation"—an energy system made up of multiple small-scale producers and consumers. In this type of grid, buildings of the future might be either producing or consuming electricity at any given time. This kind of distributed system will be the next step in the evolution of electric utilities.

Building on the new paradigm of the distributed energy grid, the "net zero energy" movement looks at buildings and communities as potential net exporters of energy. With a combined strategy of highly efficient buildings and on-site renewable energy generation, a net zero energy building or community produces more energy over the course of a year than it consumes from fossil fuel sources. Most of the early examples of this model were individual buildings, such as the Lovins house in Snowmass, Colorado, the Fraunhofer

In Sydney, Australia, Newington is a community built to serve as the Olympic Village for 15,000 athletes and coaches during the 2000 Summer Olympic Games.

ENERGY AND COMMUNITY GREENING

THOMAS L. DANIELS

The United States has about 3 percent of the world's population, accounts for about one-quarter of global energy consumption, and yet has no national energy policy. Some 80 percent of the energy Americans consume each year comes from nonrenewable fossil fuels—coal, oil, and natural gas. Oil powers more than 90 percent of the nation's transportation networks. But America has only 3 percent of the world's proven oil reserves. The nation reached its peak oil production in 1970 and now imports nearly two-thirds of the 21 million barrels it consumes each day. Moreover, the economic costs are high. Oil imports in recent years have made up more than $200 billion of the annual U.S. trade deficit. This is clearly not sustainable.

Coal provides slightly more than half of the nation's electricity. But coal is a major source of particulates, sulfur dioxide, carbon dioxide, and methyl mercury. "Clean coal" does not yet exist, and at present the phrase is an oxymoron. Natural gas is used to heat about half of the nation's homes. Natural-gas-fired electrical plants are much less polluting than coal-fired plants, but the domestic supply of natural gas in the long run is uncertain.

Nuclear power generates about 20 percent of the nation's electricity. Yet nuclear power is plagued by the difficulty of disposing of nuclear waste and the huge cost of building nuclear power plants. A new nuclear plant has not been built in the United States since the late 1970s. Hydropower is a relatively clean energy source, but the construction of new large dams does not seem likely.

Higher energy prices, along with the reality that the burning of fossil fuels produces air pollution and climate-changing carbon dioxide, have prompted communities to seek cleaner alternative energy sources. Rather than picking one energy source, communities are promoting a variety of options. Wind-generated electricity is now competitive with electricity from coal, and it would be more competitive if the health costs of air pollution were included in the price of coal-powered electricity. Wind turbines, however, are difficult to locate within cities. Nevertheless, New York City's mayor, Michael Bloomberg, proposed erecting wind turbines on skyscrapers and bridges!

Solar energy systems come in three types: a passive solar system with Trombe walls or barrels of liquid that heat up during the day and release energy at night; an active system to produce hot water; and an active photovoltaic system that generates electricity. These solar systems can help individual building owners reduce their use of nonrenewable energy and save money over time. Moreover, solar systems can reduce a community's energy bill in the long run and keep more money in the community.

To enable the use of wind turbines and solar systems, local governments must adopt siting standards in their zoning ordinances. Standards for wind turbines will depend on whether the installation is of a single turbine for home use or several turbines for a commercial wind farm. In either case, turbines should be set back from property lines so that if a turbine and its tower fall down, they will not fall onto a neighboring property. A problem with wind turbines is that they work best along ridgelines, which has led some people to oppose them for aesthetic reasons. A further problem with wind power is that wind speeds are not constant. A backup energy system is often needed, because sufficient batteries do not yet exist to store large amounts of energy generated by wind or solar systems.

A solar access ordinance helps to ensure that new buildings and alterations to existing buildings do not interfere with the access to sunlight of solar devices on neighboring buildings. The ordinance may impose restrictions on the height, bulk, and siting of new buildings and alterations to protect the exposure of existing buildings to the sun. To enable new buildings to be located to best capture the sun's rays, the ordinance may make special siting allowances, such as a zero lot line, where there are no building setbacks from a property line. The ordinance should take into consideration a building's exposure during the winter months, when the sun's rays are at a low angle.

Wind turbines and solar systems raise a debate about the merits of large centralized power systems (wind farms and solar farms) and distributed power (individual wind and solar systems). In large communities, centralized power appears to make more sense. The challenges then are to find sites where wind or solar farms can be built and to construct power lines to deliver the electricity to cities. By contrast, California has embarked on a Million Solar Roofs Initiative to install solar photovoltaic panels on one million buildings within ten years.

America's consumption of fossil fuels is directly related to climate change, which is expected to melt glaciers, raise sea levels, and threaten to flood coastal cities. Thus, decreasing the consumption of fossil fuels is imperative. The United States has not established standards to reduce emissions of carbon dioxide and other greenhouse gases that contribute to climate change, even though the U.S. Supreme Court ruled in 2007 that the Environmental Protection Agency (EPA) has the authority to regulate emissions of greenhouse gases, such as carbon dioxide, under the Clean Air Act. Nonetheless, several cities, including Columbia, Missouri, and Jacksonville, Florida, have adopted renewable portfolio standards requiring local electricity providers to obtain a certain amount of their electricity from renewable energy sources, as a way to reduce reliance on fossil fuels and thus lower carbon dioxide emissions. As yet, the federal government has not enacted renewable portfolio standards for electric utilities.

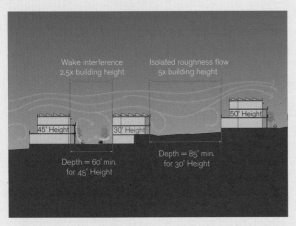

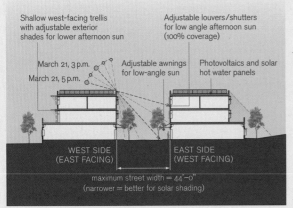

The plan and design of the Maui development Hali'imaile is responsive to local conditions. West-facing buildings need extensive adjustable shutters to keep out the late-afternoon heat. South-facing buildings have deep overhangs, which shelter the interior in the summer but also allow the low sun to enter in winter. Streets running east-west are wider than those running north-south, allowing winter sun to penetrate the public spaces while working in tandem with natural breezes.

More than 400 cities have signed the Sierra Club's Cool Cities initiative to reduce the emission of greenhouse gases that contribute to climate change, and to lower temperatures and thus lessen the need for energy to power air conditioners. Because of the extensive amount of pavement and rooftops, cities heat up more than the countryside and take longer to cool down. This is known as the "heat island effect." One of the popular ways to reduce the heat island effect is to plant trees. Trees literally green the city, but also provide shade and absorb carbon dioxide. In PlaNYC of 2007, New York City proposed to plant one million trees by 2030. Since 1992, Chicago has planted more than half a million trees. Local governments can also adopt a tree preservation ordinance to maintain existing tree cover and require developers to retain a certain percentage or number of trees and replace trees removed during construction.

Higher energy prices have encouraged city residents to seek alternative means of transportation, and transit ridership is on the rise. Mass transit systems use less energy per person than individual cars. Since 1991, metropolitan planning organizations have directed how federal transportation funds are spent. Unfortunately, federal spending on transportation has continued to favor road construction and repair over mass transit, at a split of roughly 80 percent roads and 20 percent mass transit. Even so, light-rail commuter lines now exist in more than 25 metropolitan areas and are being proposed in several others. Clearly, the development of more mass transit systems and the expansion of those already in existence would reduce America's energy use as well as air pollution and carbon dioxide emissions. But to make mass transit feasible, there needs to be a density of at least seven dwelling units to the acre. Many communities would have to change their zoning ordinances to allow this degree of density, and that may not be politically acceptable. This is one more change in lifestyle that residents of greening communities will have to make.

To promote greater energy conservation, efficiency, and use of alternative energy sources, communities can set benchmarks for improvement. An annual report can measure progress against the benchmarks. This way, elected officials can better identify successes and shortcomings in their energy efforts; and the voters can hold their elected officials accountable.

In order to create green communities, Americans will have to reduce their carbon and energy footprints. This will mean more consumption of locally grown food, less driving of cars, more use of mass transit, more walking and bicycling, the development of higher-density housing, the installation of alternative energy systems, and the planting of thousands of trees.

Federal environmental laws have provided very little direction about placemaking or community design. As a result, those communities that are going green are doing so with little help from the federal government. Moreover, the need for sustainable green communities has sparked a debate about whether the United States should continue to be a suburban nation with most of its citizens living in suburbs or return to being an urban nation with most of its people living in cities. Densely developed, walkable, and bicycle-friendly cities with mass transit systems are far more energy efficient than far-flung suburbs where residents live in single-family detached houses and depend on cars to travel anywhere. The suburban model that relies on cheap and plentiful oil supplies is simply unsustainable when the United States depends more on oil imports each year. In sum, the United States can avoid more suburban sprawl and promote urban redevelopment by "going green."

FURTHER READING

Daniels, T., and K. Daniels. *The Environmental Planning Handbook for Sustainable Communities and Regions.* Chicago: Planners Press, 2003.

Raja, S., B. Born, and J. Kozlowski Russell. *A Planners Guide to Community and Regional Food Planning: Transforming Food Environments, Facilitating Healthy Eating.* Planning Advisory Service Report No. 554. Chicago: American Planning Association, 2008.

Beddington Zero Energy Development
(BedZED), a community of 78 homes
south of London.

Institute, in Freiburg, Germany, and the Adam J. Lewis Center for Environmental Studies, at Oberlin College, in Ohio. While this strategy has been explored in Europe for about 20 years, recent concerns about energy and climate change have generated interest in net zero development within the green building movement in the United States. For example, the Architecture 2030 initiative, launched by architect Edward Mazria, promotes the goal of net zero energy for all new buildings by 2030. This effort is supported by the American Institute of Architects, the U.S. Conference of Mayors, the U.S. Green Building Council, the American Society of Heating, Refrigeration and Air-Conditioning Engineers, and other organizations. The U.S. Department of Energy also has net zero energy programs for both residential and commercial buildings. Likewise, the U.S. Department of Defense has an initiative called Net Zero Plus, which involves on-site or colocated renewable energy systems to allow military installations to continue to function after the failure of a local utility grid.

At the neighborhood scale, the first net zero energy

project to be completed was the Beddington Zero Energy Development (BedZED), a community of 78 homes south of London. Designed by architect Bill Dunster, with the involvement of several environmental groups and the Peabody Trust, a community developer, the homes use a variety of renewable energy strategies, including active solar thermal, passive solar, photovoltaic cells, and biomass. The project has served as inspiration for other net zero energy communities, including a proposal for a 2,000-home community called ZED Squared, east of London, based on a study that involved several BedZED team members and architect Norman Foster.

Subsequent to ZED Squared, Norman Foster was commissioned to design the community plan for the world's largest net zero energy project, Masdar City, in Abu Dhabi, United Arab Emirates. The project will be a complete city precinct including residences and retail, commercial, and civic buildings, totaling 66 million square feet. The entire community will rest on top of a podium containing infrastructure and an electrically powered transportation system. There will be no cars, resulting in a strong design emphasis on creating comfortable, pedestrian-friendly places. Solar energy will be the city's main source of power. Mubadala, the company responsible for developing Masdar, intends for the community to be a test site for green technologies, which can then be exported to other communities around the world.

In the United States, the Holy Cross Project in New Orleans's Lower Ninth Ward is intended to become the first net zero energy community in the country. It was the winning entry in an international design competition sponsored by Global Green USA, Brad Pitt, and the Lewis family. The design was created by Workshop/APD of New York and then further developed with residents of the Holy Cross neighborhood. The community will consist of five single-family houses, an 18-unit apartment building, a community center, corner store, and a child care center. The Holy Cross Neighborhood Association, an active participant in the project, felt strongly that the project should make a very visible statement about the United States' first urban victims of climate change and therefore supported its net zero energy goals. Construction techniques and energy technologies from the project will be used as models for rehabilitating existing houses in the Lower Ninth Ward.

The first of the houses has been completed, and work is under way to complete the community. All buildings are designed to exceed the local energy efficiency codes and will have rooftop photovoltaic arrays to generate renewable energy. These up-front investments will save residents money in the long term, in the form of lower operating costs for energy. However, the added energy efficiency and net zero energy–generating capacity comes at a cost. If not subsidized, these homes would be beyond the reach of the low-income families who plan to live there.

In the Lower Ninth Ward, as in every city and country around the world, rising and increasingly volatile energy costs put the greatest burden on low-income citizens. Not every community will be forced by natural disaster to rebuild from the ground up, but to achieve net zero and a sustainable energy future,

Masdar City, in Abu Dhabi, United Arab Emirates.

we will all need to embrace new ways of thinking about energy and carbon emissions. One mechanism for accelerating this shift is "engaged offsets," a financial vehicle jointly developed by Terrapin Bright Green, Enterprise Community Partners, JP Morgan Chase, and CTG Energetics. Unlike traditional carbon offsets, engaged offsets focus exclusively on local exchanges, using offset money as marginal financing for advanced energy measures in the funder's own community. Engaged offsets have been used to install solar energy systems on renovated homes in the Lower Ninth Ward and to fund advanced energy efficiency and wind turbines for multifamily low-income housing in New York City. This financing vehicle can benefit inner city schools, housing developments, and other community institutions. As an effective, capital-efficient step toward energy independence, engaged offsets are the kind of collaborative, win-win solution that will help us remake our existing cities for the 21st century.

Views of the Holy Cross Project in the Lower Ninth Ward of New Orleans.

NOTES

1   K. Butti and J. Perlin, *A Golden Thread, 2500 Years of Solar Architecture and Technology* (Palo Alto, Calif.: Chesire Books, 1980), 8–13.

2   A. Matzarakis and H. Mayer, "Investigations of Urban Climate's Thermal Component in Freiburg, Germany." In *Proceedings of AMS 13th Conference on Biometeorology and Aerobiology* (Albuquerque, N.M., 1998).

3   Arup, "Helping a City to Breathe," *Arup Design Yearbook 2008*, 42–43.

4   W. Becker, "Out of Harm's Way" (unpublished manuscript, 1989).

THE SPILLOVER EFFECTS OF
GROWING CROPS FOR BIOFUELS

SCOTT A. MALCOLM AND MARCEL AILLERY

Volatile petroleum prices, along with federal policies aimed at reducing the United States' dependency on oil imports and mitigating climate change, have sparked rapid growth in biofuel demand.[1] In response, production of agricultural commodities that serve as feedstock for biofuels has increased. Federal policy initiatives and private-sector investment point to continued growth in biofuel production and, consequently, increased demand for agricultural products. Rural communities dependent on agriculture face new opportunities and risks from expansion in biofuel demand. As communities adapt to adjustments across sectors of the farm economy, opportunities will emerge for market expansion and development of new industries. Growth of the biofuels sector may provide employment opportunities but may also create problems for water quality and other environmental concerns. A key policy challenge will be to manage the growth sustainably, not only for the benefit of local communities but for the broader natural environment that all communities share. Our goal here is to describe from a regional perspective how the changing economic climate may drive potential environmental consequences.

The Energy Independence and Security Act (EISA) of 2007 includes a provision for a new Renewable Fuel Standard (RFS) to increase the supply of alternative fuel sources by requiring fuel producers to use at least 36 billion gallons of biofuel annually by 2022. The RFS provision establishes a level of 15 billion gallons of conventional ethanol by 2015 and at least 21 billion gallons of cellulosic (noncornstarch) ethanol and advanced biofuels (including ethanol from sugarcane and biodiesel) by 2022.

The share of total domestic corn production supplying the ethanol market grew from 7.5 percent in 2001 to 22.6 percent in 2007. The 2007 United States Department of Agriculture (USDA) agricultural baseline, which was produced before EISA became law, assumed that annual production of corn-based ethanol will reach 12 billion gallons by 2016, or 3 billion gallons below the federally mandated target for that year.[2] By 2016, ethanol production is expected to consume more than 35 percent of U.S. corn production. To meet the EISA mandates, annual ethanol production from cellulosic feedstocks would have to grow from current pilot project levels to roughly 4.25 billion gallons in 2016 and 21 billion gallons in 2022.

The USDA's Economic Research Service (ERS) used a national agricultural sector model to estimate expected market and environmental outcomes of expanded feedstock production. The model compares the implications of producing 12 billion gallons of corn-based ethanol in 2016 (the 2007 USDA baseline estimate) with the production of 15 billion gallons (as reflected in the new RFS).

Growing demand for corn and other biomass feedstocks will transform the agricultural landscape as regional cropping patterns are adjusted and production practices adapted. While biofuels have been viewed as an environmentally preferred alternative to fossil-based fuels, there is growing concern about the potential effects of feedstock development on resource use and environmental quality. By increasing demand

An oil well in cornfield in New Haven, Illinois. The state is among the nation's leaders in ethanol production.

for agricultural feedstocks, the new RFS will encourage increased production of crops that may lead to conversion of land for use in crop production and more intensive use of fertilizers and other inputs, increasing the potential for environmental degradation.

Changes Expected in the Agricultural Landscape

Higher demand for corn—for biofuel as well as for animal feed and human food—has increased corn production in traditional corn-growing regions and elsewhere. As farmers have responded to higher corn prices, the prices and production levels of other crops have been adjusted as well. Crop producers have generally benefited from higher returns on corn and other grain crops. Some livestock and poultry producers, however, are worse off. More corn going to biofuels, together with reduced production of soybeans, sorghum, and other feed crops, has contributed to a net increase in grain feed costs for livestock producers. The availability of distillers' grains, a by-product of corn-based ethanol production that can be used as a feed supplement for some livestock, may lessen the impact on feed costs. These changing feed markets, according to ERS analysis, will prompt a slight decline in livestock production.

Given the spillover effects of expanded corn acreage on agricultural markets and the environment, technologies are being developed to produce cellulosic ethanol from a wide range of feedstocks, including crop residues and new crops dedicated to energy production, such as switchgrass. Other potential feedstocks that would not compete for existing cropland—

forestry by-products, municipal solid waste, and even algae—are under development. Since these technologies are not yet commercially operational, corn is likely to remain the major feedstock through the next decade.

Cultivated cropland is expected to expand in all U.S. regions but one, as producers respond to higher crop prices. ERS research suggests that the largest increases in cultivated cropland will likely occur in the traditional corn-producing regions of the Corn Belt (1.6 million more acres in 2016), Northern Plains (1.5 million acres), Delta (540,000 acres), and Lake States (510,000 acres). These estimated changes are conditional on model assumptions regarding corn yield growth, energy costs, ethanol conversion rates, and other factors affecting ethanol productivity and returns.

Corn accounts for roughly three-quarters of the estimated increase in national acreage cultivated under the 2016 baseline case. Corn acres are expected to expand in all regions, with the Corn Belt and Northern Plains showing the largest gains due to comparative advantage in corn production. More farmers are expected to plant corn on a continuous basis, rather than rotating corn with soybeans or other crops. Some of the additional acreage planted to corn and other crops will likely come from land enrolled in USDA's Conservation Reserve Program (CRP).

The Effects of Land Use and Management on Environmental Quality

As more of the nation's land is cultivated and as farmers adjust cropping patterns and production practices, the farm sector's impact on soil and water is likely to change. The shift to corn, for example, has largely displaced soybeans and small-grain crops that are generally less input intensive. Higher commodity prices also may intensify use of both irrigation and chemical inputs that enhance crop yield. Much of the new acreage under cultivation may be marginal lands that are more highly erodible.

ERS model results indicate that meeting biofuel targets will raise total nitrogen fertilizer use by an estimated 2 percent over previous expectations for 2016. Expected higher fertilizer use reflects increases

in both cropland cultivated and intensity of applied fertilizer in corn production. Nitrogen use is expected to rise in all regions except the Delta, where additional soybean acres will supplant more fertilizer-intensive crops. The Northern Plains area is likely to show the largest increase in nitrogen use, reflecting expanded production of corn.

Increases in applied fertilizer may lead to water quality impairment due to nutrient leaching and runoff. Nitrogen and phosphorus runoff from farm fields is a significant source of water pollution throughout the United States. Applied nitrogen on cornfields in the Mississippi River Basin is a primary cause of the hypoxic, or oxygen-depleted, zone in the Gulf of Mexico. The nature and extent of environmental damage from increased fertilizer use will vary depending on farm management practices, soil characteristics, topography, and proximity to water bodies.

While the ERS model cannot predict changes in water quality due to expanded production of corn-based ethanol, results indicate an increase in the amount of nitrogen reaching water bodies under the higher biofuel target. Annual nitrogen runoff to surface-water bodies in the United States is estimated to increase by roughly 26,500 tons by 2016, or 2.5 percent above estimated baseline levels. The projected increase in nitrogen runoff is more than proportional to the 1.5 percent increase in U.S. planted acreage, reflecting the shift to corn acreage and additional cropland expansion on marginal land. The change in nitrogen loadings over current levels will likely vary considerably by region, following the pattern of expanded nitrogen use. The Corn Belt, which accounted for 44 percent of nitrogen deposited to surface water from field crop production in 2006, shows an increase in nitrogen runoff of less than 2 percent (8,500 tons) by 2016. In percentage terms, larger increases in nitrogen runoff are expected to occur in the Northern Plains, Delta, and Appalachian regions, reflecting expansion in acreage under cultivation.

Water quality is also affected by soil erosion on cultivated cropland. Nationwide, sheet (or rainfall erosion to surface water is expected to rise 2.1 percent by 2016

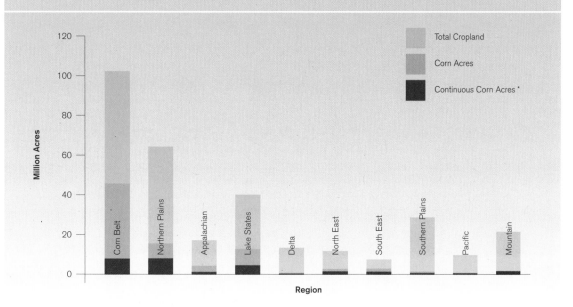

PROJECTED INCREASE IN U.S. CORN ACREAGE — 2016 USDA BASELINE

Total Cropland

Corn Acres

Continuous Corn Acres *

Million Acres

120

100

80

60

40

20

0

Corn Belt

Northern Plains

Appalachian

Lake States

Delta

North East

South East

Southern Plains

Pacific

Mountain

Region

* Acres of cropland planted to corn on a continuous basis, rather than rotating between corn and the planting of other crops, such as soybeans.

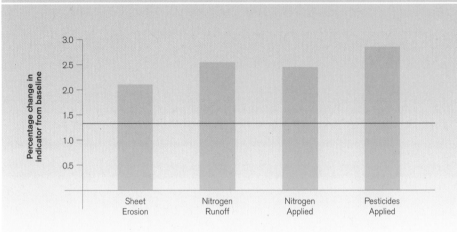

**ENVIRONMENTAL INDICATORS EXPECTED TO
INCREASE BEYOND CHANGE IN PLANTED ACREAGE**

Percentage increase in 2016 planted acres above baseline

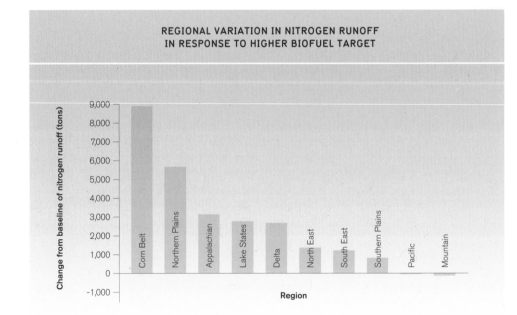

**REGIONAL VARIATION IN NITROGEN RUNOFF
IN RESPONSE TO HIGHER BIOFUEL TARGET**

under the higher biofuel target, with higher increases likely in the Northern Plains, Lake States, and Delta. Wind erosion in the United States is primarily concentrated in the Northern Plains, with lesser amounts in the Corn Belt and Southern Plains. Increased erosion reflects increases in cultivated acreage, with potential expansion on marginal croplands. Model results suggest that broader use of soil-conserving tillage systems that minimize soil disturbance at planting time—particularly no-till and reduced-till systems in the Northern Plains and Northeast and reduced-till in the Corn Belt—may help moderate the net increase in sheet and wind erosion from expanded corn acreage and continuous corn rotations.

Feedstock production for biofuels may involve additional environmental concerns. Greenhouse gas emissions from the U.S. crop sector could increase. Changes in tillage practices and conversion of land to crop production may reduce stored soil carbon. Increased use of nitrogen fertilizers can also increase emissions of nitrous oxide, another greenhouse gas. The net effect of biofuels on greenhouse gas emissions is unclear: total emissions could be higher or lower than those associated with carbon-based fuels. A life-cycle analysis, accounting for direct and indirect links along the biofuel production chain, would be needed to fully assess the net effects of biofuels on greenhouse gas emissions. Feedstock production may also increase demands on limited groundwater and surface-water resources. The net effect on agricultural water withdrawals is uncertain, however, and is likely to vary regionally and over time depending on the location of feedstock sources and local production conditions. The demand for corn ethanol would increase water use where corn feedstock production displaces crops that require less water, such as soybeans. Biofuel production could also increase water use due to expansion of irrigated cropland, both through reduced fallow acreage and conversion of nonirrigated cropland and pastureland. However, significant expansion in groundwater and surface-water withdrawals may be limited by physical supply availability, legal constraints, and economic considerations.

Land conversion for crop production may also strain local wildlife resources. Converting lands from less intensive uses—including native grasslands, forestland, and cropland set aside for environmental purposes, as through USDA's CRP—could reduce wildlife habitat and degrade habitat for fish and other aquatic species through increased delivery of sediment, nutrients, and pesticides to water bodies.

Mitigating Environmental Impacts Through Research and Policy Initiatives

The demand for corn as a biofuel feedstock has put increasing pressure on land resources and the environment. Research under way on how to increase ethanol output per acre of corn could help reduce pressure on cropland to meet federal biofuel mandates. Average U.S. corn yield per harvested acre, based on a projection of historic trends, increases by 1.8 bushels per year under the USDA baseline, to reach 170 bushels per acre by 2016. Growth in average yield depends on many factors, including availability of higher-yielding varieties, the use of irrigation, and potential expansion in less productive areas. Higher corn yields, as well as new corn cultivars with higher starch content and improved crop-ethanol conversion efficiencies, could reduce the amount of land needed for corn feedstock production. These research-driven gains in productivity also suggest potential improvements in environmental indicators, through both reduced feedstock acreages to meet biofuel mandates and indirect commodity price effects that reduce competition for land.

Cellulosic feedstocks—such as switchgrass, *Miscanthus,* and poplar—that may be grown commercially on land not currently used for crop production could further relieve pressures on land for food and feed production. Cellulosic feedstocks provide potentially more ethanol per acre of feedstock. Moreover, reduced tillage and input requirements for perennial energy crops may lessen the potential environmental impact of meeting biofuel mandates, with regional effects depending on the allocation of emerging feedstocks. However, significant challenges involving feedstock production practices, transport infrastructure, ethanol conversion technologies, and market formation must be addressed before cellulosic feedstocks become commercially viable.

Crop residues, such as corn stover and wheat straw, may serve as an important source of cellulosic feedstock in meeting mandated targets for biofuel production. Crop residues are already widely available as biomass alternatives to corn feedstock, although significant markets and processing capacity do not currently exist. Moreover, crop residues could provide an additional revenue source for grain producers. Crop residues, however, play an important role in managing soil erosion, nutrient loss, soil carbon, and soil moisture. Thus, residues are not "free"—there is a cost to residue harvesting, and soil productivity and environmental quality may suffer. The amount of residue that can be harvested while maintaining productivity—based in part on the erodibility of the soil and tillage regime used—is an important policy concern and a focus of ongoing research. Research is also needed to determine the environmental effects of large-scale cultivation of dedicated energy crops.

Conservation programs can help mitigate environmental impacts from biofuel feedstock production. USDA's Environmental Quality Incentives Program provides cost sharing and technical assistance for adoption of conserving practices that improve environmental stewardship. Nutrient and soil management measures could offset potential increases in runoff and leaching under input-intensive corn production. The use of conservation tillage systems, such as no-till, may counteract potential increases in soil erosion. Use of corn stover as a biofuel feedstock would likely promote conservation tillage systems, although guidelines would be needed to ensure sustainable harvest of crop residues. USDA conservation compliance provisions, which withhold federal farm payments to producers converting highly erodible soils or wetlands, may limit corn feedstock production on environmentally sensitive lands. The CRP, which removes environmentally sensitive cropland from production under long-term rental agreements, could also be part of a broader agricultural biofuel strategy. Riparian buffers installed

under the CRP continuous sign-up provision may help reduce soil and nutrient runoff from cropland used in feedstock production. Grazing and haying on CRP land, under an approved conservation plan, can help livestock producers facing high feed costs due in part to biofuel demand. CRP lands could also potentially be used for perennial trees and grasses harvested as biofuel feedstock, if environmental benefits are preserved. Additional research would be needed to assess the potential environmental effects of dedicated energy crops on CRP lands.

Increased production of biofuel feedstocks promises to reshape the U.S. farm sector. Higher demand for corn and other commodities has expanded the market for agricultural products, while increasing costs for food and livestock producers. At the same time, expansion in feedstock production has increased pressures on the agricultural land base, raising concerns for resource use and environmental quality. Resource effects will vary across regions, depending on the nature and distribution of feedstock expansion, resulting in changes in production practices and input use and spatial differences in climate, soil, and hydrologic conditions. In charting future directions for U.S. biofuel policy, a broad program of interdisciplinary research is needed to improve our understanding of potential outcomes and trade-offs for agriculture, energy, the environment, and rural communities. USDA conservation programs, in turn, can play an important role in encouraging farmer adoption of sustainable production systems, helping to ensure responsible development of the biofuel sector.

NOTES

1   This essay appeared in slightly different form in *Amber Waves*, March 2009. The views expressed here are those of the authors and may not be attributed to the Economic Research Service or the U.S. Department of Agriculture.

2   The 2007 USDA baseline provides long-term projections for the agricultural sector through 2016. Projections cover agricultural commodities, agricultural trade, and aggregate indicators of the sector, such as farm income and food prices. The projections are based on specific assumptions regarding macroeconomic conditions, policy, weather, international developments, and yields. The projections assume that there are no shocks due to abnormal weather, outbreaks of plant or animal diseases, or other factors affecting global supply and demand. Government programs that influence agriculture are assumed to remain in effect throughout the projection period.

Ethanol manufacturing plant, Indiana.

Scott A. Malcolm and Marcel Aillery

GREEN INFRASTRUCTURE FOR BLUE URBAN WATERSHEDS

MARY RICKEL PELLETIER

To the average American, the boundaries and planning policies of local watersheds may seem inconsequential. Water in the natural environment, municipal water-management systems, and the water in our physical bodies are locked in a closed-loop relationship that is surprisingly easy to overlook. Transportation, energy, economic development, and human services are prevailing issues that seize the attention of politicians, planners, and newspaper reporters. Yet because water can be measured across the spectrum of life, the dynamics of urban watersheds are essential to the evolution of sustainable cities. Water is a shared resource that is intricately and intrinsically linked to human health, food supplies, energy, and climate change. Green communities are learning how to incorporate "blue" design features into the urban fabric as fundamental assets of sustainable development.

Watersheds are the natural geological drainage basins through which rainwater, melting snow, and groundwater seepage flow toward a distinct watercourse, lake, or tidewater.[1] Because maps of cities are typically road maps, watersheds are difficult to visualize. Watershed maps appear strange, somewhat useless guides to places rarely seen from the comfort of our cars, buses, and trains. And because street addresses—rather than geographic landmarks—tend to structure American cities, maps that reveal the tattered tributaries of natural drainage basins are seldom a fundamental reference in municipal planning. Yet green communities are reevaluating how city planning practices and policies have shaped streetscapes, alleys, parking lots, backyards, small streams, and ponds that flow into larger scenic lakes, rivers, and coastal waters. The same policies and practices that have permitted the paving over of landscapes and waterways for automobiles are directly related to regional water quality and quantity problems. Water quality is threatened by nonpoint-source pollution: a stew of contaminants carried by stormwater runoff from roadways, parking lots, rooftops, and lawns. This runoff flows into or through an underlying maze of old and new utility lines, eventually draining into downstream waterways. The excess stormwater of sprawling metropolitan areas also causes flooding, erosion, and the backup of sewage into basements.

In addition, regional drinking water supplies are frequently depleted and aquatic environments tapped dry. As a result of this mismanagement and the broad failure to invest in infrastructure, basic water services in municipalities across America are on the brink of collapse. Even worse, according to the Natural Resources Defense Council, the United States will develop 68 million more acres by 2025.[2] We are thus failing on two critical fronts: we are neither developing and maintaining our existing systems, nor preserving the natural resources that they are meant to process, treat, and convey. These systems are at the basis of what we think of as civilization: clean, safe, disease-free, low-cost, dependable, and accessible essential resources.

Green communities are realizing that this water infrastructure crisis is also a fortuitous opportunity to revitalize municipal watersheds with green infrastructure strategies that can regenerate urban stream corridors, prioritize on-site stormwater management, expand green jobs, and encourage collaborative community planning. We can no longer afford to deplete ecosystem services—natural processes that clean water and air, reduce the urban heat island effect, replenish groundwater, and provide habitat for native vegetation. Such vegetation supports migratory birds and butterflies needed to pollinate local food supplies. Green communities are discovering how to channel rainwater runoff so that, rather than being shunted off into buried pipes, it flows through the visible urban fabric and can be incorporated into attractive and utilitarian design features. Plus, by living or working within walking distance to linear park landscapes that protect stream corridors, city residents are experiencing health benefits, as property values increase.

Yet how will we ensure that future investments will actually integrate green infrastructure into new development projects? Although green infrastructure makes economic and ecological sense, the challenge in many communities is to first change dated cultural design conventions by integrating environmental science into regional planning and into high-density municipal development projects. At present, we have too many ecologically unsound preferences embedded in our economic system. For example, new development is often premised on the availability of copious free parking, which is both an economic and ecological problem. Actually achieving a greener result requires not simply changing the parking requirements but working to shift the economic values that shape the framework of new development. Rolling back acres of asphalt will require changing prevailing transportation

planning priorities that sabotage nature in cities. Furthermore, landscapes that have conventionally served as a decorative finish to new development now need to provide measurable ecological benefits in order to promote healthy waterways, healthy communities, and reliable regional natural resources.

Green Infrastructure as a Language and a Community Value

Being green implies a variety of consumer products and practices, which may or may not directly support the natural ecosystems within an urban metropolitan area. However, green infrastructure encompasses a systemic range of local and regional cost-effective, natural best-management practices. The term "green infrastructure" includes and expands upon principles inherent in low impact development (LID) technology, which have been developed and tested by innovative nonprofit engineering and design professionals.[3]

LID weighs local site design decisions within a larger context of regional watershed. It utilizes natural hydrologic functions (interception, infiltration, evapotranspiration, soil storage, detention, and other transformative reuses) for decentralized stormwater management. Predevelopment water budgets—which establish the quantity of water absorbed by the landscape prior to development—provide a measurable benchmark for the design of on-site stormwater management features, which can enhance new development or renovation projects. This approach reduces energy costs and maintenance of mechanical pumps needed to move stormwater through

conventional underground storage systems. Green
infrastructure includes LID; landscape, architectural,
and urban design features such as eco-roofs, rainwater
harvesting systems, pervious pavement, rain gardens,
and vegetated swales; as well as regional watershed
planning strategies such as source protection for the
landscape basins surrounding drinking water sources.

A range of advanced green infrastructure projects
have been constructed by progressive municipalities,
which are frequently located near beautiful natural
landmark places—culturally significant waters such
as lakes, rivers, harbors, bays, seasides, and sounds—
that have inspired civic action. Watershed organizations have often been on the front lines in negotiating
new development parameters, engaging public interest,
conducting field research of environmental conditions,
and remedying flaws in local planning policies.
Chesapeake Bay Foundation, Johnson Creek Watershed
Council, Anacostia Watershed Restoration Partnership, Carkeek Watershed Council, Buffalo Bayou
Partnership, and Nine Mile Watershed Association are
a few of the numerous urban and regional watershed
organizations that educate citizens, while bridging
across municipal boundaries to negotiate consensus

As Chicago grew and expanded at the
end of the nineteenth century, the Calumet
wetlands offered an all-too-convenient
location for factories and garbage dumps.
Yet as early as 1909, architect Daniel
Burnham, in his influential "Plan of
Chicago," envisioned a greener future
for the Calumet wetlands even as the
area industrialized. Now a coalition of
government, environmental, and citizen
organizations, including the EPA and
the Sierra Club, is restoring the wetlands,
giving Chicagoans a new place to
connect with nature.

design solutions based on shared environmental interests. Such organizations come in many forms, whether an ad hoc "friends" group; a local chapter of Trout Unlimited; a distinct 501(c)3 nonprofit; a division of a municipal, county, or state government; or even a diverse regional alliance, such as Chicago Wilderness. Strengthened by the evolution of the Internet, these independent groups synthesize an abundance of diverse data, photographs, maps, and activities into an ongoing grassroots campaign to activate and inform the public about water quality within local natural environments, where there are numerous opportunities for greener, cost-effective design improvements.

Innovative Community Design Processes and Policy Changes

Municipal policy changes often reflect years of local community efforts conducted by watershed organizations that have formed partnerships with government agencies, academic researchers, and dedicated volunteers. For example, the Carkeek Watershed Council, in Seattle, began working in 1979 to restore salmon runs to the creek. Community interest in Carkeek encouraged Seattle Public Utilities

to build innovative projects that restore or replicate natural drainage systems. The projects, such as Street Edge Alternatives, Broadview Green Grid, and the Viewlands Cascade, have reduced stormwater runoff and demonstrated that green infrastructure can cost much less than conventional concrete sewer systems. These successes and an impressive range of other such projects that have been built and tested—especially in the Pacific Northwest, Great Lakes, and mid-Atlantic— are now national models. Such models are helping to alter dated assumptions by cultivating local green infrastructure design knowledge.

Charles River Watershed Association (CRWA) recently released the five-step "Blue Cities Guide" based on case-study project work in three Boston metro area neighborhoods: the North Allston neighborhood, where Harvard University is building an expansive new 200-acre campus; Longwood Medical Area, which borders Muddy River and Back Bay Fens; and Zakim North, a mixed residential and industrial neighborhood that falls within the Boston, Cambridge, and Somerville municipal boundaries. CRWA research began with analytical mapping of current and historical site conditions, drainage, and land uses within the subwatershed. Mapping, computer modeling of various drainage scenarios, and field research helped to identify issues and opportunities for improvements. A partnership with the Conservation Law Foundation helped to clarify the legal obligations of property owners and municipal governments. Throughout the research process, CRWA participated in numerous public meetings and reached out to stakeholders to ensure that new development projects actually improved the local natural environment and addressed community interests. CRWA research has influenced changes in the Harvard University North Allston campus plan, including the recent construction of prototype stormwater-treatment planters that can function in cold-climate streetscapes.

Thanks to advances in environmental science, building project sites are no longer the blank page or computer screen background onto which a design is imposed—rather, on-site stormwater management and ecosystem service benefits can be integrated into a watershed. Stormwater is proving to be a decentralized municipal resource that offers taxpayer cost savings and long-term quality of life benefits. As noted in the conclusion of the "Blue Cities Guide": "When policy and design innovations converge to restore natural water functions in the built environment, water quality improves, flooding is mitigated or eliminated, habitat is restored, groundwater recharge is unimpeded, and beautiful, safe networks of pedestrian corridors and open space can be built and sustained."[4]

Setting Standards for Green Infrastructure

The growth of urban watershed organizations is evidence of increasing appreciation for local, independent environmental advocates who are expanding the goals of watershed management by networking with individuals and communities to reach neighborhood, municipal, metropolitan, and regional levels. By cultivating public support, assisting with scientific and legal research, investing in community planning processes, and even building demonstration projects, local watershed organizations have managed to motivate municipal leadership. Yet aging infrastructure

The Lake Calumet region remains a landscape of contrasts, with abandoned factories and warehouses—the "silhouettes of steel industries" as Burnham called them—sharing the space with boaters and fishers.

and impaired waters require a larger long-term investment and a greater network of professional expertise. Green cities are crafting incentives and new regulations such as stormwater utility fees, accelerated permit processes, and even increased floor area ratios in order to promote on-site stormwater management features and encourage designers to think outside of the pipe.

The City of Seattle has developed the Seattle Green Factor to further green infrastructure improvements within high-density neighborhood business districts. The Seattle Green Factor scorecard calculates points for characteristics such as soil depth, tree canopy size, preservation of notable trees, permeable paving, green roofs, vegetated walls, rain gardens, drought-tolerant plants, and landscaping visible to pedestrians. The menu of green infrastructure strategies allows design flexibility for new development within the Seattle Green Factor zones.

The success of the U.S. Green Building Council's LEED rating system has prompted other specialized rating systems, including the Sustainable Sites Initiative, which is a program of the Lady Bird Johnson Wildflower Center, the U.S. Botanic Garden, and the American Society of Landscape Architects. The Sustainable Sites Guidelines and Performance Benchmarks (to be released summer 2009) will supplement the LEED rating system, which scores site-specific projects rather than municipal planning and urban design strategies. LEED for Neighborhood Development is a tool for new development projects, thus not a set of civic-scale criteria. A new partnership of ICLEI Local Governments for Sustainability, the Center for American Progress, and the U.S. Green Building Council has begun to outline a municipal rating system, the STAR Community Index, which will be developed through a two-year development and review process.[5]

Measurable municipal planning standards are needed to further green infrastructure implementation and to align municipal policies with regional integrated water resources management goals. LEED accreditation for green buildings will not result in systemic green infrastructure at the civic or regional watershed level.

Given the competing interests of various aspects of planning, green infrastructure strategies may even conflict with efforts to increase urban density. Communities seeking to increase neighborhood walkability could also inadvertently increase flooding, basement backups, combined sewer overflows, and nonpoint-source pollution problems downstream. Most noticeably, developers, municipal planners, nonprofit policy advocates, and citizens who have embraced smart growth have at times overlooked the need for on-site stormwater management to prevent excess runoff. Isolated planning decisions of upstream communities have shunted impaired waters downstream, often into older, poor urban neighborhoods located in lowlands that are vulnerable to flooding. Climate change could very well further exacerbate surges in stormwater runoff that contribute to urban and suburban flooding and degrade property values.

There are projects, however, that integrate smart growth and green infrastructure, such as the innovative rehabilitation of historic mill and factory buildings in Redding, Connecticut, known as the Georgetown Redevelopment Project.[6] A focus on green priorities has helped to qualify this brownfield redevelopment project for state and federal funding. This anti-sprawl project will include 416 residential housing units, more than 300,000 square feet of commercial space, a performing arts center, a health club, and a bed and breakfast, all within a 10-minute walk of a reopened railroad station that will link area commuters to New York City. This energy-efficient project will utilize a fuel cell system to generate clean power, and a new hydroelectric turbine will be installed in an old wire mill to provide electricity for one of the commercial buildings. In addition, the Georgetown project will daylight the Norwalk River and remediate soil and vegetation surrounding a 12-acre pond. These attributes reflect the developer's interest and effort in refining the project with respect to the surrounding community and the natural environment.

Smart growth, renewable energy, public transportation, and green infrastructure are compatible when planners recognize natural watershed drainage

Mary Rickel Pelletier

and incorporate site-specific stormwater management into their design strategies. Planning for the locations of transportation hubs and future high-density development projects ought also to evaluate whether the location is logical for high-density sewer and water utility hookups. Open space within a smart growth project can be selected to protect landscapes along stream corridors, which reduce flooding and pollution, while improving habitat connectivity that enriches biodiversity. Site design features that utilize stormwater as an on-site resource—especially for irrigation—yield long-term cost savings for the property owner, as well as reductions in energy used for water treatment and the resulting carbon emissions. Responsible municipal planners and developers can restore neighborhood waterways, manage local and regional water resources, and in turn increase the value of a smart growth project.

Investment in green infrastructure varies widely with respect to the region, state, and municipality of a project location, as well as the values of the client and surrounding community. Implementing the blue components of a truly green infrastructure requires significant policy shifts on the federal as well as the grassroots level. Overcoming the legacy of centralized, hard infrastructure conventions requires changing standards and redirecting billions of dollars into green infrastructure strategies.[7] Before 2007, Clean Water Fund investments could only be spent on conventional buried sewer systems, thus communities were forced to pay additional costs for green infrastructure. A series of memoranda and statements of intent issued by the EPA in 2007 have initiated fundamental changes in the future permit and enforcement guidelines of the National Pollutant Discharge Elimination System by recognizing the need to evaluate and compensate for green infrastructure in meeting federal Clean Water Act requirements. Motivated communities can now integrate green infrastructure strategies into visible landscape improvements for parklands and roadways, while reducing the costs of dated sewer systems.

Innovative Collaborations and Communication

These systemic changes will not happen straightaway. Urban and suburban residents need to be reminded that nonpoint-source pollution caused by American lifestyle habits is now a more pressing threat to water quality than industrial pollution. We will not create healthy metropolitan areas with vibrant natural resources and sustainable, clean drinking-water supplies simply by admiring landscapes from a car, all-terrain vehicle, snowmobile, or riding lawnmower.[8] Communities need to learn about innovative advances in professional design standards. Yet innovation can be a hard sell, however beneficial or cost effective. Taxpayers, municipal planning staff, and engineers are not always eager to embrace design strategies that have not yet been demonstrated locally, even if proven in other communities.

The new green economy will depend upon a paradigm shift in education and employment, as well as in the outlook of the general public. Creative communication professionals working with designers, scientists, and educators can quicken the transition. The Internet has become an essential tool in educating the public and encouraging people to engage in the municipal planning process. For instance, the EPA has hosted a series of green infrastructure webcasts with leading professionals, which are available in online archives.[9] PennPraxis has developed PlanPhilly, a website that posts news coverage of the existing built environment and new development proposals.[10] Chicago's Center for Neighborhood Technology has developed an online toolbox that includes green infrastructure maps and a Green Values Stormwater Calculator, which compares conventional and green interventions according to their costs and hydrologic results.[11] Another innovative tool is the Casey Trees National Tree Benefits Calculator, which can appraise the capacity of a tree to reduce stormwater runoff and atmospheric carbon, conserve energy, improve air quality, and increase property values, based on the species, site characteristics, and trunk diameter.[12]

Other websites can help size a rain garden and select appropriate plants. Websites that provide guidelines for the protection of regional water resources—such as the Low Impact Hydropower Institute Certification Program—are helping to expand awareness of the need for broader water-resource management strategies.[13]

Site design features, municipal planning policies, and maintenance practices can align with regional guidelines to protect drinking water supplies and the aquatic environments that enrich natural diversity. Intergovernmental agreements between state and municipal jurisdictions within a regional watershed can create effective watershed-scale planning. New regulations, advanced design strategies, stormwater utility fees, funding for innovative research, and academic assistance are the building blocks for the implementation of new strategies. Green infrastructure offers a catalog of cost-effective improvements that can increase regional resiliency to climate change. But the long-term goal is not simply better practices but a revised relationship between American lifestyles, our values, and nature. We are water, and water binds us—green communities are communities that take this to heart in planning for the future.

NOTES

1 See U.S. EPA watershed online resources, www.epa.gov/owow/watershed.

2 N. Stoner, ed., *Rooftops to Rivers: Green Strategies for Controlling Stormwater and Combined Sewer Overflows* (New York: National Resources Defense Council, June 2006).

3 Most notably, the Center for Watershed Protection, www.cwp.org, and the Low Impact Development Center, www.lowimpactdevelopment.org. For a further description of LID see N. Weinstein, "The Tenth Anniversary White Paper," Low Impact Development Center (May 1, 2008), www.lowimpactdevelopment.org/tenth.htm.

4 The guide also notes: "Blue Development is a water oriented approach to urban development and redevelopment. Going beyond 'green' building, 'blue' development embraces designs for the built environment that engage with every stage of the water cycle." Charles River Watershed Association, "Blue Cities Guide: Environmentally Sensitive Urban Development" (2008), www.crwa.org/projects/esud.html.

5 For LEED neighborhood development, see: www.cnu.org/leednd. For the Sustainable Sites Initiative, see www.sustainablesites.org. For STAR, see www.iclei-usa.org/programs/sustainability/star-community-index.

6 See www.georgetownland.com/index.asp.

7 U.S. EPA, "Managing Wet Weather with Green Infrastructure Action Strategy" (available at www.epa.gov/npdes/pubs/gi_action_strategy.pdf), lists future steps in transition to green infrastructure, as outlined by the Partners for Green Infrastructure: American Rivers, Association of State and Interstate Water Pollution Control Administrators, Low Impact Development Center, National Association of Clean Water Agencies, Natural Resources Defense Council, and the EPA.

8 The bottled water industry, which is less regulated than municipal tap water, charges consumers for the embedded energy costs of bottled water extraction, packaging, and transportation: See www.stopcorporateabuse.org/category/sitecategories/water.

9 U.S. EPA National Pollutant Discharge Elimination System, "Green Infrastructure," http://cfpub.epa.gov/npdes/home.cfm?program_id=298.

10 PennPraxis, "Plan Philly," www.planphilly.com.

11 Center for Neighborhood Technology, "Green Values Stormwater Toolbox," http://greenvalues.cnt.org.

12 Casey Trees, "Tree Benefits Calculator," www.itreetools.org/treecalculator.

13 Low Impact Hydropower Institute, "Certification Program," www.lowimpacthydro.org/content/certification-program.aspx.

FURTHER READING

Condition and Trends Working Group. *Ecosystems and Human Well-Being: Current State and Trends.* Vol. 1, *Millennium Ecosystem Assessment.* Washington, D.C.: Island Press, 2005.

France, R. L. *Facilitating Watershed Management: Fostering Awareness and Stewardship.* Lanham, Md.: Rowman and Littlefield, 2005.

Hawken, P. *Blessed Unrest: How the Largest Movement in the World Came into Being and Why No One Saw It Coming.* New York: Viking Press, 2007.

Pelletier, M. R. "Criteria for a Greener Metropolis." Pp. 261–77 in R. H. Platt, ed., *The Humane Metropolis: People and Nature in the 21st Century City.* Amherst: University of Massachusetts Press, 2006.

Platt, R. H. "Urban Watershed Management: Sustainability, One Stream at a Time," *Environment* 48, no. 4 (2006): 26–42.

Richards, L. *Protecting Water Resources with Higher Density Development.* Washington D.C.: EPA, 2006. See www.epa.gov/smartgrowth/water_density.htm.

Riley, A. L. *Restoring Streams in Cities: A Guide for Planners, Policy Makers, and Citizens.* Washington, D.C.: Island Press, 1998.

United Nations. "International Decade for Action: Water for Life, 2005–2015," www.un.org/waterforlifedecade.

LOCAL SUSTAINABLE ENERGY SOURCES

ERICA HELLER, AICP, AND MARK HELLER, AICP

Greening the Local Energy Supply

Global climate change and volatile energy costs demand that communities make better, greener choices about electricity generation. According to the Department of Energy's Energy Information Administration, electricity generation is the source of 40 percent of carbon emissions in the United States. Energy efficiency improvements are currently the most cost-effective means to reduce emissions of carbon dioxide and other greenhouse gases, but such efforts cannot address the bulk of the carbon dioxide problem. The vast majority of electric power supplied in the United States is derived from the burning of coal. On average, to generate a megawatt hour of electricity, the most advanced coal plants emit 519 pounds of carbon dioxide. While renewable energy sources are currently costlier and less efficient than coal, they do not generate any additional carbon dioxide; and they will become more viable as the technologies evolve, as the cost and scarcity of fossil fuels rise, and as the necessity of rapid reduction of greenhouse gas emissions sinks in. Increasingly, green communities must consider how to shift the dominance of fossil-fuel-based energy sources such coal and natural gas toward more sustainable means of energy generation, such as solar, biomass, wind, nuclear, geothermal, and hydropower.

Climate change is the ultimate challenge for planners. Compared to other major societal changes that have been managed through planning and regulation, such as transportation, housing, and pollution, climate change has no local "face" or obvious deficiency to address. At this point in time, most Americans do not personally experience climate change impacts as they do other malfunctioning symptoms of modern life, such as impenetrable traffic jams, blighted neighborhoods, or toxic spills. To complicate matters, once the effects of climate change become tangible, it will be too late to easily correct them. Therefore, planners must be proactive and persuasive in not only educating policy makers and the public about the impacts of climate change but also in providing practical advice about avoiding, mitigating, and adapting to it.

This chapter raises the key issues that local communities can and should consider regarding how to select a good match between their community's characteristics and its energy resources. To help communities balance environmental benefits and risks, we consider the potential impacts of a variety of energy generation types as well as the land-use implications of local energy choices. Throughout, examples of communities that are greening their local energy provide guidance and inspiration.

What Local Communities Can Do

Local governments that do not own the utility that supplies their citizens' power often feel powerless to green their energy supply. Although the U.S. regulatory environment favors large regional utilities, emerging information and trends suggest that local governments can increasingly influence energy generation. At least 13 states have joined other stakeholders to support state and regional initiatives that require large-scale utilities to incorporate minimum percentages of renewables in their portfolios. A number of states—including California, Massachusetts, Rhode Island, and Ohio—have passed legislation to allow community choice aggregation. This legislation gives local government the ability to aggregate local demand and collaboratively negotiate terms with utilities. Under such legislation, local governments have been able to reduce rates, capture energy savings for local reinvestment, and most important for this discussion, direct the type of new generation equipment that is brought online to serve demand.

More directly, local governments have jurisdiction over local land use and site development regulations, giving them control over the siting of new types of new generation facilities. Even national and regional energy utility decision makers that can overrule local entities, such the Nuclear Regulatory Agency and public utilities commissions that license coal plants, are required to consider local input in siting decisions. Local initiatives are gaining momentum, as large and small communities initiate and permit local wind farms, multimegawatt solar arrays, biomass incinerators, run-of-the-river small hydro facilities, and geothermal steam plants.

Local planning and zoning continue to be tools that communities can use to promote the use of natural resources for energy generation. By discouraging residential development in the windiest areas, zoning land near the best geothermal resources for heavy energy uses such as industry, or enacting development standards that allow solar-ready roofs in new developments by right, local communities can encourage desired types of energy generation. The

exact tools that should be employed depend a great deal on the type of energy that the community wishes to pursue. Local land-use planning can also encourage non-utility-scale generation by removing barriers and creating incentives for home owners and businesses to retrofit existing buildings with solar panels and small wind turbines.

Supply and Demand Considerations

Communities seeking greener local energy options must consider a wide range of energy supply and demand considerations. As a start, locals must consider what types of resources are available in the community. According to the Department of Energy (DOE), about half of the area of the United States has wind resources that are adequate for wind power, while a more limited number of communities have been identified as having utility-scale geothermal resources. Different communities have different opportunities to harness renewable energy: Coastal communities could harvest tidal river flows. The southwest United States has enough sunlight for utility-scale generation, and solar can be harvested on a smaller scale nearly everywhere. Agricultural and forested biomass feedstock can be supplied on an industrial scale in the Midwest and southeast. Municipal solid waste, methane from landfills and manure, and construction materials are available in every city.

A second set of considerations relate to the proximity of the resource to the community: Can existing transmission infrastructure deliver the energy produced, and does it have enough capacity to add the new loads? And what is the cost to deliver the energy? In Tazimina, Alaska, there is a run-of-the-river small hydro plant with a potential capacity of more than six megawatts, but because the transmission system does not yet reach to the demand center, in Anchorage, 175 miles away, the plant currently runs at only one-quarter of capacity. Before considering sources that would require significant energy loss in transmission, or other production costs, planners should first consider what kind of renewable energy source is close by and whether that source would be appropriate for the community.

A third set of considerations relate to the variability of the delivery: Must the renewable energy delivery be constant, or can it be readily increased or decreased in response to demand? If a community is already served by a relatively constant energy source such as a coal or gas plant, the potential variability in delivery from a local, lower-carbon renewable energy source could be acceptable. For example, a coal-powered community, perhaps in the Southwest, might choose a photovoltaic installation to supplement or replace peak daytime energy demands. Such a decision would allow the community to permanently set a portion of its energy costs during the day and potentially reduce carbon emissions from the plant (assuming other communites served by the same plant made similar demand reduction changes—which points out the necessity of regional collaboration).

Other important supply-and-demand consider-ations include the amount of energy a typical facility can produce, the time it takes to build a facility, the time it takes to generate electricity from the particular energy source, and the scalability of the energy pro-duced by that facility or source. Biomass energy can be generated on a range of scales, such as: a five megawatt plant the size of a pickup truck, which powers a small farm; a 50 megawatt plant that runs on wood chips or willow and provides heating and cooling for a college campus; or a regional co-fired utility plant. A single large hydro plant supplies the energy needs for all of Juneau, Alaska, population 30,000. A small in-stream hydro-generator can power a single residence or small

village. Communities need to first assess their energy needs and then determine whether the locally available sustainable energy source can meet that need. Fresno, California, found that adding a solar power plant was more cost effective than adding another traditional plant to meet extra demand on hot days.

Environmental Considerations

If the goal is to make the community more green, the full range of environmental impacts of the energy source must be assessed, and the adverse impacts mitigated or avoided. One question should be: How much would the alternative energy facility reduce greenhouse gas emissions compared to conventional energy generation or other alternatives? Options such as solar, hydro, nuclear, and wind produce no carbon emissions from production. Biomass emits carbon dioxide, but the amount is net-neutral because of what is absorbed as the feedstocks are grown.

What impacts on habitat are anticipated? Several hydro dams in Oregon have been removed due to impacts on fisheries and riparian health. The Altamont Ridge wind farm, in California, is located in raptor habitat and therefore has an unusually high number of documented avian strikes.

What waste products, emissions, or pollutants are produced, and what are their public health and environmental impacts? How can they be safely handled? Spent nuclear rods from nuclear facilities are an example of a waste product that creates a complex set of hazards, land-use impacts, and other long-term challenges. While coal can be burned cleaner, it will still release large amounts of carbon. Biofuel genera-tion creates ash and particulates.

How much land and water—precious environmen-tal and economic resources in their own right—are consumed in the process? A nuclear facility requires acres of water and a zone in a five-mile radius with low population density and excellent evacuation routes. For the growing of some biomass feedstocks, substan-tial land area and water for irrigation are required. But other feedstocks are waste from timber culling or agricultural production; and some, such as switchgrass, can be grown on land that is marginal or otherwise fallow. Wind farms may occupy low-productivity land or be colocated with agricultural uses, but may occupy valued scenic areas.

Broader land-use and social impacts should also be considered. For example, the controversy over how much corn has been diverted to ethanol production highlights the need to carefully and sustainably harvest agricultural biomass. Large-scale use of agricultural residue left after harvesting the main crop, which could be an abundant energy source, has not been fully evaluated for its impacts on soil health. Even harvesting deadwood or forests killed by pine beetles risks upsetting ecosystems. More than 150 cities in the United States, including New York City, have declared themselves nuclear-free zones, restricting the ability to transport spent radioactive materials through city limits from existing nuclear power plants to long-term storage. Communities in the vicinity of Yucca Mountain, Nevada—which is the DOE's identified site for long-term storage of spent nuclear fuel—are divided over the local risks and rewards the storage facility presents.

Other Considerations

There is a wide range of other considerations for greening local energy. At the top of the list is cost. Cost considerations include costs for initial development of the generation facilities, which depend on factors such as size and scale, existing transmission infrastructure, and connection costs; ownership of the generation equipment; state and federal permitting requirements; and available subsidies and incentives. A nuclear plant can cost $5 billion for 1,000 megawatts of capacity, compared to a $65 million wind farm that produces 50 megawatts. However, the varying life spans and realistic annual outputs (rather than capacities) of each type of energy source must also be considered, as well as the resulting price of electricity for consumers, the ability to reduce prices through demand aggregation, and local willingness to pay a premium for greener energy.[1]

Another factor is the length of time it takes to bring a new facility online. Can it be brought on incrementally? A wind farm can typically be sited and con-structed in less than five years, whereas a nuclear facility typically requires about 20 years. Once the facility is built, can production be tailored to meet fluctuations in demand? Large hydro plants are some of the most nimble facilities, as flow rate can be adjusted to match daily demand or compensate for other more intermittent sources.

Other considerations include potential local impacts; worst-case scenarios, such as noise, clashing aesthetics, negative health impacts, or radiation exposure; and the potential for benefits, such as wind turbine land leases helping independent farmers stay in business, or the shading from rooftop solar panels that reduces the urban heat island effect. Comprehensive and affordable climate data collection will be necessary so that communities can accurately forecast the likely impacts of climate change and the ability of their energy resources to adapt to those changing conditions—such as the effect of warmer water for nuclear plant cooling and warmer return water, less or more rain for biomass feedstock, and less water for hydropower.

In addition, the degree to which local government can influence or control decision making will be a factor in determining what type of green energy a community may choose to pursue. For example, a local government might not have control or ownership of the renewable resource or of the land occupied by the generating facility. Also, states vary in allowing community demand aggregation.

Specific Issues and Impacts by Energy Type

The following pages offer a matrix of local energy alternatives—hydro, nuclear, wind, solar, geothermal, and biomass—summarizing some of the unique strengths and challenges of each. There are many other energy technologies—including methane capture, waste industrial heat, and hydrogen—that are not included here because they are either not market-ready or not typically available at a utility scale.

NUCLEAR POWER

SUPPLY-AND-DEMAND CONSIDERATIONS

Quantity   Typically around 1,000 MW. Not for small
                 community applications.

Reliability Constant utility-scale baseload. Domestic
                 supply of uranium plentiful to meet foresee-
                 able future demand.

Proximity   Must be near large amount of water.
                 Should be near large demand center.

Scalability If space allows, may be able to construct
                 additional reactors after initial construction.

Flexibility Slow to power up and down. Twenty or more
                 years to approve and construct.

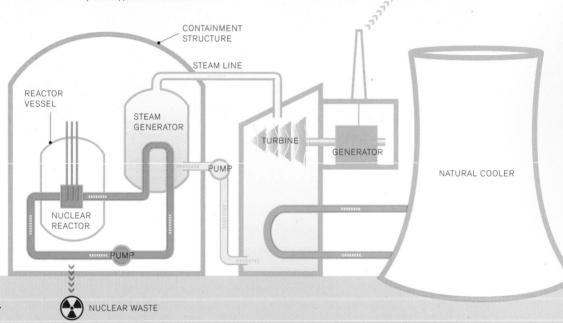

SUSTAINABILITY CONSIDERATIONS

CO2 Emissions   None.

Other Emissions   Spent fuel rods must be stored indefinitely.

Land Consumption The plant itself may be fairly compact but
                      requires a five-mile radius zone with limited
                      development and excellent evacuation
                      routes. Water needs may cause inundation.

Water Consumption Needs ready access to large quantities of
                      water for cooling, which is returned to the
                      water body at a slightly higher temperature.

Habitat Impacts   In normal operations, impacts are limited
                      to warmer water return. Remote possibility
                      for catastrophic radiation contamination.

ADDITIONAL LAND-USE CONSIDERATIONS

Local Control   Greatly limited, although the Nuclear Regu-
                    latory Commission works with localities and
                    takes concerns into consideration. Local
                    government responsible for emergency
                    management.

Local Impacts   Boom/bust cycle for construction and oper-
                    ation of the plant. Limited use of land within
                    safety zone.

Broader Impacts Nuclear storage, transport, decommissioning,
                    proliferation, and potential widespread conta-
                    mination are permanent issues.

Other Benefits One of the only proven technologies that, if
                    permitted and constructed, could substan-
                    tially reduce CO2 emissions within a decade.

SOLAR ENERGY CAPTURE

SUPPLY-AND-DEMAND CONSIDERATIONS

Quantity
Depends on location. Abundant in the Southwest. Most solar plants are relatively small (2 MW); the largest operating in the United States is 14 MW.

Reliability
Inconstant daily; seasonally predictable. Supply matches peak demand in hot sunny places. Long-term supply not expected to change much unless climate change increases cloud cover.

Proximity
Southern California and Nevada have adequate resources for utility-scale solar power. Panels can be used by individual homes and businesses almost anywhere in the United States.

Scalability
From a single photovoltaic panel to 14 MW utility installations.

Flexibility
Powers up and down easily but dependent on resource.

SUSTAINABILITY CONSIDERATIONS

CO2 Emissions
None.

Other Emissions
None.

Land Consumption
Ground installations can be land consumptive. Rooftop installations are closer to demand, with no land consumption.

Water Consumption
None.

Habitat Impacts
Limited to the impacts of shading and perhaps security fencing.

ADDITIONAL LAND-USE CONSIDERATIONS

Local Control
High degree for panel and utility-scale installations.

Local Impacts
Glare and aesthetic impacts in the immediate vicinity; burn danger is possible if someone trespasses or tampers with utility-scale solar.

Broader Impacts
Photovoltaic panel manufacturing uses silicon and other toxic materials and is energy intensive.

Other Benefits
Rooftop panels can provide shade in summer to reduce building heat absorption, cooling loads, and the urban heat island effect.

Erica Heller, AICP, and Mark Heller, AICP

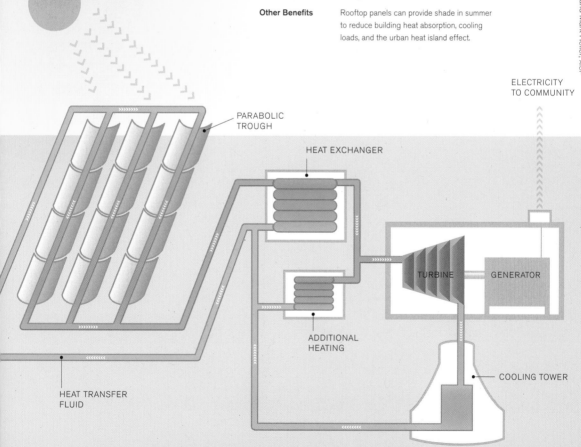

ELECTRICITY TO COMMUNITY

PARABOLIC TROUGH

HEAT EXCHANGER

TURBINE

GENERATOR

ADDITIONAL HEATING

COOLING TOWER

HEAT TRANSFER FLUID

GEOTHERMAL POWER

SUPPLY-AND-DEMAND CONSIDERATIONS

Quantity Small (250 kW) to large (1,000 MW) plants; relatively rare at utility scale. Installed capacity of about 3,000 MW in the United States. Estimates suggest it could supply up to 14% of U.S. power demand.

Reliability Constant baseload. Limited locations, and resource can be degraded by use. Depletion can be slowed by reinjection of steam after use.

Proximity Utility-scale resources limited to a few hundred communities.

Scalability Plants can be easily expanded to meet increasing demand, up to a maximum dependent on the strength of the resource.

Flexibility High. Using underground reservoir, steam can be released as needed.

SUSTAINABILITY CONSIDERATIONS

CO2 Emissions None.

Other Emissions Steam.

Land Consumption None.

Water Consumption Most are not especially consumptive. There are some steam losses in utility and industrial applications, but newer systems recapture them.

Habitat Impacts Generally, none.

ADDITIONAL LAND-USE CONSIDERATIONS

Local Control High degree if resource is within the community's jurisdiction. Must partner with landowner.

Local Impacts After electricity generation cools steam, it is still hot enough for secondary uses such as industrial applications or district heating.

Broader Impacts Plants and pipes use metals that are mined.

Other Benefits Silica removal from steam yields exceptional-quality product for high-tech applications.

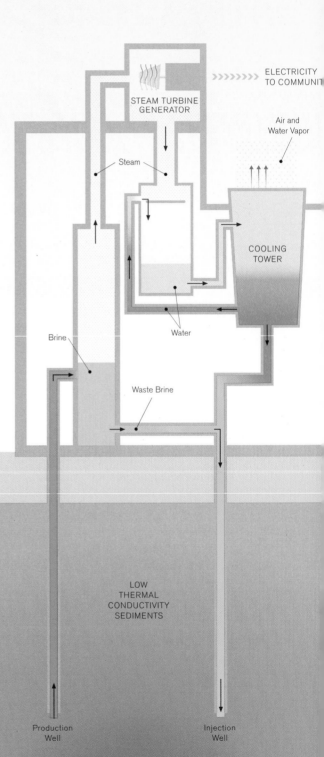

BIOMASS ENERGY CAPTURE

SUPPLY-AND-DEMAND CONSIDERATIONS

Quantity
Potentially quite large and available throughout the country. Very appropriate for community and micro applications.

Reliability
Baseload capable. Different crops could be used in different seasons and some could be stored. Supply could change somewhat with climate change, although so could selections. Municipal solid waste (MSW) and methane from manure and landfills would be constant.

Proximity
Feasible in most agricultural and forestry areas. Feedstock not viable in urban areas or slow-growth areas such as tundra or desert. MSW and methane from manure and landfills are a reliable source available everywhere.

Scalability
Power plants can range from 5 MW to utility-scale co-fired coal or gas plants.

Flexibility
Inefficient to power up or down, but possible.

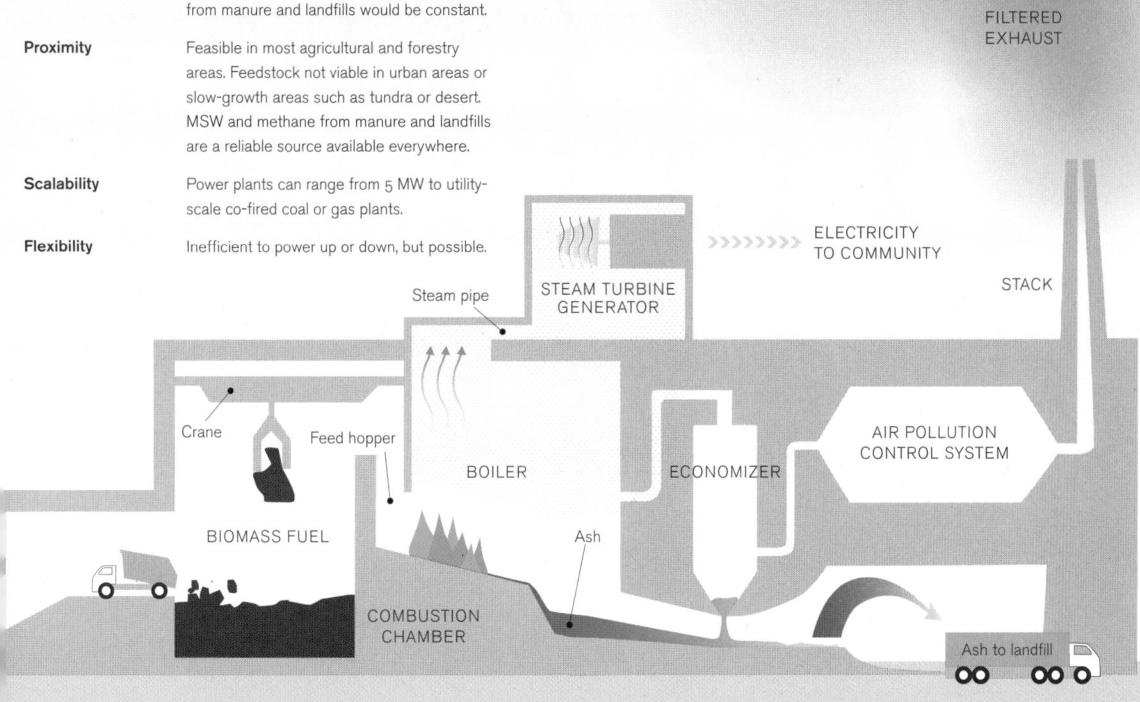

FILTERED EXHAUST

STEAM TURBINE GENERATOR

ELECTRICITY TO COMMUNITY

STACK

Steam pipe

Crane

Feed hopper

BOILER

ECONOMIZER

AIR POLLUTION CONTROL SYSTEM

BIOMASS FUEL

Ash

COMBUSTION CHAMBER

Ash to landfill

Erica Heller, AICP, and Mark Heller, AICP

SUSTAINABILITY CONSIDERATIONS

CO₂ Emissions
Yes, but generally carbon neutral since the carbon emitted from burning is equivalent to the carbon sequestered by the growth of the feedstock.

Other Emissions
No sulfur, limited nitrogen emissions. Far cleaner than coal or gas. Emits particulates (which can be filtered). Generates ash that is suitable for use in concrete.

Land Consumption
Power stations can be truck-sized or as big as a traditional coal plant. Other land consumption varies by feedstock. Use of waste materials is not at all land consumptive. Farmed feedstocks may be land consumptive but may utilize marginal or fallow land.

Water Consumption
Consumptive to the extent required to grow feedstocks.

Habitat Impacts
Some feedstocks, such as agricultural wastes or timber thinnings, may otherwise be left to return organic matter to the soil.

ADDITIONAL LAND-USE CONSIDERATIONS

Local Control
High degree if community based; less so if utility-scale.

Local Impacts
Potential for utilization of local land and water. This is beneficial if land is marginal or feedstock is a waste product, but it is negative if it displaces other productive uses. Particulates and other emissions are produced, although many fewer than from coal or gas alone.

Broader Impacts
Potential for large-scale use of land and monocultures susceptible to disease or climate change. If food crops (e.g., corn) are used for feedstock, it reduces food availability and can drive up global food prices.

Other Benefits
Could be relatively easy and cost effective to increase use in existing coal and gas plants or to construct new gasification plants. Wastes may be put to beneficial use as feedstock. Collection system for MSW and methane already in place.

HYDRO POWER

SUPPLY-AND-DEMAND CONSIDERATIONS

Quantity   Most of the best large resources in the
United States are already developed.
Continued supply at risk from climate
changes to rainfall and siltation. Small hydro
(1–30 MW) has the best expansion potential.

Reliability   Large hydro is constant. Small run-of-the-
river and short-term reservoirs depend on
flow and may be seasonal.

Proximity   Must be near fast-moving water or a
reservoir must be created. Most large hydro
is developed; some is being dismantled.
Feasible small hydro could increase total
U.S. hydro power by up to 50%.

Scalability   Hydro on the scale of 1–30 MW is a growth
area. New larger dams are not realistic in
much of the United States.

Flexibility   Very flexible. Can be controlled through flow
rate, especially when system includes
reservoir.

SUSTAINABILITY CONSIDERATIONS

CO2 Emissions   None.

Other Emissions   None.

Land Consumption   Reservoirs can be land consumptive. Small
in-stream systems are not land consumptive.

Water Consumption   Not consumptive per se, but the changes
to timing, levels, and temperature of the
flow of a river through a dam can have a
range of impacts on availability of water
for downstream and in-stream uses.

Habitat Impacts   Can be problematic for riparian habitats
downstream. The change from a river and
basin to a reservoir destroys one habitat and
creates another. Fisheries often affected.
Siltation and heavy-metal accumulation
may occur.

ADDITIONAL LAND-USE CONSIDERATIONS

Local Control   High degree for small hydro, which can be
built on free-flowing streams or outflows
from municipal reservoirs and wastewater
treatment.

Local Impacts   Large hydro: reservoir inundation of local
lands; riparian changes; economic impact
on fisheries.

Broader Impacts   For large hydro with reservoir and flow
control, there are habitat impacts on the
whole length of the river system.

Other Benefits   Reservoirs for hydro power have created
water-based recreational opportunities,
are frequented by migratory species, and
host permanent animal populations.

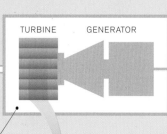

HEADPOND

WATER INTAKE

PIPELINE

ELECTRICITY
TO COMMUNITY

TURBINE   GENERATOR

POWERHOUSE

WIND ENERGY

SUPPLY-AND-DEMAND CONSIDERATIONS

Quantity Output from small turbines may be 1 to 100 kW per hour; and from wind farms may be 40–400 MW per hour. Wind is abundant, but because it is intermittent the Department of Energy estimates that it is feasible for 20 to 40% of U.S. energy supply. Wind supplies 80% of Norway's needs.

Reliability Inconstant daily; more prevalent at night. Seasonally, fairly predictable. Long-term supply constant unless climate change alters wind patterns.

Proximity Plains states, coastal areas, and the Midwest are best. Very limited in southeastern United States.

Scalability Turbines are available with output ratings from 1 kW to more than 2 MW. Wind farms may produce hundreds of MW.

Flexibility Powers up and down easily but is dependent on whether the wind is blowing.

SUSTAINABILITY CONSIDERATIONS

CO2 Emissions None.

Other Emissions None.

Land Consumption Can be somewhat land consumptive but often sited in areas that are not productive for other uses (scrublands, ridgetops) or colocated with agricultural uses.

Water Consumption No.

Habitat Impacts Limited but need to be kept out of bird migration corridors.

ADDITIONAL LAND-USE CONSIDERATIONS

Local Control High degree for both individual turbines and wind farms. Some states limit local ability to enact prohibitive regulations.

Local Impacts Noise; possible impacts on birds in some habitat areas; potential icing or flicker shadow in close proximity.

Broader Impacts Turbine and tower manufacturing uses metals that are mined.

Other Benefits In some rural areas, wind farms have been developed by leasing turbine footprints from farmers. This source of revenue can help keep family farms in operation.

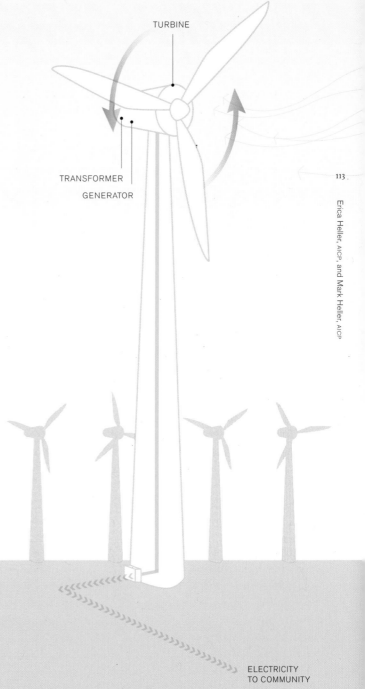

TURBINE

TRANSFORMER

GENERATOR

ELECTRICITY TO COMMUNITY

113

Erica Heller, AICP, and Mark Heller, AICP

Game Changers

There are a number of factors that could create a paradigm shift in how local communities consider green energy options. Intermittent renewable energy sources could be coupled with storage, offsetting the challenges of inconstant production. In addition to advanced batteries, one alternative being tested is to use wind power to pressurize air in giant chambers, such as underground salt beds or other geologic features, and then release the pressure to turn turbines to meet later demand. Such proprietary alternatives are being researched and developed, and several pilot tests have been approved in the United States and Europe.

Since carbon is the Achilles' heel of coal and natural gas power, much attention is being focused on keeping the carbon out of the atmosphere by sequestering it postproduction, either in the ocean or underground. Sequestration has not yet been field-tested in a meaningful way, and many experts suggest such technology will not be available for at least another 10 years. If and when sequestration becomes feasible and demonstrably secure, the use of coal and natural gas could reemerge as a green choice.

As this book went to press, the Obama administration and the 111th Congress were beginning a range of substantial revisions to the national energy policy that, when implemented, may result in a paradigm change for local energy decisions. The federal government dramatically increased subsidies for energy-efficiency implementations, increased Corporate Average Fuel Economy (CAFE) standards, began to regulate carbon dioxide, and greatly boosted the budget for research and development in renewable energy technology. A commitment by the United States to carbon reduction, whether through international agreements such as the Copenhagen successor to the Kyoto Protocol, a cap-and-trade system, or other comprehensive federal legislation would revolutionize the state and local approach to renewable energy production by combining treaty obligations and market forces with federal subsidies and progressive energy regulation.

Emerging technologies such as tidal wave energy generators, hydrogen fuel cells, small-scale nuclear fission units, and smart grids linked to electricity-generating cars and homes are under development and testing. At present, these technologies have significant hurdles to overcome before they are ready for utility-scale applications. One or more of these, or perhaps some yet-to-be conceived technology, may emerge as a cost-effective and practical source of local and sustainable energy in the years to come.

Nature waits for no one, and the possibility exists that the climate could change too quickly, severely, or in ways that we have not anticipated. New data suggests some climate changes are already outpacing predictions. Such changes could frustrate or obviate policy, funding, or energy source decisions. For example, communities throughout the country are installing, or considering installing, microturbines below reservoirs built for water retention. A change in the rate of precipitation could render those efforts useless or less productive, and an abrupt change could have far worse implications.

Communities are planning for perhaps the most uncertain times in the postindustrial era. We know that major climatic, energy, and economic shifts are under way—but we do not know the exact timing, degree, or character of these changes. This chapter has summarized the most viable types of sustainable energy sources—including nuclear, due to its zero emissions—and presented a range of issues that should be considered by communities of all sizes as they choose their energy future. To prepare for the challenges ahead, many prudent communities are working to diversify their local energy supply strategies and technologies with different capacities and limitations, each at different levels of practicality. We do not know which of these will lead us quickest to sustainable local energy supplies and national energy independence. As unpredictable as the future is, it might very well be the case that any choice toward greener local energy will be better than the status quo.

The attempt to rapidly reform energy production is complicated by the current profound economic downturn, which creates global inertia to maintain the energy status quo, at the very time when we most

need to change it. However, we are on the cusp of a
new federal approach to climate change, which could
counter that inertia and greatly advance policies,
science, technology, and funding for renewable energy.
In this new environment, planners, architects, scientists, energy developers and suppliers, policy makers,
and the public would be wise to quickly gather the tools
and the knowledge to make practical, sustainable, and
renewable energy choices.

NOTES

1   The Energy Information Administration (EIA) within DOE publishes
    official numbers for the typical cost per kilowatt hour of a variety of
    energy generation types. We have not included cost comparison numbers
    in this chapter because of the controversy created by the variability of
    the externalized costs in the EIA analyses, such as the cost of required
    transmission expansion to bring energy to the consumer. Also, industry
    and government cost calculations sometimes do not include elements
    that might, from a sustainability perspective, be appropriate to consider,
    including remediation of mines, value of habitat losses, health care costs
    of higher asthma rates, and federal payments for black lung disease.

FURTHER READING

American Wind Energy Association, www.awea.org.

Biomass Energy Resource Center, www.biomasscenter.org.

Idaho National Laboratory, www.inl.gov.

National Renewable Energy Laboratory, www.nrel.gov.

Nuclear Regulatory Commission, www.nrc.gov.

U.S. Department of Energy, www.doe.gov.

U.S. Energy Information Administration, www.eia.gov.

U.S. Conference of Mayors, www.usmayors.org.

Erica Heller, AICP, and Mark Heller, AICP

TO OPEN THE DOOR OF OPPORTUNITY
FOR HEALTH, WE MUST CLOSE THE
DOOR FOR EXPLOITATION OF LAND

—BENJAMIN MARSH, 1908

Los Angeles, California

HEALTHY COMMUNITIES, GREEN COMMUNITIES

HOWARD FRUMKIN

Almost 2,500 years ago, the legendary Greek physician Hippocrates wrote his classic *Treatise on Air, Water, and Places*. He offered careful observations on the placement of towns and cities, on wind, sunlight, soil, ground cover, and topography, and on how these factors influenced the health of people who resided there. Writing as both physician and geographer, he knew the important effects of place on health.

More than two millennia later, Frederick Law Olmsted had the same insight. The father of landscape architecture, he was keenly attuned to human health, even serving as secretary-general of the United States Sanitary Commission (forerunner of the Red Cross) during the Civil War. In such projects as New York's Central Park—the "lungs of the city"—and Boston's Back Bay Fens—a landmark in civil engineering, sewage management, and health protection—he viewed his creations as acts of public health. Working as both designer and health activist, he, too, knew the important effects of place on health.

Olmsted was prescient. Life expectancy in the United States rose from 47.3 years in 1900 to 77.8 in 2005, and historians attribute much of the increase not to medical care but to the way communities were designed, built, and operated.[1] Clean water, sewage disposal, solid and hazardous waste management, limits on overcrowding, zoning that separated homes from noxious industries—these strategies reshaped cities and helped reduce mortality from such killers as typhoid, cholera, yellow fever, and tuberculosis.

Emerging Challenges

But that was then, and this is now. We still need to combine architecture and planning with public health, but we confront a vastly different set of challenges. At least four issues are important.

First, a schism has opened, with architecture, planning, and civil engineering on one side and medicine, nursing, and public health on the other.[2,3] The two domains once overlapped considerably; believe it or not, drainage and sewage treatment were part of the medical curriculum a century ago. Now there are separate languages, separate schools, separate meetings, separate journals.

Second, health challenges have evolved. The major causes of death, suffering, and disability have changed greatly since Olmsted's time. Heart disease, cancer, strokes, injuries, asthma, diabetes, obesity, and depression have edged out such conditions as tuberculosis, dysentery, influenza, and pneumonia. Our population is far larger and older than it was a century ago. Accordingly, different public health strategies are needed.

Third, it's become clear that design strategies that once seemed modern, salubrious, and convenient have downsides.[4] For the last few generations, urban sprawl has defined our approach to community design. Cities have expanded over vast geographic areas. Land-use patterns at the urban edge have changed, from traditional farm and forest to residential subdivisions. Land-use mix has declined; housing developments are built far from schools, stores, and workplaces. Land-use density has also declined; some communities can measure residential density in acres per family

Improved connectivity plan for Starkville, Mississippi.

BIKE STARKVILLE

· · · · Rails with Trails from Wal-Mart to Research Park.

– – – A path along Lynn Lane continues on South Montgomery and Locksley Way to connect with Blackjack Road and the university.

——— Painted lanes on University Drive and Main Street continue the campus path and end at Jackson Street.

WALK STARKVILLE

– – – A sidewalk on Hospital Road connects with North Jackson Street.

· · · · Sidewalks and bike lanes on Highway 82 anticipate the opening of the bypass.

——— The Henderson School; a Starkville pilot for Safe Routes to Schools.

═══ A radius around the Henderson School that defines the Safe Routes to Schools zone.

rather than families per acre. Traditional downtowns have given way to long stretches of multilane roads lined by big box stores perched in vast parking lagoons. Transportation systems have changed as well, with the vast majority of trips—even short ones—made by automobile, with a concomitant drop in walking, bicycling, and transit use. Amenities that were routine in an earlier age—sidewalks, plazas, parks—are commonly omitted in contemporary subdivisions. At the scale of individual buildings, ever larger homes have required more and more energy to heat and cool them. Tight buildings, intended to conserve energy, have led to stubborn indoor air quality problems. Innovative building materials "bite back" by emitting volatile organic compounds.[5] From the scale of metropolitan areas, to the scale of neighborhoods, down to the scale of buildings, seemingly good ideas can be bad for health.

Fourth, the context has changed. We face global challenges that Olmsted and his contemporaries could scarcely have imagined. The energy source that powers nearly all our transportation—petroleum—is reaching a global peak in production and will become increasingly scarce and expensive in coming years.[6,7] The global climate is changing, apparently at a sharply accelerating pace, with potentially catastrophic consequences for weather, coastal lands (where many cities are built), agriculture, health, and countless other human domains.[8] The energy source that powers much of our electric grid—coal—contributes to climate change, and we need to reduce its use; no large-scale replacement source of energy is readily available. Many regions face severe shortages of water, fertile topsoil, and other natural resources. Population pressure continues to mount. Together these challenges require a commitment to sustainability.

It is not enough to design places that promote the health of those who live, work, and play in them. We also need to design places that respect ecological limits, that use resources wisely, and that thereby promote the health of our great-grandchildren.

Designing Healthy Places

Happily, there is a growing evidence base that points the way to healthy community design. The SMAR-TRAQ (Strategies for Metro Atlanta's Regional Transportation and Air Quality) study in metro Atlanta followed more than 10,000 adults, assessing their neighborhood characteristics, their means of travel, and certain health outcomes. Greater land-use mix, more walking each day, and less time spent in the car each day were each associated with a lower risk of obesity.[9] Land-use and transportation patterns predict physical activity, and physical activity is important for health.

The National Household Travel Survey, a study of more than 100,000 Americans, found that people who use mass transit benefit from substantial amounts of routine physical activity. Walking from home to the originating bus or train stop, and from the destination stop to work, school, or shopping, and reversing that journey on the way home, involves an average of 24 minutes of walking per day. Nearly one in three transit users gets the recommended full 30 minutes of daily physical activity, simply by using transit.[10] In an increasingly sedentary and overweight nation, mass transit promotes needed physical activity.

Walkable neighborhoods appear to offer benefits that extend beyond physical activity. In one study, people in more walkable neighborhoods were more likely to know their neighbors, participate politically, trust other people, and be engaged in social interactions.[11] These outcomes together reflect social capital—the glue that binds communities together and that, incidentally, is a powerful predictor of good health.[12]

A study in Atlanta during the 1996 Olympic Games took advantage of a natural experiment. Atlantans were urged to refrain from driving during the 17 days of the Games. Many complied, and peak morning traffic counts dropped by 22.5 percent. Peak daily ozone levels promptly dropped by 27.9 percent. And acute asthma events in children dropped by as much as 44.1 percent.[13] All three parameters returned to their baseline at the conclusion of the Olympics. Transportation affects air quality, and air quality affects health.

ATLANTIC STATION

Like many American cities in the second half of the 20th century, Atlanta found itself in a cycle of contamination and abandonment: downtown factories closed, leaving dirty land and water, while citizens moved farther out of the city, resulting in longer commutes, more tailpipe emissions, and worse air quality. One of those factories, Atlantic Steel, left behind a 138-acre brownfield in Atlanta's Midtown neighborhood when it closed, after nearly a century, in 1998. Now cleaned, the site is Atlantic Station, a neighborhood with 10,000 residents, green space, offices, and shops, connected to Midtown by a new bridge.

Remediation Efforts

Cleaning the site's contaminated soil and water was only part of the challenge. Developers were also committed to cleaning the air by creating a transit-oriented neighborhood to reduce reliance on private automobiles. A nearby rapid-transit stop was inaccessible across the interstate. Thus, the project hinged on constructing a bridge across the highway, which would require permission from the federal government. But Atlanta's air quality at the time did not meet federal standards, prohibiting the city from spending funds on any project requiring federal permission—even if it was intended to improve air quality. The Environmental Protection Agency broke this impasse using an innovative program, Project XL, to address the complex relationships among transportation, land use, and environmental and public health.

New Site

By 2000, the last toxic traces of Atlantic Steel were removed. A one-acre pond is part of the project's stormwater management system to reduce runoff and provides a centerpiece for the community commons. Generous sidewalks, car-sharing programs, and the new pedestrian bridge connecting to the rapid-transit station and the attractions of Midtown all help to wean Atlantic Station's residents from their car dependence, improving personal health as well as that of the natural environment.

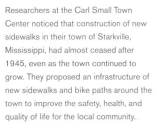

Researchers at the Carl Small Town Center noticed that construction of new sidewalks in their town of Starkville, Mississippi, had almost ceased after 1945, even as the town continued to grow. They proposed an infrastructure of new sidewalks and bike paths around the town to improve the safety, health, and quality of life for the local community.

In sprawling communities where people spend much time in their cars, motor vehicle fatality rates and pedestrian fatality rates are high.[14] This is a pressing public health challenge; motor vehicle crashes are the leading cause of death among young people nationwide. Not surprisingly, reducing driving can help prevent these tragedies. In fact, when gasoline prices rise, people drive less, and highway death rates decline[15]—an effect that seems to have operated to save lives during the summer of 2008.[16] With less driving there are fewer traffic deaths.

Common sense suggests that parks are an asset for communities. They provide a venue for physical activity, social interaction, and relaxation, which all promote health and well-being. But a recent study of parks in Copenhagen provided further evidence of health benefits. People who live near parks not only use the parks more frequently than those at a distance, but they have lower stress levels and weigh less—an effect *not* fully explained by visits to the park![17] Nearby parks are salutary.

And it isn't just parks that promote health. Simply the presence of nearby trees offers benefits. In a landmark series of studies at a former low-income housing complex in Chicago, researchers at the University of Illinois compared buildings with and without trees nearby. People living in buildings with trees showed a remarkable range of social and psychological benefits: a greater sense of community,[18] higher levels of attention and greater effectiveness in managing major life issues,[19] substantially lower levels of aggression and violence among women (both as victims and as perpetrators),[20] and less crime.[21]

Community design, then, can do a great deal to promote health. Good sidewalks and trails, mass transit, nearby destinations, parks and other green spaces, safety, and the presence of other people all play a role. To support these design features, many of the principles of "smart growth" are relevant: density, connectivity, mixed land use, vibrant activity centers, transportation alternatives, and preservation of green spaces. Community design is increasingly recognized as a public health strategy.[22]

Planning and Public Health: Different Toolboxes, Shared Tools

Planners and public health professionals have available a set of common tools that permit them to work together to reach shared goals. One example is the "health impact assessment," a set of methods used to evaluate the impact on health of policies and projects in community design, transportation planning, and other areas outside traditional public health concerns.[23] Another example is a walkability audit, one of several methods that convene planners, health officials, and members of the public to evaluate community infrastructure and identify opportunities for improvement. Charrettes accomplish a similar goal, but prospectively instead of retrospectively. Mapping exercises using GIS can pinpoint hot spots of motor vehicle crashes, asthma, and other health outcomes and help identify space-based solutions. Health professionals can serve as members of planning commissions, and planners can serve on boards of health.[24]

The Beauty of Synergy

One appeal of this approach is the synergy it offers. We don't have a drug that prevents heart disease, cancer, asthma, diabetes, depression, or injuries. (If we did, we'd be adding it to the water supply!) But we do have community design strategies that offer all of this and more. The simple act of a child walking to school—with all the precursors, environmental and behavioral, that lie behind it—reduces the risk of each of the conditions listed above. The simple intervention of planting trees in a community offers many of these health benefits, directly and indirectly. At a time when health care costs are rising and health care coverage eludes many Americans, such synergistic preventive strategies are more important than ever.

The beauty of this synergy extends beyond direct health benefits. In many cases, the interventions that define healthy communities also define green communities. Shifting transportation from driving to walking, bicycling, and transit does more than promote health. It improves air quality, and it reduces carbon dioxide emissions. Building more compact communities, balanced by the preservation of green space, does more than promote health. It protects waterways and floodplains, conserves rural and agricultural land, and promotes biodiversity. At a smaller scale, "green" buildings that utilize sustainably produced, nontoxic materials and effective insulation do more than improve indoor air quality; they reduce energy consumption, which in turn reduces pollutant and carbon dioxide emissions from power plants.

The benefits of green, healthy communities do not accrue only to those who live in them, or even to their contemporaries. They accrue over time. The decisions we make today—not only in community design but in energy, transportation, agriculture, and a host of other arenas—will have implications for our grandchildren and their grandchildren. The United Nations Commission on Environment and Development in 1987 defined sustainable development as development that "meets the needs of the present without compromising the ability of future generations to meet their own needs"—a recognition that we need to be good stewards, for the

The Bike Starkville & Walk Starkville initiative proposes adding sidewalks and bike lanes to link many adjacent but currently disconnected town neighborhoods. For instance, by connecting the Mississippi State University campus to downtown, to shopping, and to a proposed new business park, the organization hopes to make it easier for people to leave their cars in their garages.

sake of those who will follow us. This is a recognition found in many cultures and credos. The Great Law of Peace of the Hau de no sau nee (the Six Nations Iroquois Confederacy) mandated that chiefs consider the impact of their decisions on the seventh generation yet to come.[25] Contemporary religious leaders have called for "creation care"—stewardship of the earth as both a religious obligation and an obligation to future generations.[26] Ethicists have asserted intergenerational justice as a moral basis for action on climate change.[27] We need to look to the future.

Green communities, then, are in many ways healthy communities—promoting good health and well-being directly for those who reside in them, indirectly for their neighbors, and indirectly for those who come after. They offer a wide range of health benefits, corresponding to the major contemporary causes of morbidity and mortality. They offer "co-benefits" that extend beyond health to the environment and the economy. Those who care about health, and those who work in design, architecture, and planning, can celebrate their growing convergence of interest and the enormous opportunities to collaborate in achieving shared goals: green, healthy, and sustainable communities for all people.

NOTES

1 J. Duffy, *The Sanitarians: A History of American Public Health* (Champaign: University of Illinois Press, 1992).

2 J. Corburn, "Confronting the Challenges in Reconnecting Urban Planning and Public Health," *American Journal of Public Health* 94 (2004): 541–46.

3 M. F. Greenberg et al. "Linking City Planning and Public Health in the United States," *Journal of Planning Literature* 8 (1994): 235–39.

4 H. Frumkin, L. Frank, and R. J. Jackson, *Urban Sprawl and Public Health* (Washington, D.C.: Island Press, 2004).

5 E. Tenner, *Why Things Bite Back: Technology and the Revenge of Unintended Consequences* (New York: Knopf, 1997).

6 K. S. Deffeyes, *Hubbert's Peak: The Impending World Oil Shortage* (Princeton, N.J.: Princeton University Press, 2008).

7 D. Goodstein, *Out of Gas: The End of the Age of Oil* (New York: Norton, 2004).

8 M. Parry et al., eds., *Climate Change 2007: Impacts, Adaptation and Vulnerability. Contribution of Working Group II to the Fourth Assessment Report of the Intergovernmental Panel on Climate Change* (Geneva: IPCC and Cambridge: Cambridge University Press, 2007). Available at: www.ipcc-wg2.org/.

9 L. Frank, M. Andresen, and T. Schmid, "Obesity Relationships with Community Design, Physical Activity, and Time Spent in Cars," *American Journal of Preventive Medicine* 27 (2004): 87–97.

10 L. M. Besser and A. L. Dannenberg, "Walking to Public Transit: Steps to Help Meet Physical Activity Recommendations," *American Journal of Preventive Medicine* 29 (2005): 273–80.

11 K. M. Leyden, "Social Capital and the Built Environment: The Importance of Walkable Neighborhoods," *American Journal of Public Health* 93 (2003): 1546–51.

12 L. Kawachi, S. V. Subramanian, and D. Kim, eds., *Social Capital and Health* (New York: Springer, 2008).

13 M. S. Friedman et al., "Impact of Changes in Transportation and Commuting Behaviors During the 1996 Summer Olympic Games in Atlanta on Air Quality and Childhood Asthma," *Journal of the American Medical Association* 285 (2001): 897–905

14 R. Ewing, R. A. Schieber, and C. V. Zegeer, "Urban Sprawl as a Risk Factor in Motor Vehicle Occupant and Pedestrian Fatalities," *American Journal of Public Health* 93, no. 9 (2003): 1541–45.

15 D. C. Grabowski and M. A. Morrissey, "Gasoline Prices and Motor Vehicle Fatalities," *Journal of Policy Analysis and Management* 23 (2004): 575–93.

16 M. Sivak, "Is the U.S. on the Path to the Lowest Motor Vehicle Fatalities in Decades?" Report no. UMTRI-2008-39, University of Michigan Transportation Research Institute (July 2008), http://deepblue.lib.umich.edu/bitstream/2027.42/60424/1/100969.pdf.

17 T. S. Nielsen and K. B. Hansen, "Do Green Areas Affect Health? Results from a Danish Survey on the Use of Green Areas and Health Indicators," *Health & Place* 13 (2007): 839–50.

18 F. E. Kuo et al. "Fertile Ground for Community: Inner-City Neighborhood Common Spaces," *American Journal of Community Psychology* 26 (1998) 823–51.

19 F. E. Kuo, "Coping with Poverty: Impacts of Environment and Attention in the Inner City," *Environment and Behavior* 33 (2001): 5–34.

20 F. E. Kuo and W. C. Sullivan, "Aggression and Violence in the Inner City: Effects of Environment via Mental Fatigue," *Environment and Behavior* 33 (2001): 543–71.

21 F. E. Kuo and W. C. Sullivan, "Environment and Crime in the Inner City: Does Vegetation Reduce Crime?" *Environment and Behavior* 33 (2001): 343–67.

22 More information on this strategy is available at CDC's website, www.cdc.gov/healthyplaces

23 A. L. Dannenberg et al., "Growing the Field of Health Impact Assessment in the United States: An Agenda for Research and Practice," *American Journal of Public Health* 96 (2006): 262–70.

24 These and other tools are described in depth in M. Morris, ed., *Integrating Planning and Public Health: Tools and Strategies to Create Healthy Places*, Planning Advisory Service Report no. 539/540 (Chicago: American Planning Association and National Association of County and City Health Officials, 2006).

25 W. LaDuke, *All Our Relations: Native Struggles for Land and Life* (Cambridge, Mass.: South End Press, 1999).

26 Evangelical Environmental Network, "On the Care of Creation: An Evangelical Declaration on the Care of Creation," www.creationcare.org/resources/declaration.php.

27 A. Dobson, ed., *Fairness and Futurity: Essays on Environmental Sustainability and Social Justice* (Oxford: Oxford University Press, 1999).

CLIMATE CHANGE
AND PUBLIC HEALTH

JAMES A. LaGRO JR.

Climate change could be the catalyst that finally focuses society's attention on ensuring the sustainability of the built environment.[1] But what can communities do about the challenges—and uncertainties—of a changing climate? What design decisions at the local level would have positive effects on a larger scale? And what does climate change mean for community sustainability and livability? Addressing these challenges—and opportunities—will require a mix of adaptation and mitigation strategies that span a range of scales.

Climate Hazards, Vulnerabilities, and Risks

The Intergovernmental Panel on Climate Change (IPCC) is a scientific consortium created by the World Meteorological Organization and the United Nations Environment Program. The IPCC—whose role is "to assess on a comprehensive, objective, open and transparent basis the latest scientific, technical and socio-economic literature produced worldwide relevant to the understanding of the risk of human-induced climate change, its observed and projected impacts and options for adaptation and mitigation"—has issued four climate assessment reports since 1990. The 2007 assessment concludes that (1) warming of the climate system is unequivocal; (2) a wide array of adaptation options is available, but more extensive adaptation than is currently occurring is required to reduce vulnerability to climate change; and (3) adaptive capacity is intimately connected to social and economic development but is unevenly distributed across and within societies. There are barriers, limits, and costs, which are not fully understood.[2]

This challenge is particularly acute because the biophysical environment has always influenced settlement patterns and human health. Many of the world's largest cities are on coastlines or at the confluence of major rivers, and these communities face increasing risks from global climate change. In addition, projected rapid population growth will increase the potential risks to public health.

Between 1970 and early 2009, the U.S. population increased from 205 million to 305 million, and the Census Bureau projects a population of 405 million by 2040. The implications of this growth for community sustainability—given the challenges of climate change—are profound. Climate hazards will also potentially entail dramatic changes in temperature, precipitation, and wind regimes, as well as an increased incidence of more extreme weather events. Yet since climate hazards vary spatially and temporally within the built environment, they pose heightened risks to vulnerable segments of society, especially infants and young children, the elderly and infirm, and the poor. These public health risks include infectious diseases, heat exhaustion, respiratory disorders, water shortages, malnutrition, obesity, drowning, stress, and social unrest and conflict.[3]

Some of these effects of climate change will be exacerbated by the way we have designed—or failed to design—our physical environment. Millions of acres of forests, grasslands, and wetlands in the United States have been converted to urban and suburban development. This dramatic expansion of the built environment, with very little attention to its sustainability,

NATIONAL (CONTIGUOUS U.S.) TEMPERATURE, 1895–2007

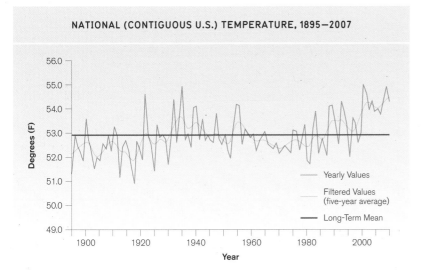

NATURAL HAZARD

**Sudden Events and
Chronic Issues:**

Past recurrence intervals
Future probability
Speed of onset
Magnitude
Duration
Areal extent

**RISK OF
DISASTER**

VULNERABLE SYSTEM

**Exposure, Sensitivity,
and Resiliance of:**

Population
Economy
Land use and development
Infrastructure and critical facilities
Cultural assets
Natural resources

has destroyed productive natural areas and fragmented many of the linkages between remaining terrestrial and aquatic ecosystems. Nature's infrastructure—air, water, soil, plants, animals, and microbes—provides the ecosystem services that we humans need to survive on this planet. Yet this infrastructure has a finite capacity to dilute and detoxify pollutants from agriculture, industry, and other activities without impairing human health and safety.[4] Climate change compounds the human impacts on land, water, and air, threatening ecosystem services and the sustainability and livability of our communities.[5]

These effects are local, regional, and global. Crab and oyster fisheries have declined in the nation's largest estuary, Chesapeake Bay, partly as a result of polluted runoff from the region's built environment. Air pollution from coal-burning power plants and contaminated stormwater runoff from streets, parking lots, and construction sites contribute to the problem. During heavy rainstorms, combined stormwater and sanitary sewer overflows spill tons of raw sewage into the bay and its tributaries.[6] Oxygen-depleted "dead zones" in the Chesapeake and other locations worldwide are among the many signs that nature is increasingly out of balance.

On a regional scale, climate scientists project that today's 100-year heat waves—which by definition are supposed to occur only once per century—will occur, on average, about once every two years by 2050. The harsh European heat wave of 2003, our worst recent exemplar, resulted in more than 30,000 deaths in France, Italy, and Spain.[7] Warming associated with climate change could, of course, lead to substantial shifts in the causes and rates of human mortality and morbidity. Deaths from freezing and hypothermia, for example, may decline. But if, as expected, the geographic range of tropical diseases expands, the global net health effects are not likely to be positive.

Climate Change Mitigation and Adaptation
Communities can pursue a broad, multifaceted strategy to reduce their vulnerability to climate

extremes. The most effective strategies entail both climate mitigation and adaptation.[8]

Mitigation reduces or eliminates greenhouse gas (GHG) emissions and potentially slows or reverses climate change by removing carbon dioxide and other GHGs from the atmosphere. Thus, for example, a local policy of planting and protecting trees and natural areas can directly mitigate climate change impacts. Urban and suburban forests sequester carbon in their biomass, protect aquatic ecosystems and potable water supplies, and improve air quality.

Similarly, adapting building codes can have significant mitigating effects. Buildings account for about 40 percent of both the energy consumed and carbon dioxide emitted in the United States, according to the U.S. Department of Energy. Thus, insulating buildings to reduce energy consumption for heating and cooling has mitigative benefits. Improving energy efficiency and conservation can be as simple as increasing insulation and replacing old furnaces, hot-water heaters, and household appliances.

Building smaller and more energy-efficient homes is another effective measure. The average floor area in new single-family houses built in the United States has increased steadily for decades, from 1,645 square feet in 1975 to 2,434 in 2005.[9] By 2007, 26 percent of all new single-family houses in the United States were 3,000 square feet or larger. Whether this supersizing of America's suburbs was driven by consumer demand or by a home-building industry fueled by lax mortgage-lending practices and sprawl-inducing zoning codes, the results have been unsustainable.

Adaptation to climate change reduces society's vulnerability to future climate hazards. One way to do this is to stop building in unsustainable and threatened areas. The U.S. National Flood Insurance Program has provided substantial financial subsidies for development on barrier islands, in floodplains, and in other flood-prone locations—even areas that have experienced repeated property losses. This policy is unsustainable and is unlikely to persist into the future as the sea level continues to rise. In most cases, buildings and infrastructure that are substantially damaged by storm surges and beach erosion should be removed, conserving public fiscal resources and protecting public health by creating coastal buffers. Consequently, adapting to climate change will require politically difficult—but ecologically and economically sound—policy decisions to retreat from the sea.

Policy, Planning, and Design Implications

Public policy responses to climate change range from doing nothing to attempting to control nature with "brute force" geo-engineering. Skepticism, institutional inertia, and vested financial interests are among the substantive barriers that communities face in reducing GHG emissions and adapting to a changing climate. Yet the purpose of government is to protect public health, safety, and welfare, and much can be done by federal, state, and local governments to reduce the risks of climate change and increase both community sustainability and livability.

Increasing community awareness is an important strategy. Climate change is a mounting concern of the U.S. Centers for Disease Control and Prevention (CDC) and other public health agencies.[10] CDC policy on climate change and public health identifies 11 "priority health actions for climate change."[11] These include monitoring environmental conditions, disease risks, and disease occurrence, and identifying population groups and locations at greatest risk. Other key goals are communicating the health risks of climate change to policy makers, health care providers, and the public, and developing and implementing plans to respond to climate-related health threats. Monitoring indicators of both public health and environmental quality is essential in helping communities assess progress toward, and threats to, desired outcomes.

Smarter growth and infrastructure are essential. The key opportunity that communities can now take advantage of is the fact that policies that reduce GHG emissions can also promote community sustainability and livability, or quality of life. These policies require good planning but also careful consideration of the design, or spatial configuration, of the built environment. Broad-scale patterns—such as the location of high-

ways, schools, and open spaces—are important design decisions. Fine-scale patterns—such as walkway connectivity, the presence of street trees, and the infiltration of stormwater runoff from parking lots—are equally important design details. Pursued holistically, design decisions can drive a sustainable GHG policy.

Community leaders need informed guidance to reform public policies that overtly—though perhaps inadvertently—make communities less sustainable, less livable, and more vulnerable to climate change. Understanding both the initial and life-cycle costs of low-density urban fringe development—including its economic, social, and environmental impacts—can help communities achieve balanced and sustainable growth while protecting essential services provided by nature's infrastructure.[12] With this knowledge, planning commissions and city councils might be more inclined to encourage retrofitting of vacant and underutilized sites served by existing streets and utilities, instead of subsidizing scattered fringe development.

Smarter land-use policy—such as creating human-scaled, pedestrian-friendly mixed use redevelopment served by transit, with landscaped public plazas and streetscapes—will go a long way toward improving community livability. Transit-oriented development and other neighborhood nodes with shops, restaurants, libraries, and other services can also significantly limit household GHG emissions by reducing vehicle miles traveled, which also has community-wide safety and health benefits. Vehicles also produce other air pollutants: nitrous oxides, carbon monoxide, hydrocarbons, and particulate matter.[13] Pollution taxes could provide a price incentive to reduce GHG emissions. Not unlike taxes on cigarettes, a pollution tax on gasoline and diesel fuels also could generate billions of dollars each year for treating asthma and other respiratory disorders linked to traffic-related air pollution.

Restoring nature's infrastructure should be another goal. America's shopping malls, commercial strips, and office complexes generally have too few trees, little green space, and large impervious surfaces that shed rather than conserve rainwater. By contrast,

TREE BENEFITS CALCULATOR

STORMWATER

Urban stormwater runoff (or "nonpoint-source pollution") washes chemicals (oil, gasoline, salts, etc.) and litter from surfaces such as roadways and parking lots into streams, wetlands, rivers, and oceans. The more impervious the surface (e.g., concrete, asphalt, rooftops), the more quickly pollutants are washed into our community waterways. Drinking water, aquatic life, and the health of our entire ecosystem can be adversely affected by this process.

Trees act as mini-reservoirs, controlling runoff at the source. Trees reduce runoff by: 1. Intercepting and holding rain on leaves, branches and bark. 2. Increasing infiltration and storage of rainwater through the tree's root system. 3. Reducing soil erosion by slowing rainfall before it strikes the soil.

ENERGY

Trees modify climate and conserve building energy use in three principal ways (see figure below): 1. Shading reduces the amount of heat absorbed and stored by buildings. 2. Evapotranspiration converts liquid water to water vapor and cools the air by using solar energy that would otherwise result in heating of the air. 3. Tree canopies slow down winds thereby reducing the amount of heat lost from a home, especially where conductivity is high (e.g., glass windows).

Strategically placed trees can increase home energy efficiency. In summer, trees shading east and west walls keep buildings cooler. In winter, allowing the sun to strike the southern side of a building can warm interior spaces. If southern walls are shaded by dense evergreen trees there may be a resultant increase in winter heating costs.

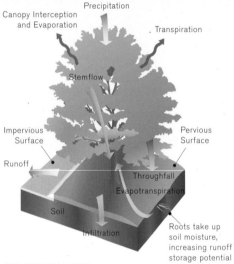

Precipitation
Canopy Interception and Evaporation
Transpiration
Stemflow
Impervious Surface
Pervious Surface
Runoff
Throughfall
Evapotranspiration
Soil
Infiltration
Roots take up soil moisture, increasing runoff storage potential

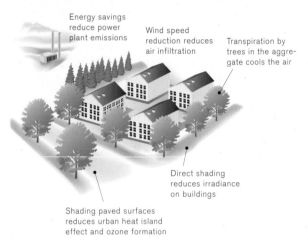

Energy savings reduce power plant emissions
Wind speed reduction reduces air infiltration
Transpiration by trees in the aggregate cools the air
Direct shading reduces irradiance on buildings
Shading paved surfaces reduces urban heat island effect and ozone formation

PROPERTY VALUE

Trees in front of single-family homes have a greater property value benefit than those in front of multifamily homes, parks, or commercial properties. Real estate agents have long known that trees can increase the "curb appeal" of properties thereby increasing sale prices. Research has verified this by showing that home buyers are willing to pay more for properties with ample versus few or no trees.

This model uses a tree's Leaf Surface Area (LSA) to determine increases in property values. That's a researcher's way of saying that a home with more trees (and more LSA) tends to have a higher value than one with fewer trees (and lower LSA). The values shown are annual and accumulate incrementally over time because each tree typically adds more leaf surface area each growing season.

CO2

Trees can have an impact by reducing atmospheric carbon in two primary ways. 1. They sequester ("lock up") CO_2 in their roots, trunks, stems, and leaves while they grow, and in wood products after they are harvested. 2. Trees near buildings can reduce heating and air-conditioning demands, thereby reducing emissions associated with power production.

Combating climate change will take a worldwide, multifaceted approach, but by planting a tree in a strategic location, driving fewer miles, or replacing business trips with conference calls, it's easy to see how we can each reduce our individual carbon "footprints."

AIR QUALITY

Air pollution is a serious health threat that causes asthma, coughing, headaches, respiratory and heart disease, and cancer. Over 150 million people live in areas where ozone levels violate federal air quality standards; more than 100 million people are impacted when dust and other particulate levels are considered "unhealthy." We now know that the urban forest can mitigate the health effects of pollution by:

- Absorbing pollutants like ozone, nitrogen dioxide, and sulfur dioxide through leaves
- Intercepting particulate matter like dust, ash, and smoke
- Releasing oxygen through photosynthesis
- Lowering air temperatures which reduces the production of ozone
- Reducing energy use and subsequent pollutant emissions from power plants

It should be noted that trees themselves emit biogenic volatile organic compounds (BVOCs) which can contribute to ground-level ozone production. This may negate the positive impact the tree has on ozone mitigation for some high-emitting species (e.g., willow oak or sweetgum). However, the sum total of the tree's environmental benefits always trumps this negative.

WILLOW TREE
25" Diameter
Northeast Climate

Stormwater   3,183 gallons of stormwater runoff intercepted this year

Property Value   Property value raised by $44 and will add 73 square feet of LSA this year

Energy   144 Kilowatt / hours of electricity conserved for cooling and reduce consumption of oil or natural gas by 53 therm(s)

Air Quality   "Dep" stands for deposition. This is your tree absorbing or intercepting pollutants. "Avd" stands for avoided. This is your tree lessening the need for creation of these pollutants in the first place by reducing energy production needs.

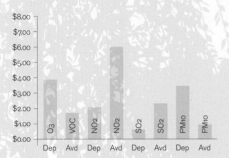

CO2   Atmospheric carbon reduced by 645 pounds

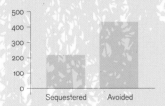

Overall Benefits $185 every year

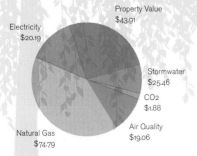

Property Value $43.91
Electricity $20.19
Stormwater $25.46
CO2 $1.88
Air Quality $19.06
Natural Gas $74.79

BLACK ASH TREE
30" Diameter
Northeast Climate

Stormwater   4,330 gallons of stormwater runoff intercepted this year

Property Value   Property value raised by $78 and will add 130 square feet of LSA this year

Energy   198 Kilowatt / hours of electricity conserved for cooling and reduce consumption of oil or natural gas by 67 therm(s)

Air Quality   "Dep" stands for deposition. This is your tree absorbing or intercepting pollutants. "Avd" stands for avoided. This is your tree lessening the need for creation of these pollutants in the first place by reducing energy production needs.

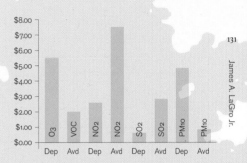

CO2   Atmospheric carbon reduced by 1,042 pounds

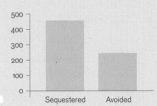

Overall Benefits $266 every year

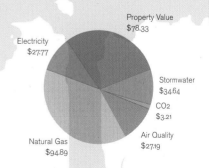

Property Value $78.33
Electricity $27.77
Stormwater $34.64
CO2 $3.21
Air Quality $27.19
Natural Gas $94.89

James A. LaGro Jr.

Web-based tree-benefit calculators allow anyone to use basic inputs of location, tree species, and size to approximate the annual environmental and economic value provided by individual street-side trees. This rendering is drawn from a web-based calculator that is based upon the U.S. Forest Service's street-tree assessment tool, STRATUM, which is part of a free software suite called i-Tree. Rather than offer a scientific accounting of precise values, this simple and accessible calculator makes clear the aesthetic and economic value trees contribute to communities.

green streets and parking lots have pervious pavement and are bordered by shade trees and bio-infiltration swales that filter stormwater runoff and allow rainwater to percolate into the ground. These plantings, and similar ones within highway medians and rights-of-way, can benefit public health and the environment.[14] Eliminating mowing on these thousands of acres would cut carbon emissions and create vital ecological "bridges" for plant and animal species displaced by climate change.

Greener approaches to managing floodplains and riparian zones can reduce the quantity, and improve the quality of, stormwater runoff entering streams, rivers, lakes, bays, and estuaries. Greenways encompassing drainage corridors and wetlands also can provide opportunities for outdoor recreation and meaningful nature experiences for children. Moreover, restoring native vegetation along shorelines and within riparian corridors—and protecting them, ideally, with conservation easements—can sequester carbon and provide needed refuge for birds and other wildlife.

Greening the built environment is a key element, because healthy urban forests perform valuable functions that enhance community livability and increase resilience to climate change. Trees have multiple benefits, including moderating microclimate to reduce urban heat island effects.[15] Trees improve air quality and aesthetics, increase biodiversity, and can even increase outdoor physical activity and reduce the severity of heat-related respiratory disorders. By reducing summer air temperatures in the built environment, trees can also mitigate climate change by lessening the need for air-conditioning.

On commercial and industrial buildings, green roofs can reduce heating and cooling costs, provide usable outdoor space, and reduce urban heat island effects.[16] About 14 percent of the total roof surface in Germany is now green, and notable efforts are also evident in the United States.[17] For example, the City of Chicago offers grants, and New York City offers tax credits to spur green-roof retrofits.

Community Sustainability and Livability

Many complementary actions on many different scales must be taken to reduce GHG emissions and adapt buildings, neighborhoods, communities, and regions to the realities of climate change. Urban design guidelines, smart electrical grids, green building codes, and tree preservation ordinances are among the many diverse policy tools that communities can employ to create climate-resilient neighborhoods. Retrofitting communities to make them more resilient to climate change can, with foresight and effective interdisciplinary collaboration, also make them more sustainable and more livable. In the century ahead, urban planners, landscape architects, architects, engineers, and members of allied professions will play crucial roles in protecting public health, safety, and welfare from the deleterious effects of climate change.

NOTES

1 The author completed this work while serving as an American Association for the Advancement of Science (AAAS) Science & Technology Policy Fellow with the U.S. Environmental Protection Agency's Global Change Research Program.

2 See www.ipcc.ch/about/index.htm. In the United States, the Climate Change Science Program (www.climatescience.gov) seeks to enhance understanding of "changes in the Earth's global environmental system . . . and to provide a sound scientific basis for national and international decision making."

3 J. Patz et al., "Impact of Regional Climate Change on Human Health," *Nature* 438, no. 17 (2005): 310–17; G. Lin et al., "Climate Amenity and BMI," *Obesity* 15, no. 8 (2007): 2120–27.

4 G. Daily, "Management Objectives for the Protection of Ecosystem Services," *Environmental Science & Policy* 3 (2000): 333–39; Kates et al., "What Is Sustainable Development? Goals, Indicators, Values, and Practice," *Environment: Science and Policy for Sustainable Development* 47, no. 3 (2005): 8–21.

5 P. Vitousek et al., "Human Domination of the Earth's Ecosystems," *Science* 277 (1997): 494–99; Millennium Ecosystem Assessment, *Ecosystems and Human Well-Being: Synthesis* (Washington, D.C.: Island Press, 2005).

6 U.S. Environmental Protection Agency, "National Pollutant Discharge Elimination System (NPDES): Combined Sewer Overflows" (2008), http://cfpub.epa.gov/npdes.

7 J. P. Holdren, "Meeting the Climate-Change Challenge" (eighth annual John H. Chafee Memorial Lecture on Science and the Environment, National Council for Science and the Environment, Washington, D.C., 2008).

8 N. Stern, *The Economics of Climate Change: The Stern Review* (Cambridge: Cambridge University Press, 2006).

9   U.S. Census Bureau, 2008. "New Housing Characteristics.
    Manufacturing, Mining, and Construction Statistics,"
    www.census.gov/const/www/newresconstindex.html.

10 H. Frumkin et al., "Climate Change: The Public Health Response,"
    American Journal of Public Health 98, no. 3 (2008): 435–45.

11 Centers for Disease Control and Prevention, U.S. Department of Health and
    Human Services, "CDC Policy on Climate Change and Public Health" (2007),
    www.cdc.gov/climatechange/policy.htm.

12 J. A. LaGro Jr., *Site Analysis: A Contextual Approach to Sustainable Land Planning
    and Site Design*, 2nd ed. (Hoboken, N.J.: John Wiley and Sons, 2008).

13 U.S. Environmental Protection Agency, "Mobile Source Emissions:
    Past, Present, and Future" (2009), www.epa.gov/otaq/invntory/overview/
    pollutants/index.htm.

14 U.S. Environmental Protection Agency, "Biodiversity and Human Health"
    (2008), http://es.epa.gov/ncer/biodiversity.

15 K. L. Wolf, *Trees, Parking and Green Law: Strategies for Sustainability* (Stone
    Mountain, Ga.: Georgia Forestry Commission, Urban and Community
    Forestry, 2004). See also James C. Schwab, ed., *Planning the Urban Forest*,
    Planning Advisory Service report no. 555 (Chicago: American Planning
    Association, 2009).

16 S. Peck and M. Kuhn, *Design Guidelines for Green Roofs* (Toronto:
    Ontario Association of Architects and the Canada Mortgage and
    Housing Corporation, 2002).

17 G. Ngan, "Green Roof Policies: Tools for Encouraging Sustainable
    Design," prepared with funding from the Landscape Architecture
    Canada Foundation, 2004.

FURTHER READING

Snover, A., et al. *Preparing for Climate Change: A Guidebook for Local, Regional,
    and State Governments*. Oakland, Calif.: ICLEI and Local Governments
    for Sustainability, 2007.

At the very northwest edge of Chicago, suburban development gives
way to the rural landscape of the Liberty Prairie Reserve, comprising
more than 5,000 acres of publicly and privately held forests,
grasslands, farms, and trails. Within the reserve sits Prairie Crossing,
founded in 1987, a community of residences, shops, and a charter
school. While still very much a commuter suburb, Prairie Crossing
offers a different vision from most such communities, one committed
to local agriculture and the stewardship of its unique landscape.

TOWARD SITOPIA

CAROLYN STEEL

The feeding of cities is arguably the greatest planning challenge of our time. With three billion people living in cities now, and a further three billion expected to join them by 2050, the question of how so many are going to be fed is urgent. Yet in urban planning circles, food remains a peripheral issue: an adjunct to the more familiar subjects of housing, transport, shopping, open space, and so on. Given that feeding cities is probably the most powerful human activity shaping the planet, this is paradoxical. Cities, like people, are what they eat—so why do we fail to recognize this?

The answer is partly cultural. To live in a postindustrial Western city is to have a strange relationship with food. A historically unparalleled cornucopia is available to us all year round at our local supermarket, yet the logistical miracle that makes this possible—that delivers, say, enough food for 30 million meals each day to a city the size of New York—is invisible. We just take it for granted that the food will be there. It's fresh, cheap, and convenient, right? Well actually, wrong.

We have become so used to modern food systems that it can be hard to step outside the bubble and realize that they are not quite as wonderful as their adverts suggest. More often than not, the "fresh" food we eat has been harvested weeks or months before it reaches us, and gassed or chilled to keep it edible. Meanwhile, processed foods contain substances to improve their industrial "performance" that wreak havoc on our bodies. For instance, palm oil, a fat so artery-clogging that it goes by the nickname "tree-lard," is commonly added to cakes and biscuits in order to improve their

mouthfeel and shelf life. Think about that next time you reach for the cookies.[1]

So, what about convenience? Is driving to a large shed and filling up with enough goodies to last us a fortnight really that convenient? The convenience, it seems to me, is all on behalf of the retailers.

Then, what about industrial food's much-trumpeted cheapness? Another myth. Whatever price one pays for it in the supermarket, our food's hidden costs in terms of ecological destruction, resource depletion, carbon emissions, pollution, and health-care burdens are many times as great. Each year, 4.2 million acres of Amazonian rain forest are destroyed for farmland, yet globally, 49.4 million acres of existing arable land are lost to salinization and erosion. A billion people worldwide are obese, while 850 million starve. An estimated four planet earths would be needed to sustain the world on an American diet, yet half of the food produced in the United States is wasted. None of it makes much sense, but then very little about the modern food industry does.

Industrialized food systems and the supermarkets they supply are the products of an evolutionary logic that has everything to do with profit and little to do with the sorts of values—sociability, sustainability, equality, health, happiness—that most of us would probably sign up to as reasons for living in a civilized society. So, how have we arrived at such a pass? And what, if anything, can we do about it?

The first point to grasp is that, in social terms, cities and supermarkets are essentially at odds. Although both are shaped by food, their relationship with it is

Les Halles Market, Paris, ca. 1860.

entirely different. To supermarkets, food is simply a reliable source of profit. (In hard times, people may stop buying televisions, but they never stop buying food.) In this context, all the natural characteristics of food—irregularity, squishiness, seasonality, perishability—are just an annoyance. If supermarkets could do nothing but sell us cans of mush with the word food written on the label, they would. In contrast, cities embrace every aspect of food, not just as the key to survival, but to conviviality, fellowship, identity. Put another way, supermarkets reduce food to a commodity, whereas cities express it as culture.

The relationship between cities and food goes back to the parallel evolution of agriculture and urbanity in the ancient Near East after the last ice age. The earliest cities considered by most archaeologists to deserve the title—the Sumerian city-states of Uruk, Ur, and Kish, in modern-day southern Iraq—were compact urban centers surrounded by productive farmland, dominated by large temple complexes. The temples held yearly cycles of festivals, which mirrored the agricultural seasons, and also organized the gathering of the harvest, ritually offering the grain to the gods before redistributing it to the people.[2] With their public granaries and bakeries, the temples effectively functioned as central food distribution hubs, while

imbuing daily life in the city with a sense of the divine. Physically and spiritually, they expressed the vital bond between city and country that, despite appearances, remains fundamental to all urbanity.

Sustaining the food supply remained every city's biggest headache throughout the preindustrial era. Evidence of the struggle was everywhere: roads were full of carts and wagons carrying vegetables and grain; rivers and docksides were packed with barges and fishing boats; streets and backyards were full of cows, pigs, and chickens. Preventing monopolies from forming was the most vital concern of every urban authority, and most enacted laws to prevent producers and suppliers from gaining too great a share of the market.[3] As a result, most cities were fed by hosts of small producers, who often sold directly to their customers. Since markets were generally the only places where one could buy fresh food, everyone went to them, not just to buy bread but to swap news and gossip, to laugh and to gawp, to protest or to celebrate. Markets were the social, commercial, and political cores of cities. From the Roman forum and Athenian agora to Les Halles and Covent Garden, markets tied city to countryside, and people to one another.

Food's role in shaping preindustrial cities is easy to see, yet food is still shaping postindustrial ones, albeit

FOOD AND COMMUNITY GREENING

THOMAS L. DANIELS

Safe, reliable, and affordable supplies of food are essential for community prosperity as well as national security. Yet the federal government has not staked out a national food policy. Meanwhile, the days of cheap and abundant food may be ending, thanks to rising energy prices driven by global demand. In response, elected officials, planners, and citizens are making changes in land-use planning to promote local food production for local consumers.

American agriculture depends heavily on petroleum to power its machinery and create pesticides, and on natural gas for fertilizers. Remarkably, the average meal in the United States travels more than 1,500 miles from where it is grown to where it is consumed. Overall, about 10 calories of fossil fuel are used to produce just one calorie of food. This situation is not sustainable in the long run.

Higher energy prices have opened up new opportunities for local and regional food production. Growing food in America is a more than $290 billion a year industry, not including the costs of food processing, packaging, transportation, and marketing. The United States has about two million farms, but the top 200,000 farms produce roughly 90 percent of the domestically grown food

supply. Local food production is an excellent example of community greening as well as an import substitution strategy: keeping more money within a city or region, while using less energy to produce and distribute fresh, healthy food.

The past decade has seen a marked increase in the number of small farms, less than 50 acres in size. Small farmers are taking advantage of niche markets for products such as organic fruits and vegetables or specialty livestock, which can be profitably produced on small tracts of land because of the proximity of local markets. Small farmers can earn a higher return by selling directly to consumers rather than selling wholesale to middlemen. In addition, consumers' concerns about their health and the quality of the food they eat have been a major boost for small farms.

Small-scale organic farms use less farm machinery than conventional farms and virtually no fossil-fuel-based pesticides and fertilizers. Because small farms supply local markets, they consume less energy in transporting, processing, packaging, and refrigerating food. Sales of organically grown food have been increasing by about 20 percent a year since 2000 and are now worth more than $20 billion annually. However, grain and meat may be difficult to produce locally in many metro regions because of high land costs—grain being a relatively low-value crop—and because of the closing of regional slaughterhouses.

Urban food production is likely to meet only a small proportion of a community's total food needs. Still, local food production can improve environmental quality and social ties and encourage

San Francisco was the first large city in the United States to collect food scraps for composting. Now the city is striving to exceed a state-mandated 50 percent recycling goal by diverting 75 percent of all waste to recycling programs by the year 2010. Toward this end, San Francisco provides residents with green carts for compostable materials like food scraps and yard waste. These materials go to a processing plant, which closes the recycling loop by turning waste into a valuable resource of organic compost. Almost all of the resulting compost is distributed to vineyards within a 100-mile radius of the city. The rest is returned to local agriculture, to grow fresh produce for farmer's markets throughout the area. The 75,000 households and hundreds of restaurants that contribute over 300 tons of organic waste daily for composting reconnect city and farm, two communities once intimately related but now split by industrial food and fertilizer production.

sustainable local economic development. For instance, urban farms can reclaim vacant land, such as in Buffalo and Philadelphia, and provide a local source of fruits and vegetables in what were previously "food deserts"—neighborhoods without grocery stores—where local residents had little to no access to nutritious food. In cities with large amounts of vacant land and low-income residents, such as Baltimore, Detroit, and New Orleans, urban farming could greatly help with greening the city and revitalizing neighborhoods.

Urban farms come in three forms: privately owned plots, city-owned plots leased to private producers, and city-owned land made available for community gardens for a small fee or on a first-come-first-served basis. To promote urban farming, Milwaukee changed its zoning ordinance to allow agricultural uses in any residential zone. Madison, Wisconsin, has 30 city-funded community gardens with more than 1,600 plots. Locally grown food can be consumed by the growers, sold to local restaurants and grocery stores, or sold directly to consumers through farmers markets or through Community Supported Agriculture (CSA) schemes in which consumers pay the farmer up front at the beginning of the season and collect the produce as it is grown.

Urban farms have the advantage of low start-up and operating costs. But these enterprises are labor intensive, and the jobs are seasonal. Also, processing organic foods into products with a longer shelf life remains a challenge. Moreover, organic produce typically commands a higher price than nonorganic produce, potentially putting organically grown food out of the reach of low-income consumers. In addition, "organic" doesn't necessarily mean food grown and sold by small farmers. Large growers, such as 26,000-acre Earthbound Farm, produce organic crops, and large companies, such as Whole Foods and Wal-Mart, sell organically grown food.

Cities can work together with nonprofit groups to set up local farmers markets. City zoning ordinances can allow farmers markets in certain zoning districts, as in Madison, and cities can streamline the permitting process for food vendors. The popularity of farmers markets has soared over the past 15 years. Nationwide, there were 1,755 farmers markets in 1993, and the number had more than doubled by 2008, exceeding 4,000.

Metropolitan counties with a central city of at least 50,000 people offer the best opportunities for local and regional food production. Metro counties produce most of the nation's fruits and vegetables and dairy products. Four out of five Americans live in a metro county, and most of the nation's population growth up to 2050 is expected to occur in metro counties.

Links between farms within a 50-mile radius of a major city and urban consumers are important for the success of regional food production. In addition to the setting up of city farmers markets, the preservation of farmland through the purchase or donation of development rights from willing landowners will be key to managing growth in metro areas, as well as essential for assuring regional food supplies. Over the past 20 years, farmland preservation efforts by local and state governments and nonprofit land trusts have resulted in the preservation of more than two million acres of metropolitan area farmland.

In Marin County, California, the Marin Agricultural Land Trust has preserved 42,000 acres of farmland. The county has zoned its agricultural land at a very low density of only one house per 60 acres, and it included policies supporting farmland protection and access to food in its 2007 county comprehensive plan. In addition, more than 150 local governments—such as Sonoma County, California, and Baltimore County, Maryland—have adopted urban growth boundaries to limit the extension of central sewer and water lines into rural areas. Thus, government land-use policies, investment in development rights along with the nonprofit sector, and assistance with farmers markets are helping to create more sustainable regional food systems. But the key will be consumer willingness to "buy fresh, buy local."

Modern green markets from around the
United States. From the top, Reading
Terminal Market, Philadelphia; Cathedral
Square Market, Milwaukee; Union Square
Green Market, New York City; and
Downtown Market, Los Angeles.

in a far less obvious way. Industrialization has eman-
cipated cities from geography and disguised the effort
of feeding them, but that doesn't mean the problem
has gone away. On the contrary, the unprecedented
explosion of city-building in the last two centuries has
exacerbated the problem beyond measure. In 1800, just
3 percent of the world's population lived in urban areas;
now more than half of us live in conurbations so vast
that they redefine the very meaning of "urban." Quite
apart from the dubious desirability of living in such
places, the questionable ecological wisdom of doing
so would be obvious to any time-traveling companion
from the preindustrial past.

The great irony, or tragedy, of modern food delivery
is that it has made the very thing it promised to make
easier—feeding cities—infinitely more complex. By
enabling the metropolitan carpet to roll out across
field, forest, and desert, it has created a burgeoning
population who live not merely remote from their
sources of food but utterly dependent on unsustainable
systems and processes to feed them. Equally damaging

is the way in which industrial food production has obscured our vital relationship with the land. Divorced from nature, we are in danger of losing a sense of what, deep down, it means to be human. That is why the *cultural* import of food, so powerful in the ancient world, so debased in ours, is crucial. The rituals of growing and tending, buying and selling, cooking and eating, sharing and celebrating, are markers of the obligations and aspirations that distinguish us from the merely animal. It is such rituals, and not merely the physical mechanisms of subsistence, that shape our civilization.

The distinction is important, because it shifts the debate about what might constitute a "good" food system away from the dead-end polarity of industrial versus organic, into far more fruitful territory. The essential role of food systems should not just be to feed us adequately and sustainably (no mean feat in itself) but also to nourish our quality of life. If all we are concerned with is survival, then a series of largely scientific calculations about diet, soil, sunlight, water, and energy should indicate how best to arrange our lives. But if we also care about such things as joy, ethics, culture, and freedom, we are faced with a far more difficult—yet far more worthwhile—problem to solve. How best to reconcile the satisfaction of our animal needs with our higher aspirations? That is the ultimate dilemma of civilization, and a question that people have long struggled to answer.

The concept of utopia—a theoretical ideal community—has long been a favorite way of attempting to do just that. Utopias have come in many different guises, but their fundamental themes are essentially those we encountered earlier in our "good society" checklist: sociability, sustainability, equality, health, happiness. Utopia is a concept that allows us to imagine a better world, but as a practical tool for change, it is effectively useless. If we actually want to *build* a better world, what we need is a model that aims not at perfection but at something human and attainable. My suggested alternative is *sitopia* (from the ancient Greek *sitos*, food, and *topos*, place). Whether we realize it or not, we already live in a world shaped by food—so why

not harness food's power in order to shape it better?

Sitopia, then, is a society shaped by food. Nothing unusual in that. What distinguishes sitopia, however, is that it shapes itself *consciously*, using food as a tool. The first step toward sitopia, therefore, is to understand the nature of this tool. What immediately strikes us when we contemplate food in this context is that its influence is everywhere: from the Amazonian rain forest to our own backyard. Food affects everything—the way we work, play, and socialize; how and where we build cities, houses, and roads; the way we walk and talk; the way we inhabit land, sea, and sky. Food is the great connector: that is what makes it such a powerful agent. So, how might we harness it to best effect? There are clues in the past. Arguably, all preindustrial cities were sitopias of sorts: societies that recognized and celebrated the primacy of food. Even today, in places where rural traditions remain strong, respect for food and the land where it is grown is paramount. That respect is what we who live in postindustrial societies must regain. We need to rebuild a sense of our vital bond with the earth: something our ancestors lived by, yet we seem to have forgotten. Once we have restored that sense, we are ready to create sitopia. It really is that simple.

The wonderful thing about food is that its influence is so ubiquitous and profound that one can start almost anywhere and make an immediate difference. In our electronic age, food has the unique quality of being the one thing we must *physically* encounter every day in order to survive. This gives it an unparalleled capacity to bring people together—an opportunity we regularly squander whenever we shop in a supermarket or have lunch sitting alone at our desk with a sandwich. How different it is when we buy food from a local market or share a meal with friends! How we choose to eat, shop, and cook is up to us, but our choices, multiplied many times, represent almost limitless potential to forge personal connections, support local businesses, animate public space—in short, to foster sociability, the first item on our "good society" checklist.

Of course, the range of choices in America and Britain is often limited by decades of neglect of food.

Unplanned growth results in suburban sprawl, encroaching on agricultural land and increasing the distance between a city and its sources of food. Alternatively, there is no reason why agriculture could not be brought into the city, as in this proposal for a vertical farm by the firm Mithun. The Center for Urban Agriculture, envisioned for Seattle, constructs an entire ecosystem of solar and water collection, native plants and bird habitat, and agriculture, squeezing one and a third acres onto a three-quarter-acre site by building upward instead of outward. Affordable housing, a produce market, and a café serving food grown on site complete the vision of a small farming town reshaped into a single building.

Many of us live miles from any food source other than a supermarket, and many more have never learned to cook—serious flaws for any would-be sitopian. We must work far harder than, say, the average Roman, to become what the founder of Slow Food, Carlo Petrini, calls "co-producers," knowledgeable consumers who actively promote local, sustainable, ethical food networks through their everyday actions.[4] Yet the counterrevolution is already under way on both sides of the Atlantic. A surge of interest in farmers markets, box schemes, in which farmers provide householders with regular deliveries of seasonal fruit and vegetables, and urban allotments where one can grow one's own indicates that we are starting to take food seriously once again. The trick now is to find ways of building up such initiatives so that they present a viable alternative to the behemoths of modern food delivery.

Part of the process of recalibrating our relationship with food involves learning how to frame the right questions. Instead of asking how we can feed cities most efficiently—a question that, by its very nature, can only yield one result—we should be asking what sort of communities we want to live in and designing our food systems to match. Once you put the question that way round, everything changes. Industrial food systems, seen as diagrams, are what the architect Christopher Alexander calls a tree: supply chains in which many roots (producers) are channeled through a single trunk (supermarkets) to feed many branches (us).[5] In such a system, the trunk exerts a stranglehold over the entire chain, keeping producers and consumers well apart. But what if those of us living in cities became co-producers, forging direct relationships with those who grew our food? That would create a very different system, one that Alexander calls a semi-lattice: a complex network of local, personal, flexible connections, each of which affects the others. That, as Alexander points out, is much closer to the way traditional cities functioned in the past. It is also a model far more likely to foster the sorts of personal relationships necessary for a successful community.

In countries such as France and Spain, where traditional food cultures remain largely intact, such

networks still exist. However, it is increasingly recognized that if they are to survive the forces of globalization, they will need government protection. Hence, half of the 70,000 independent stores in Paris are protected by law, so that local butchers or bakers cannot be replaced by mobile phone companies. Similarly, Barcelonan supermarkets are prohibited from selling fresh food within a certain range of any of the city's 43 food markets. For the time being, in cities such as these, the traditional pleasures of shopping, cooking, and sharing good food remain at the very core of urban life.

Paris and Barcelona preserve something of the traditional role of food in the West. But it is in countries where mass urbanization is yet to occur, such as India, that food retains its ancient power. In Indian cities, the influence of rural life can still be felt. Harvest festivals are widely celebrated; food markets spill onto pavements; vegetable-sellers wheel carts through the streets; cyclists deliver lunch boxes from country wives to their husbands at work; people cook on pavements, buy spicy snacks from stands, smear sweetmeats on holy shrines. India remains an inherently sitopian nation, yet such cultures are increasingly under threat. Half of India's 700,000 small farms are expected to disappear over the next 20 years, raising the question of where their ex-owners will live and what they will do. As the example of China has recently demonstrated, the mass abandonment of the countryside for cities is no guarantee of a better life. Rather the opposite, in fact. At the start of 2009, 26 million of China's migrant workers found themselves unemployed, leaving the Chinese government facing a social time bomb. If the credit crunch has taught us anything, it is that there has never been a better time to rethink the urban-rural balance and its vital role in shaping communities.

All of which brings us to the last item on our "good society" checklist: happiness. Notoriously difficult to measure, happiness is increasingly seen as something that no amount of progress in the form of electronic gadgetry or accumulated wealth can buy. Indeed, the latest thinking suggests that a modest income—enough to enjoy a simple life, no more—is all that

most of us need to be content.[6] And that is where
food can make its most valuable contribution to
solving our oldest dilemma. Wielded as a weapon,
food can make our lives a misery. Yet embraced as
our most essential shared necessity, it can guide us
to a new approach to dwelling.

So, where might such an approach lead us? What,
in other words, might sitopia be like? Clearly, its
urban-rural ties would be strong. There would be
active markets and local shops. Houses would have
large, comfortable kitchens, and children would
learn to grow food and cook and would eat meals
with their parents from an early age. There would be
neighborhood allotments, community farms, a local
abattoir. Government regulation would prevent the
formation of food monopolies, ensuring that regional
and small-scale networks thrived, and farmers would
get a fair price for their produce. Kitchen waste would
be composted, and urban areas would form part of the
local organic cycle. Above all, food would bring people
together and help them trust one another. Food would
be central to life, valued, enjoyed, and celebrated.

Such a community, in its ideal form, is clearly
utopia. But we don't have to aim at perfection. Sitopia
is primarily a state of mind, so it can exist anywhere—
even in New York City. Park Slope Food Coop in
Brooklyn is an ethical food cooperative with 14,000
members, who each work a few hours' shift every
month in exchange for substantial savings on their
groceries. Established in 1973, the co-op has a strong
ethical code enforced through frequent members'
meetings, spot checks on suppliers, and long-term
relationships with around 40 small-scale farms within
a 200-mile radius of the city. The co-op is also a neighborhood social center, hosting a program of events
including lectures, debates, cookery classes, and so on.
The co-op is, in effect, a mini-sitopia in the midst of the
metropolis. Along with emergent international movements such as Transition Towns and Città Slow, such
projects show what can be done. There are elements of
sitopia everywhere. All we need to do now is join up
the dots and see how, together, they can become much
more than the sum of their parts.

NOTES

1 G. Critser, *Fat Land* (London: Penguin, 2003).

2 M. Symons, *A History of Cooks and Cooking* (Champaign: University of
Illinois Press, 2004).

3 S. Kaplan, *Provisioning Paris: Merchants and Millers in the Grain and Flour Trade
During the 18th Century* (Ithaca, N.Y.: Cornell University Press, 1984).

4 C. Petrini, *Slow Food Nation: Why Our Food Should Be Good, Clean and Fair,*
trans. C. Furlan and J. Hunt (New York: Rizzoli, 2007).

5 C. Alexander, "A City Is Not a Tree," *Architectural Forum* 122, no. 1
(April 1965) (Part I) and no. 2 (May 1965) (Part II).

6 R. Layard, *Happiness: Lessons from a New Science* (London: Penguin, 2005).

143

FURTHER READING

Hopkins, R. *The Transition Town Handbook: From Oil Dependency to Local Resilience.*
Totnes, U.K.: Green Books, 2008.

Pollan, M. *The Omnivore's Dilemma.* London: Bloomsbury, 2006.

Schumacher, E. F. *Small Is Beautiful.* New York: Vintage, 1973.

Steel, C. *Hungry City: How Food Shapes Our Lives.* London: Chatto and Windus, 2008.

Carolyn Steel

THE IMPACT OF THE BUILT ENVIRONMENT ON HEALTH — THE BRAIN'S STRESS RESPONSE AND THE BRAIN-IMMUNE CONNECTION: IMPLICATIONS FOR HEALTH CARE AND URBAN DESIGN

ESTHER M. STERNBERG

The World Health Organization has defined health as "a state of complete physical, mental and social well-being and not merely the absence of disease." In this regard, the built environment is as important as any other physical factors that might trigger disease, such as infectious or inflammatory agents or toxins. Indeed, the physical environment is often central to fostering these ailments, as it can harbor the vectors of disease, such as vermin or insects that carry viruses or bacteria. But beyond this, the physical environment also impacts the emotional responses of people in those spaces. Through the emotions, the physical environment can trigger or worsen stress-related diseases, or it can do the opposite: calm and prevent stress and thus enhance healing and health. Healthy environments must, then, be those that sustain both the emotions and physical health.

Physicians and scientists in previous eras typically focused on improving health by ridding the environment of infectious agents. Throughout the 19th century, especially after germ theory was proved, public health leaders worked to improve sanitation in cities and hospitals, provide clean drinking water and cleaner air, and reduce crowding. This effort was largely successful and not only removed the urban penalty of higher mortality in cities, but actually reversed it. However, we are now faced with a growing rural or suburban penalty, as a result of the pendulum having swung too far in the opposite direction. Thus, crowding in cities is being replaced by isolation in the suburbs. Infectious diseases that resulted from crowding are being replaced by illnesses related to

isolation and lack of exercise: depression and obesity and all the attendant illnesses that come with these, such as diabetes, metabolic syndrome, osteoporosis, and cardiovascular disease.

The built environment—whether individual buildings, entire neighborhoods, cities, or regions of the world—deeply affects the functioning and health of the people who occupy it. In order for professionals to plan and design spaces that optimize people's functioning, they must take into account features of the physical environment that might positively or negatively impact both physical and emotional health. In order to do so, it is important to have some knowledge of the workings of the body's physiological systems that mediate health.

Our body's first-line interface with the external environment occurs through two main organ systems: the nervous system and the immune system. The reason that the environment has such far-reaching effects on health is that the brain and immune system are closely linked. This connection plays a vital role in either supporting mental and physical health or predisposing a person to disease. The built environment can directly affect each of these systems, or, by affecting one, it can impact the other through their communication routes.

The built environment can directly foster the spread of infections through the growth of germs in contaminated areas or through the expansion of populations of insects or other animals that harbor disease. Also, toxins in the environment, such as pollutants and allergy-producing proteins, called allergens, can trigger asthma and other lung diseases such as bronchitis.

The built environment can also indirectly affect the immune system and health through its impact on the brain. We perceive the world around us through all our senses: vision, hearing, touch, smell, and even taste. Once we recognize an aspect of the environment through any or all of these senses, memories and emotions are triggered, which in turn, through the nerve chemicals and hormones that are released, can affect how the immune system functions to fight disease.

Thus, when we are stressed, the brain's stress center (the hypothalamus) releases a hormone called corticotropin releasing hormone, or CRH. This in turn, through a cascade of other hormones, causes the release of cortisol from the adrenal glands. At the same time, the adrenal glands and certain nerves release adrenaline and noradrenaline. Together, these compounds make us feel what we feel when we are stressed, including anxiousness, racing heart, sweating, having the urge to defecate, and so on. This is the brain and body's stress response, which in the short term is a highly effective means of getting us out of danger, because in addition to making us feel all those negative symptoms, the stress response also gives us the energy and focused attention to fight or escape. This is called the "fight-or-flight response." The stress response operates according to the principle of an inverted U-shaped curve. That is, there is an optimum level of the stress response that permits optimum functioning of the organism. Too little and the animal is sluggish, inattentive, and not alert. Too much and it freezes and is unable to perform the task at hand. Just right

and it performs optimally. This is true for all animals, including humans.

There is a center in the brain stem called the locus ceruleus where nerve cells that contain adrenaline become active with increasing amounts of stress. This center is particularly important in governing attention and optimal performance. Researchers, recording from single nerve cells in this region in awake primates, have shown that electrical activity in individual nerve cells increases as performance improves. However, when the animal is stressed, there is across-the-board firing of nerve cells, and the animal's performance fails. Much like when e-mail spam jams a computer, the only way to regain optimum functioning is to shut down and reboot.

Those same stress hormones and nerve chemicals also affect how well immune cells can fight infection and heal wounds. In general, stress hormones are anti-inflammatory, especially the adrenal glands' cortisol. Thus, people who are chronically stressed have been shown to have more frequent and severe colds and viral infections, a less-effective response to vaccines, and much slower wound healing than people who are not stressed. This is largely because the excess cortisol released from the adrenal glands of people who are stressed suppresses their immune systems' ability to fight infections and heal wounds.

Features of the physical environment that have long been known to trigger the stress response in rodents include: novelty, rapid change, unpredictability, multiple choice points (such as in mazes), crowding, isolation, excessive heat or cold, lack of landmarks to use for navigation, and environments that the animal has previously learned to associate with a noxious stimulus. In fact, many of these features are incorporated into standard tests for the development of antianxiety drugs. A novel environment, called an "open field" (a clear Plexiglas box), is used to measure stress-related behaviors such as freezing and reduced exploration, stress-induced release of nerve chemicals, and the ability of drugs to prevent or reverse such responses. Mazes are also used in a similar manner, as is a swimming apparatus resembling a small wading pool. When an animal finds itself in such environments without landmarks, stress levels and stress-related behaviors increase. Placing simple visual cues around the edges of such devices allows the animal to more easily find its way and reduces the stress response. Finally, sudden loud noises will also trigger the stress response and a rapid reflex called the "startle response," in which the animal jumps in response to the sound. An apparatus that delivers a loud noise and measures the intensity of the startle response is also a standard method for testing the efficacy of antianxiety drugs.

Humans respond similarly to rodents in all these situations. Clearly, features of the built environment that create such conditions could trigger the stress response in humans in a similar manner. In cities, lack of landmarks, crowding, isolation, noise, and novel or threatening environments can all cause both physical and mental distress and could eventually contribute to the development of stress-related illnesses.

Many of the features in the modern physical environment that trigger the stress response are the result of the efforts of previous generations of planners and designers to clean and sanitize the environment. Public health measures were instituted that improved sanitation, such as providing better sewer systems and a clean water supply, and the removal of all physical elements in the environment that could foster infection. In hospitals, surfaces were stripped of decoration and fomites—features that could harbor infection, dirt, and dust, such as draperies and carpets. Surfaces were covered with metal, stone, or tile, which could be easily doused with antiseptics to keep them clean and sterile.

In cities, people fled to the suburbs, which were built to reduce population density, with houses farther and farther apart.

These measures greatly improved sanitation and health and greatly reduced infection rates. In hospitals in the United States, the Mayo Clinic led the way, with a reduction of postsurgical infections to approximately 2 percent, down from the average of 25 percent or more in most hospitals the late 19th century. In cities, the urban penalty gradually reversed, with less and less urban mortality and eventual equalization of mortality compared to rural areas. The cholera epidemics were stopped, and tuberculosis spread was curtailed.

One exception to this reversal in urban penalty is in inner city areas, where health disparities still abound. In particular, asthma is increasing at an alarming rate, and the precise reason for this is as yet unknown. Certainly socioeconomic factors play a role, with the inner city tending to lack adequate health care to treat such illnesses. It could also be related to greater exposure to cockroaches, dust, and pollution. Some postulate that the violence in inner city areas leads to stress and related behaviors that might exacerbate asthma, such as keeping children indoors, where they might be more exposed to asthma-inducing allergens.

The enthusiastic embracing of measures to reduce infection has now led to other illnesses—illnesses of the emotions, which are fostered by the design features imposed on hospital and city environments in the attempt to remove all possible sources of infection. Rates of infection were reduced, but conditions related to a dearth of support and stimulation of the emotions were exacerbated. In hospitals, the shiny hard surfaces that were so easy to keep clean turned out to be highly reflective of sound, resulting in noise levels in intensive care units sometimes reaching 98 decibels—the level of a motorcycle at close range. Not only is loud noise a powerful stressor, but the associated sleep disruption that results also negatively impacts health. Lack of sleep is associated with increased cortisol release and associated illnesses, including obesity and metabolic syndrome, which predisposes a person to diabetes. Changes in mood occur, including increased

Above: Founded in 1882, the Adirondack Cottage Sanitarium (later known as the Trudeau Sanitorium) was the first North American institution for the treatment of tuberculosis patients. It prescribed patients a regimen of rest and clean mountain air, prior to the availability of antibiotics. Below: In the Kirkbride Plan, mental asylums of the late 19th and early 20th centuries were designed expressly to support the emotions, with beautiful views, places for social congregation, and places where patients and staff could work side by side in bucolic rural estates.

irritability, lack of ability to concentrate, aggressiveness, and depression. It is conceivable that such sleep disruption and its associated effects on the brain and body might be a mediator or amplifier of some of the problems of lack of attention, difficulty coping, and even violence seen in the inner city.

The attempt to isolate patients from one another and family members who might carry and spread infection led to the design of hospitals without spaces for family and friends, reducing the social support that is so important in maintaining health. All these factors, coupled with the unfamiliar and often frightening diagnostic and therapeutic equipment that has increasingly populated hospitals, have compounded hospitals' already stressful and anxiety-provoking nature. The pendulum has swung from an environment that fostered infection to one that is sterile in every sense of the word. Hospitals indeed have become places where the emotions are ignored, except for hospitals for the mentally ill.

In the Kirkbride Plan, mental asylums of the late 19th and early 20th centuries were, in fact, designed expressly to support the emotions, with beautiful views, places for social congregation, and places where patients and staff could work side by side in bucolic rural estates. Unfortunately, these institutions became primarily custodial in nature and were overtaken by the more primitive treatments used at that time for mental illness. In keeping with the trend then to separate illnesses of the mind and body, the notion that hospitals might be designed to support the emotions was not applied to hospitals for the physically ill.

In cities, attempts to reduce crowding have led to social isolation and the attendant illnesses of the emotions that can come with it, such as depression. At the same time, the long winding roads and the lack of sidewalks in suburbs, designed more for the automobile than for walking, have provided barriers to natural exercise. The bland suburban environment has removed attractors such as shops and parks that might encourage walking. The Centers for Disease Control recently reported that obesity is increasing across the United States at an alarming rate. This is particularly evident in suburban and rural areas, where driving is the primary mode of transportation. New York City now enjoys a distinct body weight advantage, especially when compared to more rural or suburban areas in upstate New York. New Yorkers are not only on average five to 10 pounds lighter than those who live in more rural surroundings, but they also live longer and are healthier. Some interpret this urban advantage as a reflection of the choices made by people who choose to live in urban settings because they like to walk. On the other hand, it is known that place shapes behavior, and the more features of the environment that encourage walking and discourage driving, the more likely it will be that people who live there will walk and exercise to a greater degree.

Not only does place shape behavior, but behavior shapes place. Thus, the growth of the suburbs and cities is cutting into surrounding natural habitats, forcing forest creatures into areas inhabited by people. This has brought about a rise in illnesses carried by such animals, such as Lyme disease, which results from exposure to *Borrelia burgdorferi*, carried by deer ticks. Human behavior, including driving, use of greenhouse-gas-producing energy sources, and growth of cities are all affecting global warming, which in turn is affecting health.

The impact of cities on global warming, as well as regular climate cycles such as El Niño, can result in periods of extreme drought followed by heavy rain, which give rise to epidemics due to the increase in populations of animals, including insects, that harbor disease. One example is an outbreak of hantavirus that occurred in the early 1990s in the Four Corners region of New Mexico. This virus, which causes pneumonia, respiratory failure, and death, is carried by mice whose population exploded in the Four Corners area as a result of extremely wet conditions. Global warming is also bringing with it the spread of other infectious diseases, including cholera, malaria, and dengue fever, in areas previously not affected because they were too cold or too high in altitude or too dry to support the vectors that spread them. Thus, malaria is marching up the slopes of mountains in Africa to higher and

higher altitudes, because the *Anopheles* mosquito is able to survive at higher altitudes as the temperatures in these regions rise. Similarly, cholera outbreaks are occurring earlier in the summer and lasting later into the fall as the warm and wet seasons extend because of global warming. Indeed, the World Health Organization has declared climate change and the resulting emerging infectious diseases the defining health issue of the 21st century.

It is clear from this mounting evidence that whether at an individual, city, or global level, the built environment greatly affects all aspects of health of individuals and communities. Views of nature in hospitals are important and have been shown to speed recovery from surgery and reduce the need for pain medication. Whether it is the colors, the calming views, or the light itself that helps healing is not known. It is known that exposure to sunlight improves mood and can reverse certain forms of depression. Light also speeds healing, the latter in part by stimulating vitamin D production in the skin. It may well be a combination of all of these factors that help.

Similarly, the presence of nature in inner city environments has been shown to positively impact the functioning of people in those spaces. In a landmark study of the Robert Taylor Homes, in Chicago, Kuo and colleagues showed that the presence of green spaces—as little as some grass and a few trees—significantly increased residents' attention and ability to cope with larger problems. The study was rigorously designed and took advantage of the fact that residents were randomly assigned to units in identical apartment buildings, where the only difference was the presence of paved barren areas or green spaces nearby. The specific features of the green spaces that accounted for this difference were not addressed, but the study provided convincing evidence that green spaces in the inner city can help improve people's functioning. One might postulate, based upon the knowledge of how the brain's stress and attention centers work, that such spaces allowed the residents to temporarily escape from stress and move back along the inverted U-shaped curve to a more optimal level of functioning.

Via Verde was the winning entry in the 2007 New Housing New York Legacy Project design competition for affordable and sustainable housing. Planned for a brownfield site in the South Bronx, the heart of the project is a garden that begins at street level as a courtyard and plaza and spirals upward through a series of landscaped terraces and roof gardens, leading to a sky terrace. These green spaces provide stormwater control and insulation for the building, enable residents to grow their own fruits and vegetables, and strengthen the local community by providing residents with common outdoor living space.

149

These studies suggest that urban planners and design professionals should consciously incorporate elements that include views of nature, adequate and appropriate lighting, sound abatement, adequate spaces for social support and socialization, and adequate areas for exercise—in sum, features that support the emotions and mental health. Elements and systems must be incorporated that encourage walking, including sidewalks and public transportation, to help combat the obesity epidemic in America. And we need to incorporate green elements at an individual, regional, and global level, because what is good for the environment is also good for individual health. More research is also needed in all these domains to identify and measure the elements of the built environment that impact both the brain and immune system, to ultimately understand not only whether but also how these features affect our health.

Those professionals who plan our urban environment should be aware that their work can either harm us or help us heal. Thus, thoughtful attention to the features of space that have a positive impact on the health of the people within it can help professionals play a vital and active role in sustaining the public health.

FURTHER READING

Books on Related Topics by Esther M. Sternberg

Sternberg, E. M. *The Balance Within: The Science Connecting Health and Emotions.* New York: Holt, 2001.

Sternberg, E. M. *Healing Spaces: The Science of Place and Well-being.* Cambridge, Mass.: Harvard University Press, 2009.

Hospitals' Impact on Health

Cohen, S., et al. "Psychological Stress and Disease." *Journal of the American Medical Association* 298, no. 14 (2007): 1685–87.

———. "Social Ties and Susceptibility to the Common Cold." *Journal of the American Medical Association* 277, no. 24 (1997): 1940–44.

Devlin, A. S., and A. B. Arneill. "Health Care Environments and Patient Outcomes: A Review of the Literature." *Environment and Behavior* 35 (2003):665–94.

Glaser, R., and J. K. Kiecolt-Glaser. "Stress-induced Immune Dysfunction: Implications for Health." *Nat Rev Immunol* 5, no. 3 (2005): 243–51.

The presence of nature in inner city environments has been shown to positively impact the functioning of people in those spaces. In a landmark study of the Robert Taylor Homes, in Chicago, Francis Kuo and colleagues showed that the presence of green spaces—as little as some grass and a few trees—significantly increased residents' attention and ability to cope with larger problems. The new design for the site will include an extensive urban tree canopy.

Kellert S. R., J. Heerwagen, and M. Mador. *Biophilic Design: The Theory, Science and Practice of Bringing Buildings to Life.* Hoboken, N.J.: John Wiley, 2008.

Kohn, L., J. M. Corrigan, and M. S. Donaldson. *To Err Is Human: Building a Safer Health System.* Washington, D.C.: Institute of Medicine, National Academy of Sciences, National Academies Press, 2000.

Marques-Deak, A., et al. "Brain-Immune Interactions and Disease Susceptibility." *Mol Psychiatry* 10, no. 3 (2005): 239–50.

Tomes, N. *The Art of Asylum-Keeping: Thomas Story Kirkbride and the Origins of American Psychiatry.* Cambridge: Cambridge University Press, 1994.

Urban Design and Health

Brody, H., et al. "Map-Making and Myth-Making in Broad Street: The London Cholera Epidemic, 1854." *Lancet* 356, no. 9223 (2000): 64–68.

Camagni, R., M. C. Gibelli, and P. Rigamonti. "Urban Mobility and Urban Form: The Social and Environmental Costs of Different Patterns of Urban Expansion." *Ecological Economics* 40, no. 2 (2002): 199–216.

Caracci, G. "General Concepts of the Relationship Between Urban Areas and Mental Health." *Current Opinion in Psychiatry* 21, no. 4 (2008): 385–90.

Centers for Disease Control and Prevention, "State-Specific Prevalence of Obesity Among Adults—United States." *MMWR* 55, no. 36 (2006): 985–88.

Cervero, R., and M. Duncan. "Walking, Bicycling, and Urban Landscapes: Evidence from the San Francisco Bay Area." *American Journal of Public Health* 93, no. 9 (2003): 1478–83.

Colwell, R. R. "Infectious Disease and Environment: Cholera as a Paradigm for Waterborne Disease." *Int Microbiol* 7, no. 4 (2004): 285–89.

Crutzen, P. "New Directions: The Growing Urban Heat and Pollution 'Island' Effect—Impact on Chemistry and Climate." *Atmospheric Environment* 38 (2004): 3539–40.

Dannenberg, A. L., et al. "The Impact of Community Design and Land-Use Choices on Public Health: A Scientific Research Agenda." *American Journal of Public Health* 93, no. 9 (2003): 1500–1508.

Eid, J., et al. "Fat City: Questioning the Relationship Between Urban Sprawl and Obesity." *Journal of Urban Economics* 63, no. 2 (2008): 385–404.

Ewing, R., et al. "Relationship Between Urban Sprawl and Weight of United States Youth." *American Journal of Preventive Medicine* 31, no. 6 (2006): 464–74.

Frank, L. D., et al. "Obesity Relationships with Community Design, Physical Activity, and Time Spent in Cars." *Am J Prev Med* 27, no. 2 (2004): 87–96.

Giles-Corti, B., and R. J. Donovan. "The Relative Influence of Individual, Social and Physical Environment Determinants of Physical Activity." *Soc Sci Med* 54, no. 12 (2002): 1793–812.

Grimm, N. B., et al. "Integrated Approaches to Long-Term Studies of Urban Ecological Systems." *Bioscience* 50, no. 7 (2000): 570–84.

Haines, M. R. "Mortality in Nineteenth-Century America: Estimates from New York and Pennsylvania Census Data, 1865 and 1900." *Demography* 14, no. 3 (1977): 311–31.

Handy, S. L., et al. "How the Built Environment Affects Physical Activity: Views from Urban Planning." *Am J Prev Med* 23, Suppl. no. 2 (2002): 64–73.

Hedley, A. H., et al. "Prevalence of Overweight and Obesity Among U.S. Children, Adolescents and Adults, 1999–2002." *Journal of the American Medical Association* 291, no. 23 (2004): 2847–50.

Jackson, L. "The Relationship of Urban Design to Human Health and Condition." *Landscape and Urban Planning* 64 (2003): 191–200.

Kerr, R. A. "Climate Change. Scientists Tell Policymakers We're All Warming the World." *Science* 315, no. 5813 (2007): 754–57.

Kuo, F. E. "Coping with Poverty: Impacts of Environment and Attention in the Inner City." *Environment and Behavior* 33, no. 1 (2001): 5–34

Lopez, R. "Urban Sprawl and Risk for Being Overweight or Obese." *American Journal of Public Health* 94, no. 9 (2004): 1574–79.

Lopez, R. P., and H. P. Hynes. "Obesity, Physical Activity, and the Urban Environment: Public Health Research Needs." *Environ Health* 5 (2006): 25.

Mokdad, A. H., et al. "Prevalence of Obesity, Diabetes, and Obesity-Related Health Risk Factors, 2001." *Journal of the American Medical Association* 289, no. 1 (2003): 76–79.

Morgan, W. J., et al. "Results of a Home-Based Environmental Intervention Among Urban Children with Asthma." *New England Journal of Medicine* 351, no. 11 (2004): 1068–80.

Patz, J. "Satellite Remote Sensing Can Improve Chances of Achieving Sustainable Health." *Environ Health Perspect* 113, no. 2 (2005): A84–85.

Patz, J. A., et al. "Impact of Regional Climate Change on Human Health." *Nature* 438, no. 7066 (2005): 310–17.

Phipatanakul, W., et al. "Effect of Environmental Intervention on Mouse Allergen Levels in Homes of Inner-city Boston Children with Asthma." *Ann Allergy Asthma Immunol* 92, no. 4 (2004): 420–25.

Saelens, B. E., et al. "Neighborhood-Based Differences in Physical Activity: An Environment Scale Evaluation." *American Journal of Public Health* 93, no. 9 (2003): 1552–58.

Simonsick, E. M., et al. "Just Get Out the Door! Importance of Walking Outside the Home for Maintaining Mobility: Findings from the Women's Health and Aging Study." *J Am Geriatr Soc* 53, no. 2 (2005): 198–203.

Staropoli, J. F. "MSJAMA: The Public Health Implications of Global Warming." *Journal of the American Medical Association* 287, no. 17 (2002): 2282.

Stone, R. "Air Pollution: Counting the Cost of London's Killer Smog." *Science* 298, no. 5601 (2002): 2106–7.

Vlahov, D., et al. "The Urban Health 'Advantage.'" *Journal of Urban Health* 82, no. 1 (2005): 1–4.

Ward, S. "A Framework for Incorporating the Prevention of Lyme Disease Transmission into the Landscape Planning and Design Process." *Landscape and Urban Planning* 66 (2004): 91–106.

Wenzel, R. P. "A New Hantavirus Infection in North America." *New England Journal of Medicine* 330, no. 14 (1994): 1004–5.

Wright, R. J., et al. "Community Violence and Asthma Morbidity: The Inner-City Asthma Study." *American Journal of Public Health* 94 (2004): 625–32.

Zimring, C. A., et al. "Influences of Building Design and Site Design on Physical Activity: Research and Intervention Opportunities." *Am J Prev Med* 28, no. 2, Suppl. no. 2 (2005): 186–93.

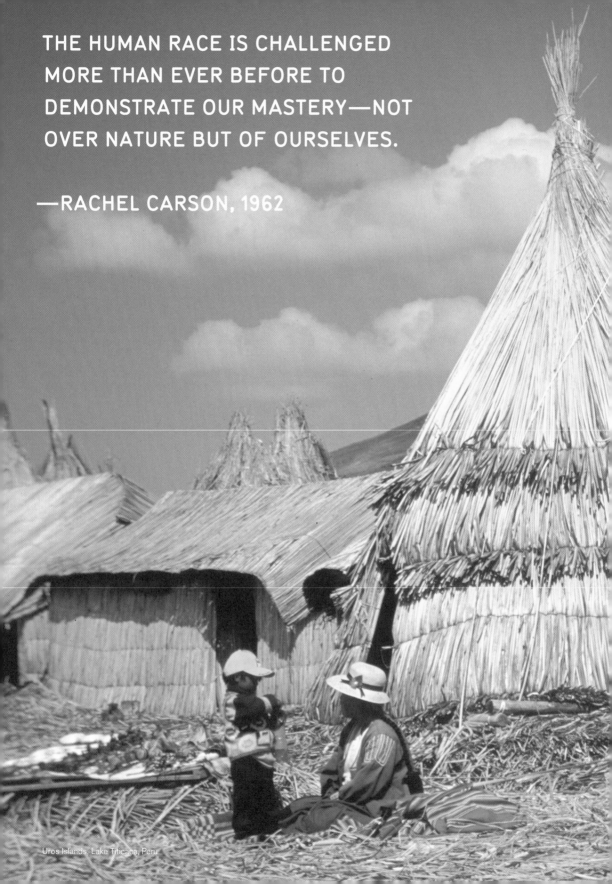

THE HUMAN RACE IS CHALLENGED
MORE THAN EVER BEFORE TO
DEMONSTRATE OUR MASTERY—NOT
OVER NATURE BUT OF OURSELVES.

—RACHEL CARSON, 1962

Uros Islands, Lake Titicaca, Peru

CONCLUSION

REPRESENTATIVE
EARL BLUMENAUER

I have spent my entire public service career promoting livable communities as places where families are safe, healthy, and economically secure. Each passing year confirms my belief that this issue is one that touches people of all ages, political persuasions, income levels, educational backgrounds, and professions.

Since I was elected to Congress in 1996, I've used the term "livable communities" as a way to get people's attention and to engage them in seeing beyond the traditional terminology. Even terms like "smart growth" tend to alienate people at both ends of the discussion, garnering resistance from those who advocate "no growth" as well as those who promote growth at any speed, regardless of the consequences. I wanted people to think about the issues that make a difference in their daily lives—their children's safety as they walk or bike to school; the traffic on their streets; their access to jobs, parks, schools, and shopping. I wanted people to realize that they had the ability and capacity to make their own communities better places, regardless of geographic location, cultural background, demographics, or size. Most important, I wanted to focus on what people were *for*, rather than what they were against.

It has been exciting to watch these concepts take hold and even become mainstream. "Green communities" has evolved into an accepted term for livable communities—places where we can live in safety and good health, with a wide range of housing and transportation choices, based on economies that rely on sustainable processes and products, in a manner that enhances rather than destroys the natural world on which we depend.

This evolution of "green communities" concepts has been remarkable. We have moved beyond concerns about the dominance of the automobile in community design to an understanding of the vital connection between

land use and transportation. The EPA's earliest Smart Growth programs
and Vice President Al Gore's leadership in the Clinton administration
helped more people realize how government policies, programs, and
investments in our infrastructure, environmental protection, public
health, and even agriculture can impact our daily lives, the well-being
of our communities, and the ability of our environment to sustain us
in the long term.

Today, many people realize that green communities are not just a
good idea—they are essential to our very survival. Climate change, our
dependence on imported oil, and the global economic meltdown all
illustrate the fundamental flaws in how we've built our communities
for the last 60 years.

Instead of scaling back our efforts in the face of these challenges,
I believe that now is the perfect time to focus on green communities.
The current instability and uncertainty make it impossible to continue
on our same trajectory; a "business as usual" approach will no longer
work. If our communities, our way of life, and our planet are to survive,
we must tackle these daunting challenges in new and resourceful ways.

Our nation's history is one of looking at the big picture. In 1808,
President Thomas Jefferson's secretary of the Treasury, Albert Gallatin,
developed a plan to address the transportation and economic needs of a
vast new nation. One hundred years later, President Teddy Roosevelt, in
response to environmental abuses from industry, a growing economic
crisis, and the fact that natural areas were disappearing, developed his own
plan with Gifford Pinchot. They convened the first White House conference of governors to draw up a national plan that created the National
Park Service, established vast irrigation and hydro projects, and laid the

foundation for later infrastructure investments, such as Eisenhower's interstate highway system.

Are we ready to deal with today's challenges on such a grand scale? The indictors are very positive, but it will take some serious rethinking of our objectives, our priorities, and our approach. Focusing on green communities enables us to avoid the shortsighted assumptions and flawed processes that have helped create our current crises. It means focusing instead on a more sustainable economy, healthier lifestyles, and more-livable communities.

In fact, we're well on our way. While my hometown of Portland, Oregon, is often cited as a successful green community, we've recently seen numerous other communities throughout the country stepping up to the plate, making significant progress toward a more sustainable future. Mayors from more than 900 U.S. cities, representing more than 81 million Americans, have signed on to the Mayors' Climate Protection Agreement. Rather than wait for the federal government, they decided to move ahead on policies that help people move, work, and live more sustainably, while revitalizing their own communities.

The progress we have made on green communities is building a sense of cooperation and collaboration, as we realize we have valuable lessons to teach—and learn—from one another. The traditional competition is a race to the bottom that benefits no one. More and more communities are discarding the approach that mortgaged their future in return for questionable benefits. The promised new jobs and higher tax bases, even when realized, required costly concessions that often destroyed valuable and beloved open space, generated more traffic and pollution, and created greater homogenization but less livability.

Fortunately, we have discovered that choosing between jobs and our quality of life, between the economy and the environment, are false choices. Investing in programs and projects that improve our quality of life actually makes our communities more attractive for the economy of the future. If we actively engage the public and tie the pieces together by focusing on long-term sustainable solutions, we can make the most of our existing resources.

Many communities are rethinking the function and design of their street networks, for example. Rather than addressing traffic congestion by building more lanes for more cars, they are finding that by providing a greater range of safe and reliable transportation options—biking, walking, and frequent transit service—they can not only save money, but reduce neighborhood noise and local traffic. A similar focus on streets as green and inviting public places rather than as throughways has drawn pedestrian traffic of all ages to city centers and businesses. Green streets also encourage social and civic interaction and filter stormwater efficiently, reducing the load on aging water and sewer systems.

Communities are also rethinking outdated zoning codes, to allow a mixture of residential and commercial zoning. This change enables people to live close to their work, eliminating traffic congestion and the need to provide additional roadway and transit capacity. In addition, encouraging appropriate new development and redevelopment in existing areas well served by transit reduces the need to build auto-dependent greenfield sprawl. This eliminates the need to build new freeways and local streets, new water and sewer infrastructure, new schools and institutions—while reducing traffic congestion and commute times.

By aligning zoning, design, tax, and historic preservation policies, communities both large and small are encouraging location-sensitive development while enabling developers to create products appropriate to the community. Communities are also finding that aligning local, state, and federal policies on the same objective can speed the development process, saving money for jurisdictions and developers alike.

Finally, communities are discovering the power of effective public participation. Engaging citizens as equal partners in necessary changes not only results in better projects but creates valuable support in the future. While public participation takes more time up front, it can actually speed the development process and almost always ensures long-term success.

The good news is that green communities can be created regardless of community size, location, diversity, demographics, or economics; thoughtful land-use and transportation policies and investments have the potential to transform communities everywhere. In fact, recent studies of "green dividends"—the economic, environmental, and personal benefits of policies that create green communities—have demonstrated significant impacts in cities as varied as Chicago and Portland.

For instance, because of the Portland region's investment in sound land-use and transportation policies and projects, Portlanders drive 20 percent less per capita than residents of other U.S. metro areas. Region-wide, this translates to a reduction of 28 billion miles per year, saving residents $1.1 billion in out-of-pocket transportation costs and bolstering the local economy to the tune of $800 million, money that would have otherwise left the region in car and gasoline purchases.

Chicago, a much larger and more mature region, has experienced similar "green dividends" from its land-use and transportation investments. Chicago-area residents drive 10 percent fewer miles than their counterparts in other large metro regions, resulting in 5.8 billion fewer miles per year, regionwide. This amounts to a total of $2.3 billion in out-of-pocket transportation expenses for metropolitan Chicago residents and a whopping $2 billion that stays in the regional economy instead of leaving to pay for gas and car purchases.

Such benefits are not unique to these two cities; the policies that create green communities have the potential to transform and strengthen communities and economies across the nation. Think about it: each of the 156 million Americans who live in the largest 51 metropolitan regions drives, on average, 24.9 miles per day. If we could reduce that daily mileage figure by a single mile per day—4 percent—we could reduce driving in these metro areas by 57 billion miles per year. At $3.50 a gallon for gasoline, this reduction could save Americans $10 billion a year on fuel costs alone. If we include auto purchasing and maintenance costs, the savings leap to $28.6 billion per year—money that becomes available to be invested in local economies.[1]

Green communities' time has obviously come. Demonstrating that our economic recovery is inextricably tied to environmental sustainability, green communities provide us all with the means to revitalize our communities, refresh our economy, strengthen our nation, and save our planet.

NOTES

1   J. Cortright, "City Dividends: Gains from Improving Metropolitan Performance," Impresa Consulting (November 2008), www.ceosforcities.org/files/City_DividendsFINAL.pdf.

A powerful tornado struck the town of Greensburg, Kansas, in May 2007, flattening 90 percent of its buildings. The physical town was almost completely destroyed, but the community was not. Greensburg's 1,400 citizens determined to rebuild in as sustainable a manner as possible. Greensburg's new plan will concentrate development in a compact and walkable downtown, maintaining a distinct boundary between the town and the agricultural land upon which it depends. Its new town center includes extensive planting and pervious paving that forms a treatment train to capture and cleanse the water, allowing it to seep gradually into the ground and recharge the High Plains Aquifer, a vast underground reservoir stretching from the Dakotas to Texas.

CONTRIBUTORS

Timothy Beatley is the Teresa Heinz Professor of Sustainable Communities at the University of Virginia, where he has taught for more than 20 years. He has authored or coauthored 15 books, including *The Ecology of Place*, *Green Urbanism*, *Native to Nowhere*, and *Ethical Land Use*. He holds a Ph.D. in city and regional planning from the University of North Carolina at Chapel Hill.

F. Kaid Benfield is director of the smart-growth program at the Natural Resources Defense Council in Washington, D.C. He supervises research, public education, and works with all levels of government and the private sector on behalf of sustainable land development in America. He cofounded LEED-ND, a national process for defining and certifying smart-growth development, under the auspices of the U.S. Green Building Council. He is also a founder and board member of Smart Growth America, a nation-wide coalition of organizations working together on smart-growth strategies. Benfield has authored or coauthored many publications, including *Smart Growth in a Changing World* (APA Planners Press, 2007) and *Solving Sprawl*.

Earl Blumenauer. Throughout a public-service career that has spanned more than 35 years, U.S. Representative Earl Blumenauer of Oregon has focused on livable communities—places where families are safe, healthy, and economically secure. He served three terms in the Oregon State Legislature starting in 1972, followed by two terms as a Multnomah County commissioner and 10 years on the Portland City Council before being elected to Congress in 1996. He now serves as the vice chair of the Select Committee on Energy Independence and Climate Change and is a member of the Ways and Means Committee.

William Browning is a partner in Terrapin Bright Green LLC, which crafts environmental strategies for corporations, government agencies, and large-scale developments. In 1991, he founded the Rocky Mountain Institute's Green Development Services, the recipient of the 1999 President's Council for Sustainable Development/Renew America Prize. He is a founding member of U.S. Green Building Council's board of directors and Greening America. He served on the Department of Defense's Defense Science Board Energy Task Force and the State Department's Industry Advisory Panel.

Thomas L. Daniels is a professor in the Department of City and Regional Planning at the University of Pennsylvania. He teaches courses on environmental planning, land-use planning, and growth management. His latest book is the third edition of *The Small Town Planning Handbook* (APA Planners Press, 2007).

Howard Frumkin is director of the National Center for Environmental Health/Agency for Toxic Substances and Disease Registry at the U.S. Centers for Disease Control and Prevention. He is an internist, environmental and occupational medicine specialist, and epidemiologist. Previously, Dr. Frumkin was professor and chair of the Department of Environmental and Occupational Health at Emory University's Rollins School of Public Health and professor of medicine at Emory Medical School. Currently serving on the Institute of Medicine Roundtable on Environmental Health Sciences, Research, and Medicine, he is a Fellow of the American College of Physicians and the American College of Occupational and Environmental Medicine.

Sir Peter Hall is Bartlett Professor of Planning and Regeneration at the Bartlett School of Architecture and Planning, University College London. He is also president of the Town and Country Planning Association. He was a member of Richard Rogers's Urban Task Force and of the Department of Communities and Local Government's Eco-Towns Challenge Panel.

Fred Hansen. As general manager of TriMet, the regional transit authority in the Portland, Oregon, metro area, Hansen is a recognized leader in the transit industry, having lectured and participated on panels throughout the United States and around the world. He has carried the message that land use and transportation must be fully integrated if we are to address global climate change and the livability needs of our citizens. He chairs the American Public Transportation Association's Sustainability Task Force. Previously, he served as deputy administrator of the U.S. EPA in the Clinton administration and directed the Oregon Department of Environmental Quality for more than 10 years.

Erica Heller and Mark Heller. Erica Heller, AICP, is an associate with Clarion Associates, a land-use zoning and planning firm based in Denver. She writes zoning codes and comprehensive plans for communities of all sizes. She has published and spoken about land-use regulations for wind turbines and other local renewable-energy issues. Mark Heller, AICP, has professional expertise in community planning, economic and real estate development, environmental advocacy, and law. He serves as the executive director of the Golden Urban Renewal Authority in Golden, Colorado. He led that community in developing an award-winning sustainability plan with broad citizen support.

James A. LaGro Jr. is a professor in the Department of Urban and Regional Planning at the University of Wisconsin–Madison, with more than 25 years of professional experience. His research and teaching

seek to advance the sustainable redevelopment of the built environment. He is the author of *Site Analysis: A Contextual Approach to Sustainable Land Planning and Site Design.*

Robert E. Lang and Mariela Alfonzo. Robert E. Lang is director of the National Capital Region Urban Affairs and Planning Program, codirector of the Metropolitan Institute, and a professor in Urban Affairs and Planning at Virginia Tech. He is the editor of *Housing Policy Debate*. Lang's research specialties include suburban studies, world cities, demographic and spatial analysis, housing and the built environment, and metropolitan governance. His publications include *Boomburbs: The Rise of America's Accidental Cities* and the three-volume *Redefining Urban and Suburban America: Evidence from Census 2000*. He received a Ph.D. in sociology from Rutgers University. **Mariela Alfonzo** is an urban-design researcher and consultant specializing in the "triple bottom line"—the social, environmental, and economic value—of urban design. She is a postdoctoral fellow at the Metropolitan Institute at Virginia Tech, in the Department of Urban Affairs and Planning. Her current projects include a research study with the Brookings Institution on real estate value and community design and an assessment of the value of public spaces within regenerated retail environments in Europe.

Scott A. Malcolm and Marcel Aillery. Scott A. Malcolm is a research economist with the Economic Research Service, U.S. Department of Agriculture. His recent research examines the role of renewable energy and climate policy on agricultural land, resources, and markets. Recent publications include contributions to "Increasing Feedstock Production for Biofuels" (2008) and "Weaning Off Corn: Crop Residues and

Contributors

the Transition to Cellulosic Ethanol" (2008). **Marcel Aillery** is an agricultural economist with the Economic Research Service, U.S. Department of Agriculture. His research has addressed agricultural conservation and environmental policy, with a focus on water use and quality. Recent articles include "Integrating Commodity and Conservation Programs: Design Options and Outcomes," "Contrasting Working-Land and Land Retirement Programs," and "Managing Manure to Improve Air and Water Quality."

Timothy Mennel is senior editor and acquisitions manager for Planners Press and Planning Advisory Service Reports at the American Planning Association. He coedited *Block by Block: Jane Jacobs and the Future of New York* and developed the exhibition *Growing and Greening New York: PlaNYC and the Future of the City* at the Museum of the City of New York. He has been an editor at Random House, the Andy Warhol Foundation for the Visual Arts, *Artforum*, and elsewhere, as well as a consultant to the Rockefeller Foundation. He has a Ph.D. in geography from the University of Minnesota.

Richard Moe, with Patrice Frey. Richard Moe is the president of the National Trust for Historic Preservation, whose mission is to save the nation's diverse historic places and create more livable communities for all Americans. A member of the board of the Ford Foundation, Moe was the recipient of the Vincent Scully Prize from the National Building Museum in 2007. He is coauthor of *Changing Places: Rebuilding Community in the Age of Sprawl* and author of *The Last Full Measure: The Life and Death of the First Minnesota Volunteers.* Moe graduated from Williams College and received a law degree from the University of Minnesota. **Patrice Frey** is the deputy director for the Sustainability Program at the National Trust for Historic Preservation.

She is a graduate of the University of Pennsylvania's program in historic preservation, where she received a master's degree in preservation planning and a certificate in real estate design and development through the Penn School of Design and Wharton Business School.

Mary Rickel Pelletier provides independent design research, writing, and advocacy for innovative green projects. Since 2004, she has focused on the evolution of green infrastructure while working as director of the Park River Watershed Revitalization Initiative. Pelletier has a B.Arch. from the Rhode Island School of Design, as well as a master's in design theory from the Harvard University Graduate School of Design. She edited *The Sustainable Architecture White Papers*. Her essay "Criteria for a Humane Metropolis" in *The Humane Metropolis: People and Nature in the 21st-Century City*, described the need for a municipal green rating system.

Susan Piedmont-Palladino is an architect, a curator at the National Building Museum, and a professor of architecture at Virginia Tech's Washington/Alexandria Architecture Consortium (WAAC). She was the curator of the exhibition *Green Community* at the National Building Museum. Previously she served as a guest curator for *Tools of the Imagination: Drawing Tools and Technologies from the Eighteenth Century to the Present*. She is the author of *Devil's Workshop: 25 Years of Jersey Devil Architecture* and *Tools of the Imagination*, the companion book to the exhibition, both published by Princeton Architectural Press. She is the former national president of Architects/Designers/Planners for Social Responsibility.

Douglas R. Porter, FAICP, is president of the Growth Management Institute in Chevy Chase, Maryland. His work as a consulting planner, researcher, and writer spans many aspects of regional and community development. He is currently completing a book on green development. Other recent publications include *Urban Design and the Bottom Line* (coauthor) and the second edition of *Managing Growth in America's Communities*. In prior positions, he directed the public-policy research program of the Urban Land Institute and was a principal of a planning consulting firm. He has degrees in urban and regional planning from Michigan State University and the University of Illinois.

Jonathan Rose's business, not-for-profit, and public-policy work focuses on integrating transportation, housing, environmental and open-space policies to create healthy, equitable metropolitan regions. Jonathan Rose Companies LLC—a multidisciplinary real estate development, planning, consulting, and investment firm—is a leading green urban solutions provider. Rose is a trustee of the Urban Land Institute, the Natural Resources Defense Council, and Enterprise Community Partners. He chairs the Metropolitan Transit Authority's Blue Ribbon Sustainability Commission and the Trust for Public Land's National Real Estate Council. He also serves on the leadership councils of both Yale University's School of Forestry and Environmental Studies and the School of Architecture.

Carolyn Steel is an award-winning architect, lecturer, and writer whose work has focused on the everyday lives of cities. A director of Cullum and Nightingale Architects and a Rome Scholar, she has run successful design units at the London School of Economics, London Metropolitan University, and Cambridge University, where her lecture series "Food and the City" is an established part of the architectural degree. Her first book, *Hungry City: How Food Shapes Our Lives*,

won the Royal Society of Literature Jerwood Award for Non-Fiction.

Esther M. Sternberg received her medical and rheumatology training at McGill University and was on the faculty at Washington University, St. Louis, before joining the National Institutes of Health in 1986. Currently chief of the Section on Neuroendocrine Immunology and Behavior at the National Institute of Mental Health, Dr. Sternberg is also director of the Integrative Neural Immune Program, NIMH/NIH, and a research professor at American University. She is internationally recognized for her discoveries in brain-immune connections and the role of the brain's stress response in diseases, including arthritis. She has authored two books, most recently *Healing Spaces: The Science of Place and Well-being*.

ACKNOWLEDGMENTS

The editors wish to thank the following individuals
for their input and support of *Green Community*. At the
American Planning Association: Susan Deegan, Monica
Groh, Dennis Johnson, Sylvia Lewis, Richard Lukas,
Roberta Rewers, Suzanne Rynne, Jeffrey L. Soule, FAICP,
Carolyn Torma, and Lois Tucker. At the National Building
Museum: Cathy Frankel and Shar Taylor. In addition,
this book was vastly improved by the efforts of Martha
Malnor, Vanessa Mickan, Marya Morris, and Evan Stone.
We particularly thank Asad Pervaiz and Sarah Gephart
of mgmt. design for their dedication and care.

We reserve our deepest appreciation for Reed Haslach,
whose patient management of so many details has
made this book not just better but possible at all.

Susan Piedmont-Palladino
Timothy Mennel
September 2009

164

IMAGE CREDITS
AND PERMISSIONS

165

INDEX